Lecture Notes in Computer Science 3527

Commenced Publication in 1973
Founding and Former Series Editors:
Gerhard Goos, Juris Hartmanis, and Jan van Leeuwen

T0223546

Ron Morrison   Flavio Oquendo (Eds.)

Software
Architecture

2nd European Workshop, EWSA 2005
Pisa, Italy, June 13-14, 2005
Proceedings

 Springer

Volume Editors

Ron Morrison
University of St Andrews, School of Computer Science
St Andrews, Fife KY16 9SX, UK
E-mail: ron@dcs.st-andrews.ac.uk

Flavio Oquendo
University of South Brittany
VALORIA - Formal Software Architecture and Process Research Group
B.P. 573, 56017 Vannes Cedex, France
E-mail: flavio.oquendo@univ-ubs.fr

Library of Congress Control Number: 2005926937

CR Subject Classification (1998): D.2

ISSN   0302-9743
ISBN-10   3-540-26275-X Springer Berlin Heidelberg New York
ISBN-13   978-3-540-26275-6 Springer Berlin Heidelberg New York

Springer is a part of Springer Science+Business Media

springeronline.com

Typesetting: Camera-ready by author, data conversion by Scientific Publishing Services, Chennai, India
Printed on acid-free paper   SPIN: 11494713   06/3142   5 4 3 2 1 0

Preface

The 1st European Workshop on Software Architecture (EWSA 2004) was held in St Andrews, Scotland on 21–22 May 2004. The workshop provided an international forum for researchers and practitioners from academia and industry to discuss a wide range of topics in the area of software architecture and to jointly formulate an agenda for future research. We were pleased to continue this forum in EWSA 2005.

The importance of software architecture as a fundamental area of software engineering continues to grow. In addition to describing the underlying structure of software systems, architectures are now being used to model and understand dynamic behavior. New areas of study, which have their roots in control systems, are beginning to emerge. The field of autonomics requires an underlying software architecture to describe the executing computation as does any control system that involves system evolution. The range of papers in EWSA 2005 reflected both the traditional and new applications of software architecture techniques.

EWSA 2005 distinguished between three types of papers: research papers (which describe authors' novel research work), a case study (which describes experiences related to software architectures) and position papers (which present concise arguments about a topic of software architecture research or practice).

The Programme Committee selected 18 papers (12 research papers, 4 position papers, 1 case study, and 1 unrefereed invited paper) out of 41 submissions from 20 countries (Australia, Belgium, Brazil, Chile, China, Czech Republic, Finland, France, Germany, India, Italy, Ireland, Korea, Netherlands, Pakistan, Portugal, Spain, Switzerland, UK, USA). All submissions were reviewed by at least three members of the Programme Committee. Papers were selected based on originality, quality, soundness and relevance to the workshop. Credit for the quality of the proceedings goes to all authors of papers.

We would like to thank the members of the Programme Committee for providing timely and significant reviews and for their substantial effort in making EWSA 2005 a successful workshop.

As with EWSA 2004, the EWSA 2005 submission and review process was extensively supported by the Paperdyne Conference Management System. We are indebted to Volker Gruhn, Dirk Peters and Clemens Schfer for their support.

Finally we acknowledge the support from Springer, which published these proceedings in printed and electronic volumes as part of the Lecture Notes in Computer Science series.

April 2005

Ron Morrison
Flavio Oquendo

Programme Committee

Programme Chairs

Ron Morrison
    University of St Andrews, UK
    ron@ dcs.st-andrews.ac.uk
Flavio Oquendo
    South Brittany University, France
    Flavio.Oquendo@ univ-ubs.fr

Committee Members

Dharini Balasubramaniam
    University of St Andrews, UK
    dharini@ dcs.st-and.ac.uk
Isabelle Borne
    South Brittany University, France
    Isabelle.Borne@ univ-ubs.fr
Jan Bosch
    Nokia Research Center, Finland
    Jan.Bosch@ nokia.com
Carlos E. Cuesta
    University of Valladolid, Spain
    gcecuesta@ infor.uva.es
Harald Gall
    University of Zurich, Switzerland
    gall@ iì.un.izh.ch
Mark Greenwood
    University of Manchester, UK
    markg@ cs.man.ac.uk
Volker Gruhn
    University of Leipzig, Germany
    gruhn@ ebus.informatik.uni-leipzig.de
Jon Hall
    The Open University, UK
    J.G.Hall@ open.ac.uk
Paola Inverardi
    Università dell'Aquila, Italy
    inverard@ di.univaq.it

Valrie Issarny
    INRIA Rocquencourt, France
    Valerie.Issarny@inria.fr
Jeff Kramer
    Imperial College London, UK
    j.kramer@imperial.ac.uk
Philippe Kruchten
    University of British Columbia, Canada
    pbk@ece.ubc.ca
Nicole Levy
    University of Versailles, France
    nicole.levy@prism.uvsq.fr
Jeff Magee
    Imperial College London, UK
    j.magee@ic.ac.uk
Radu Mateescu
    INRIA Rhne-Alpes, France
    radu.mateescu@inria.fr
Carlo Montangero
    University of Pisa, Italy
    carlo.montangero@di.unipi.it
Mourad C. Oussalah
    University of Nantes, France
    Mourad.Oussalah@lina.univ-nantes.fr
Dewayne Perry
    University of Texas at Austin, USA
    perry@ece.utexas.edu
Frantisek Plasil
    Charles University, Czech Republic
    plasil@nenya.ms.mff.cuni.cz
Fausto Rabitti
    ISTI, Italy
    Fausto.Rabitti@isti.cnr.it
Bradley Schmerl
    Carnegie Mellon University, USA
    schmerl@cs.cmu.edu
Brian Warboys
    University of Manchester, UK
    bwarboys@cs.man.ac.uk
Michel Wermelinger
    The Open University, UK
    m.a.wermelinger@open.ac.uk

Organizing Committee

John Favaro (Chair)
    Consorzio Pisa Ricerche, Italy
    jfavaro@ tin .it
Concettina Larosa
    Consorzio Pisa Ricerche, Italy
    c .larosa@ cpr .it
Hilary Hanahoe
    Consorzio Pisa Ricerche, Italy
    h .hanahoe@ trust-itservices .com

Sponsorship

EWSA 2005 was sponsored by the ArchWare European R&D Project: Architecting Evolvable Software – www .arch-ware.org. ArchWare is partially funded by the Commission of the European Union under Contract No. IST-2001-32360 in the IST-V Framework Programme.

Table of Contents

Research Papers

Case Study

Position Papers

Invited Paper

Managing Dynamic Reconfiguration in Component-Based Systems

Thais Batista[1,2,*], Ackbar Joolia[2], and Geoff Coulson[2]

[1] Computer Science Department,
Federal University of Rio Grande do Norte (UFRN),
59072-970, Natal – RN, Brazil
thais@ufrnet.br
[2] Computing Department, InfoLab21, Lancaster University,
LA1 4WA, Lancaster, UK
{t.batista, a.joolia, g.coulson}@lancaster.ac.uk

Abstract. We propose a meta-framework called 'Plastik' which i) supports the specification and creation of runtime component-framework-based software systems and ii) facilitates and manages the runtime reconfiguration of such systems while ensuring integrity across changes. The meta-framework is fundamentally an integration of an architecture description language (an extension of ACME/Armani) and a reflective component runtime (OpenCOM). Plastik-generated component frameworks can be dynamically reconfigured either through programmed changes (which are foreseen at design time and specified at the ADL level); or through ad-hoc changes (which are unforeseen at design time but which are nevertheless constrained by invariants specified at the ADL level). We provide in the paper a case study that illustrates the operation and benefits of Plastik.

1 Introduction

Software architecture modeling using Architecture Description Languages (ADLs) is becoming increasingly popular in the *early phases* of system development [1, 2, 3]. Such languages facilitate the construction of high-level models in which systems are described as compositions of components. They play an important role in developing high quality software by supporting reasoning about structural properties early in the development process. This can make it easier to produce more extensible structures, locate design flaws, and better maintain consistency.

At the same time there has been a parallel development of *runtime* component models which are targeted at the actual construction and deployment of systems [4,5,6,7]. These component models are becoming quite sophisticated in their capabilities for runtime reconfiguration. For example, they use reflective or runtime aspect-oriented programming techniques to allow software to inspect, adapt and extend itself while it is running. This is particularly useful in inherently adaptive software environments such as mobile computing and adaptive real-time systems [8].

---

* Thais Batista is supported by the Brazilian Research Council (CAPES) project BEX0680/04-4.

R. Morrison and F. Oquendo (Eds.): EWSA 2005, LNCS 3527, pp. 1 – 17, 2005.

It is clear that an integration of the two above-mentioned strands of development holds significant potential. Some early work has attempted to do this (see related work discussion in section 5) but this has typically suffered from two main limitations: *i*) it has not taken a sufficiently comprehensive approach to formally specifying and constraining runtime reconfiguration at the ADL level, and *ii*) it has not leveraged the most recent developments in reconfigurable runtime component technologies. The 'Plastik' meta-framework described in this paper is an ADL/ component runtime integration that attempts to address such limitations.

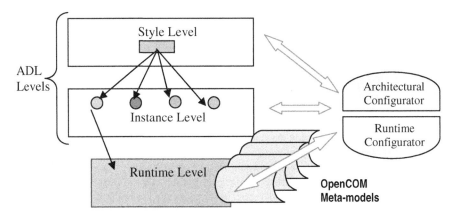

Fig. 1. Plastik's system architecture

The Plastik architecture, illustrated in figure 1[1], supports formally-specified runtime reconfiguration of systems through an integration of an ADL and a reflective, component model runtime. The ADL level is based on ACME/ Armani [9,10] which we have enhanced with new constructs for dynamic reconfiguration; and the runtime level is based on our OpenCOM component model [7] and its association notions of component frameworks and reflective meta-models [12].

Plastik supports both programmed and ad-hoc reconfiguration:

* *Programmed reconfiguration* pertains to changes that can be foreseen at system design time. In Plastik, this is supported at the ADL level in terms of 'predicate-action' specifications. For example, consider a PDA-based video application that needs to run over both fixed and wireless networks. In such an environment, one could specify a programmed reconfiguration that switches from a MPEG decoder to an H.263 decoder ('action') when the PDA detects a drop in the quality of network connectivity ('predicate') [12]. In this example, the predicate could be expressed in our extended ADL as a function of a dynamic property of an underlying protocol component, and the associated action would take the form of (extended) ADL statements that replace the old component with the new one.

---

[1] Section 3 expands on the various entities depicted in figure 1.

- *Ad-hoc reconfiguration*, on the other hand, is intended for changes that are not and cannot be foreseen at system design time. The approach here is to build general invariants into the specification of the system and to accept any change as long as the invariants are not violated. As an example, the above mobile computing scenario might be enhanced by the insertion of a jitter-smoothing buffer which, despite not having been considered at design time, could nevertheless be usefully inserted at runtime.

In addition, Plastik allows both programmed and ad-hoc reconfiguration to be initiated from multiple architectural levels (see section 3) which enables considerable flexibility.

The remainder of this paper is structured as follows. Section 2 provides background on ACME/ Armani and on the OpenCOM component runtime; it also considers the relationship between the two technologies. Section 3 then details our approach to programmed and ad-hoc reconfiguration, and section 4 presents a case study which exemplifies the approach. Finally, section 5 discusses related work, and section 6 offers our conclusions.

2   Background on ACME/Armani and OpenCOM

2.1   The ACME/Armani ADL

The Plastik meta-framework's ADL level provides the basis for specifying systems and enabling and constraining their reconfiguration. We have selected ACME [9] as our ADL because:

- Unlike many ADLs it offers sufficient generality to straightforwardly describe a variety of system structures. Most ADLs are domain-specific so they do not provide generic structures to cope with a wide range of systems.
- It comes with tools that provide a good basis for designing and manipulating architectural descriptions and generating code.

The basic elements of ACME are as follows: *Components* are potentially composite computational encapsulations that support multiple interfaces known as *ports*. Ports are bound to ports on other components using first-class intermediaries called *connectors* which support so-called *roles* that attach directly to ports. *Attachments* then define a set of port/role associations. *Representations* are alternative decompositions of a given component; they reify the notion that a component may have multiple alternative implementations. The ACME type system provides an additional dimension of flexibility by allowing type extensions via the *extended with* construct. *Properties* are <*name, type, value*> triples that can be attached to any of the above ACME elements as annotations (apart from attachments). Finally, *architectural styles* define sets of types of components, connectors, properties, and sets of rules that specify how elements of those types may be legally composed in a reusable architectural domain (see example below).

In addition, we adopt the *Armani* [10] extensions to ACME. Armani is a FOPL-based sub-language that is used to express architectural constraints over ACME architectures. For example, it can be used to express constraints on system composition, behavior, and properties. Constraints are defined in terms of so-called *invariants* which in turn are composed of standard logical connectives and Armani predicates (both built-in and user-defined) which are referred to as *functions*. Although Armani appears to introduce an element of dynamicity, it is important to emphasise that ACME/Armani does *not* currently support dynamic runtime reconfiguration of systems (see also section 5).

The ACME fragment below illustrates the main ACME/Armani concepts. The style definition includes two port types and two roles types. The *OSIComp* component type then defines the central player in a layered communications system environment. This definition includes a connector type which is used to connect protocol layers and an Armani invariant that states that a system must comprise a four-level stack.

```
Style PlastikMF {
        Port Type ProvidedPort, RequiredPort;
        Role Type ProvidedRole, RequiredRole;
        ....
};

Component Type OSIComp: PlastikMF {
    ProvidedPort Type upTo, downTo;
    RequiredPort Type downFrom, upFrom;

    Property Type layer =
        enum {application, transport, network, link};
};

Connector Type conn2Layers: PlastikMF {
    ProvidedRole Type source;
    RequiredRole Type sink;
};

Invariant
    Forall c:OSIComp in sys.Components
            cardinality(c.layer = application) = 1 and
            cardinality(c.layer = transport) = 1 and
            cardinality(c.layer = network) = 1 and
            cardinality(c.layer = link) = 1 and

Property Type applicationProtocol;
Property Type transportProtocol;
Property Type networkProtocol;
Property Type linkProtocol;
```

Fig. 2. An example definition in ACME

2.2   The OpenCOM Reflective Component Model

The OpenCOM component runtime has been extensively used over the past few years to build reconfigurable systems software elements such as middleware and programmable networking environments [11]. A high-level view of its programming model is given in figure 3. Components (the filled rectangles) are encapsulated units of functionality and deployment that interact with their environment (i.e. other components) exclusively through interfaces (the small circles) and receptacles (the small cups). A component may support multiple interfaces and receptacles and may be internally composite (i.e. composed of other components). Components are deployed at runtime into environments called capsules (the outer dotted box) which support a runtime 'capsule API' containing operations to load/ unload components (and also to bind/ unbind interfaces and receptacles; see below). The loading of components into a capsule can be requested by any component inside or outside the capsule (this is referred to as third-party deployment). Interfaces are units of service provision offered by components; they are expressed in terms of sets of operation signatures and associated datatypes. For programming language independence, OMG IDL is used as an interface definition language. Receptacles are 'anti-interfaces' used to make explicit the dependencies of components on other components: whereas an interface represents an element of service provision, a receptacle represents a unit of service requirement. Receptacles are key to supporting a third-party style of composition (to complement the third-party deployment referred to above): when third-party deploying a component into a capsule, one knows by looking at the component's receptacles precisely which other component types must be present to satisfy its dependencies. Finally, bindings, which are created via the capsule API, are associations between a single interface and a single receptacle. As with loading, the creation of bindings is inherently third-party in nature; it can be performed by any party inside or outside the capsule.

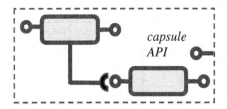

Fig. 3. The OpenCOM component model

In implementation, the OpenCOM programming model is supported by a small runtime of around 17KB in size. Components are written in C++ by default. As well as supporting the programming model concepts described above, the OpenCOM runtime also supports a set of so-called *reflective meta-models* [12] which facilitate reconfiguration of systems by permitting different system aspects to be inspected, adapted and extended at runtime. In particular, OpenCOM employs the following meta-models:

- an *architecture meta-model* which exposes the compositional topology of a system of deployed components in terms of a causally-connected graph structure;
- an *interception meta-model* which allows one to interpose interceptors at bindings between component interfaces; and
- an *interface meta-model* which allows one to discover information about interfaces at runtime and to invoke interface types that are dynamically discovered at runtime.

The final key aspect of OpenCOM is that it supports building systems in terms of the medium granularity (i.e. between components and whole systems) notion of *component frameworks* (hereafter, CFs) [12]. CFs are tightly-coupled clusters of components that cooperate to address some focused domain of functionality, and which accept 'plug-in' components that tailor or extend functionality in that domain. The idea is that one constructs systems by composing and configuring appropriate CFs. For example, one might develop a middleware system by composing CFs that address independent functionality domains such as protocol stacking, thread scheduling and request-handling [12]. Importantly, CFs incorporate policies and constraints that determine how and to what extent the CF can be runtime reconfigured. Typically, per-CF constraints are also imposed on the use of the reflective meta-models. Essentially, reflection provides maximal openness and flexibility, whereas CFs channel and constrain this expressive 'power' into useful and safe forms.

2.3   Mapping from ACME/Armani to OpenCOM

As can readily be observed, there is a close correspondence between concepts in ACME/Armani and in OpenCOM. This correspondence is summed up in table 1.

Table 1. ACME/Armani to OpenCOM correspondences

ACME/Armani	OpenCOM
component	*(composite) component*
connector	*(composite) component*
port	*interface/ receptacle*
role	*interface/ receptacle*
attachment	*binding*
representation	*(composite) component*
property	*interface operation*
style	*CF*
invariant	*CF constraints*

The style-to-CF correspondence is central. As domain-specific units of re-usable and dynamically reconfigurable functionality, OpenCOM CFs are the natural target abstraction for ADL-specified styles whose specification incorporates programmed reconfiguration and constraints on ad-hoc reconfiguration. This observation forms the basis for Plastik's approach to reconfiguration as detailed in the next section. The fact that OpenCOM supports third-party deployment and binding is also crucial in enabling the runtime to be manipulable from the ADL level.

3 Approach to Reconfiguration

3.1 Architecture

Before discussing our approach to programmed and ad-hoc reconfiguration, we briefly expand on the architecture diagram presented in figure 1.

Note first that figure 1 has *two* ADL sub-levels: a style level and an instance level. The style level is used to define generic patterns—an example could be a 'protocol stacking' style which defined a basic set of elements and constraints for describing linear compositions of 'protocol' components. The instance level then particularises a style for a specific context while honouring any constraints imposed by the style. For example, one could define an 'TCP/IP stack' CF that imposed the additional constraints that the maximum number of levels was 4, that a stack can only be reconfigured when a connection is dormant, and that a "TCP" component must always be placed above an "IP" component.

Figure 1 also illustrates Plastik's *system configurator* which is divided into two levels: an *architectural configurator* responsible for accepting and validating reconfiguration requests at the ADL levels, and a *runtime* configurator responsible for managing the OpenCOM/ runtime level. There is one instance of the architectural configurator in the whole Plastik system, but there is one instance of the runtime configurator for each deployed CF. Both parts of the configurator are implemented in an interpreted scripting language called Lua [13]. The link between the ADL and the runtime levels is realised as an ACME/ Armani compiler (we use AcmeLIB [22] as the basis of this). The output of the compiler is a Lua program that instantiates OpenCOM elements that correspond to the ADL-level specifications. The compiler also generates finite state machines that implement Armani invariants as discussed below. These are located in the runtime configurator of each CF. More detail is given below.

3.2 Programmed Reconfiguration

3.2.1 Limitations of ACME/ Armani

As indicated in the introduction, we address programmed reconfiguration by providing appropriate extensions to ACME/Armani. Before introducing these extensions, we will briefly motivate them by analysing the limitations of 'standard' ACME/ Armani with respect to dynamic programmed reconfiguration.

Programmed reconfiguration *could potentially* be expressed using the following existing ACME/Armani concepts as a basis:

- The Armani 'invariants' are potentially useful in ensuring that a system preserves the constraints imposed by the software architecture despite the dynamic insertion or removal of ACME elements.
- The 'extend with' construct enables type extension, and could conceivably be applied to extend types at runtime.

- The 'representation' construct could be used as a basis of switching from one representation of a component to another at runtime.
- The 'properties' construct could also be used to describe how components may be changed at runtime.

Nevertheless, these features are insufficient as a basis for runtime reconfiguration. First, the 'extend with' and 'representation' constructs do not address the most general reconfigurations that might be required—e.g. those involving removal of components or other elements. Second, 'properties' on their own are severely limited by the fact that they have no inherent semantics—which means that their interpretation is intuitive and depends on a shared understanding. Furthermore, neither properties nor any of the other constructs mentioned provide any way of specifying *when* reconfiguration should take place or *what* should be changed in any particular configuration operation.

3.2.2 ACME Extensions for Programmed Reconfiguration

The first extension is a conditional construct that allows the ADL programmer to express runtime conditions under which programmed reconfigurations should take place, together with a specification of what should change. The syntax of the construct is as follows:

On (<predicate>) **do** <actions>

The 'predicate' is expressed using the standard Armani predicate syntax, and refers to properties attached to ACME components. Composite predicates involving multiple properties are supported. As will be explained later, it is these properties that 'ground' the predicate in the OpenCOM runtime system. The 'actions' are arbitrary ACME statements[2] that are instantiated when the predicate becomes true. These statements could, for example, declare additional components and connect them into the existing architecture by declaring additional attachments. Where more than one action is specified, it is assumed that the set of actions will be instantiated in sequence and atomically.

The second extension is a pair of constructs that specify the destruction of existing ACME elements:

detach <element>
remove <element>

Detach is used to remove an attachment between a port and a role; and *remove* is used to destroy an existing component, connector or representation. Removal of elements is only possible when they are no longer involved in an attachment. The idea is that *remove* and *detach* can be used as *On-do* actions to enable architectures to be dismantled as well as constructed. Given this capability, fully general runtime changes are possible, ranging from simple replacement of an element to a wide-ranging reconfiguration that can modify the whole architecture. The use of *remove* and *detach* in conjunction with *On-do* is illustrated in figure 4:

---

[2] In this and the following extensions, we build on existing ACME constructs but apply them (such as here) in novel syntactical contexts. The semantics are, however, maintained.

```
On (net_bandwidth = low) do {
    detach MPEG-dec.req to conn-dec.p;
    remove MPEG-dec;
    Component H263-dec : decoder = new decoder extended with {
        Property decoder-type = "H263";
    };
    Attachments
            H263-dec.r to conn-dec.p;
}
```

Fig. 4. Example of use of the *On-do* statement

When the given predicate becomes true (i.e. when the *net_bandwidth* property transits to the value *low*), the following reconfiguration sequence takes place: component *MPEG-dec* is detached from connector *conn-dec* and removed; and then a new H.263 component is instantiated and attached to the same connector.

The third extension that we propose is intended to express runtime dependencies between architectural elements. Managing dependencies among first-class entities is especially important to dynamic reconfiguration to avoid architectural mismatches when a new element is inserted in a system. The syntax of this extension is as follows:

dependencies <statements>

The *dependencies* statement allows expression of the fact that dynamic instantiation/ destruction components is dependent on the creation/ destruction of other components. Here is an illustration of the use of *dependencies*:

```
Component transport: OSIComp = {
        ...
    dependencies {
            extended with {RequiredPort bufport};
            Component bm: bufferManager;
            Invariant
            forall p:ProvidedPort in bm.Ports
                    p.rate > 1000
            }

            Connector transtobuf {
            ProvidedRole pr;
            RequiredRole rr;
            }
            Attachments {
            transport.bufport to transtobuf.rr;
                    bm.pp to transtobuf.pr;
            }
        }
}
```

Fig. 5. Example of use of the *dependencies* statement

This specifies that the *transport* component depends on a buffer manager; therefore an instance of the latter is instantiated and attached whenever an instance of the former is created. (The example also includes an invariant that requires that the buffer manager must be able to accept data at a certain rate.)

The fourth and final extension allows attachments to be specified for a *type* as well as for an instance (only instances are supported by standard ACME). The precise instance to be used is selected at runtime according to a policy specified by the associated connector[3]. The syntax of the construct is as follows:

```
<connector> to dynamic <componentport>
```

An example of the use of the dynamic statement is shown in figure 6. This assumes that *ConnX* contains a policy that determines which instance of the *Network* component type will be attached.

Attachments {ConnX.r **to** dynamic Network.p}

Fig. 6. Example of use of the *dynamic* statement

Note that there is an analogue to this sort of dynamic component instantiation in Darwin [14]. However, in Darwin it is not possible to declare an attachment to a specified 'provided' port of a dynamic component. We consider that this makes the architectural description unclear and can lead to unexpected bindings at runtime.

3.2.3 Supporting Programmed Reconfiguration at Runtime

This largely amounts to providing runtime support for the above-described ACME extensions for programmed reconfiguration. First, the predicate element of each *On-do* statement is compiled into a runtime finite state machine (FSM) representation. All the FSMs for each Plastik CF are contained in the associated per-CF runtime configurator. As mentioned, the ADL-level predicates are 'grounded' into the OpenCOM runtime through their embedded property elements. In particular, it is required that each ADL-level property is supported by corresponding 'property operations' in a distinguished interface of the OpenCOM component that underpins the ADL-level component to which the property is attached. There are simple lexical conventions that tie ADL-level property names to runtime level property operations, and the property operation are discovered and bound to by the configurator at runtime using OpenCOM's interface meta-model. Given this machinery, the FSMs are evaluated every time a runtime property operation reports (via a callback) a change in the value of the runtime property. This evaluation may then trigger an execution of the *On-do* statement's 'actions' clause.

Execution of the actions clause is carried out transactionally in case the whole sequence cannot be completed (e.g. if an attempt is made to remove an element that is still attached to some other element). It is also important to confirm that the proposed reconfiguration will not violate any general Armani-specified constraints elsewhere in the CF (whether at the style or the instance levels). These general constraints are discussed further in section 3.3.

---

[3] We are also considering alternative means of specifying these policies.

Implementation of the *detach* and *remove* actions make use of OpenCOM's architecture meta-model to ensure that the required preconditions of these actions (see section 3.2.2) are satisfied. The load/unload and bind/unbind APIs of OpenCOM's capsule API are then used to effect each actions. The *dependencies* statement causes the runtime to dynamically load (and bind) any dependent components whenever it instantiates an OpenCOM component whose ADL-level analogue specifies such a dependency. Finally, the implementation of the *dynamic* construct also builds directly on OpenCOMs load/ bind APIs. It involves the prior evaluation of an associated policy to select the appropriate instance—this is performed by Lua code generated from the policy statement.

3.3 Ad-Hoc Reconfiguration

By definition, ad-hoc reconfiguration is not specified at the ADL level. Rather, our approach is to *constrain* at the ADL-level the allowable range of permissible ad-hoc reconfigurations. For this we again rely on Armani invariants and similarly ground the invariants using property values that refer to the runtime level.

In Plastik, ad-hoc reconfiguration can be initiated either at the ADL level or at the runtime level. ADL level ad-hoc reconfiguration involves submitting an *architecture modification script* to the architectural configurator. This script is written in our extended ACME and specifies a set of proposed runtime changes to a target ADL specification. The script may not include invariants at the top level. The changes are applied to the target specification which is then recompiled to produce a Lua *diff script* that is (transactionally) executed to reconfigure the runtime CF. As in the case of programmed reconfiguration, the runtime system confirms before making any changes that running the diff script will not violate any architectural constraints specified in the target ADL specification. Both style and instance level invariants are taken into account. Notice that because the architecture modification script is written in extended ACME, it is possible to dynamically add new programmed reconfiguration clauses to a running CF.

Reconfiguration requests at the runtime level take the form of operations directly applied the OpenCOM reflective meta-models. This is the 'traditional' means of exploiting OpenCOMs reconfiguration capabilities. In Plastik, however, the meta-model APIs are hidden by automatically-generated per-CF wrappers so that calls on them are first validated by an evaluation of the invariants as discussed above.

Supporting ad-hoc reconfiguration at both the ADL and runtime levels raises issues of *causality*—i.e. to what extent are changes at one level reflected in the other? Our current approach is to provide full causality in the ADL-to-runtime direction, but not in the other direction. An implication of this is that a runtime-level ad-hoc reconfiguration may cause rejection of a subsequent ad-hoc reconfiguration at the ADL level due to an inconsistency having being introduced—e.g. if the ADL-level reconfiguration request refers to some component that has previously been removed by the runtime-level reconfiguration. In practice, we expect that most CFs will employ *either* ADL-level *or* runtime-level ad-hoc reconfiguration but not both. Use of the runtime level is appropriate in low-level system environments that are driven primarily by dynamic events in other low-level CFs. Use of the ADL-level, on the other hand, is more appropriate for higher-level CFs that are primarily driven by applications or GUIs.

4   Case Study

To further illustrate the use of Plastik, we extend the running *OSIComp* example to demonstrate both programmed and ad-hoc reconfiguration of the example protocol stack illustrated in figure 7.

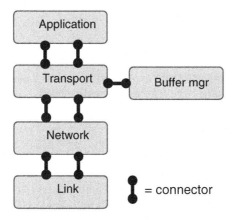

Fig. 7. Example of a reconfigurable protocol stack

4.1   Programmed Reconfiguration

To illustrate programmed reconfiguration consider changing the Application component of our system from an MPEG decoder to an H.263 decoder on the basis of a change in available bandwidth (as outlined in the introduction and specified in figure 4). The definition of the MPEG component, which derives from *decoder* which in turn derives from *OSIComp*, is as follows:

```
Component Type decoder:OSIComp = new OSIComp extended with
{};
Component MPEG-dec: decoder = new decoder extended with {
  ProvidedPort transportProtocol:downTo = {
    Property protocol:string="tcp";
    Invariant
      Forall p in self.ProvidedPorts
                    p.protocol = transportProtocol
  };
  Property layer = 'application';
  Property decoder-type="MPEG";
};
```

(Note the invariant that requires that the component can only be connected to a transport protocol.) The programmed reconfiguration is specified in the below definition of the complete system.

```
System OSIStack : PlastikMF {

Component MPEG-dec:OSIComp; // Application Level
Component Transport:OSIComp;
Component Network:OSIComp;
Component Link:OSIComp;

Connector AppToTrans: conn2Layers;
Connector TransToNet: conn2Layers;
Connector NetToPhys: conn2Layers;

Attachments{
      //connecting the Application to Transport layer
      Application.dataTo to AppToTrans.source;
      Transport.dataFrom to AppToTrans.sink;

      //connecting the Transport to Network layer
      Transport.dataTo to TransToNet.source;
      TransToNet.sink to dynamic Network.dataFrom;

      //connecting the Network to Physical layer
      dynamic Network.dataTo to NetToPhys.source;
      Link.dataFrom to OuterApplication;
};
On (Link.net_bandwidth = low) do
{
      detach MPEG-dec.downTo to AppToTrans.source;
      remove MPEG-dec;
      Component H263-dec : decoder = new decoder extended with
      {
          Property decoder-type = "H263";
      };
      Attachments
              H263-dec.downTo to AppToTrans.source;
};
};
```

The key part of this is the *On-do* statement, the predicate of which includes a *Link.net_bandwidth* property. This is a property of the link layer component and, as outlined in section 3.2.3, is realised at the runtime level as a dynamic 'property operation'. Depending on its value, this property will trigger a programmed reconfiguration that replaces the MPEG-decoder component with an H.263-decoder component.

4.2 Ad-Hoc Reconfiguration

As mentioned, ad-hoc reconfiguration can be initiated from either the ADL level or the runtime level.

As an example of ad-hoc reconfiguration at the ADL level consider changing the Transport component's BufferManager with a larger BigBufferManager. The change script to achieve this is as follows:

```
//inserting new Component BigBufferManager
Component BigBufferManager{
  ProvidedPort pp;
  RequiredPort rp;
      ...
};

detach BufferManager.pp to transtobuf.pr;
remove BufferManager;

Component bbm: BigBufferManager = new BigBufferManager;
Attachments{
      BigBufferManager.pp to transtobuf.pr;
};
```

The script detaches and removes the old component, and then creates and attaches an instance of the new component.

As an example of reconfiguration at the runtime level consider inserting a logging component between the Network and the Link layers. This could be implemented using the OpenCOM meta-models [7] as follows.

```
Component_instance loggingI;
Loaded_component logging; //new component to be loaded

logging = load(comp_type_logging);
loggingI = instantiate(logging);
//use the Architecture meta-model to inspect and insert the
Logging component

if(ArchMM.connected(Network-comp, Link-comp))
{
      ArchMM.unbind(Network-comp,Link-comp);
      ArchMM.bind(NEWBINDER,Network-comp,loggingI);
      ArchMM.bind(NEWBINDER,loggingI,Link-comp);
      ArchMM.insert(loggingI,CLSID);
      ArchMM.updateLink(CLSID,Network-Comp);
}
```

This pseudo-C code uses the architecture meta-model to discover the current topology of the system and then uses the OpenCOM's capsule API to insert the logging component. Recall that the calls to the meta-model are 'wrapped' by Plastik so that it can be ensured that they do not break any architectural constraints that were specified at the ADL level.

5 Related Work

Relevant areas of related work are as follows: software architecture, frameworks that support reconfiguration, and component runtime systems.

Software Architecture. Dynamic ACME [15] is an ACME extension that models dynamic architectures. However, it is focused on constraining evolution of specifications rather than providing support for runtime reconfiguration.

ArchWare [16] shares some similarities with Plastik as it implements dynamic change via reflection and reification, and is driven by an ADL with formal support. ArchWare uses *hyper-code*, an active executing graph with a programmable interface, as a representation, for purposes of reflection, of the executing system.. In contrast, Plastik adopts a efficient component runtime as its execution element and focuses on the mapping from an (extended) ADL to this runtime.

Mae (Managing Architectural Evolution) [17] is an architectural evolution environment that uses xADL to specify architectures. Its basis for reconfiguration is a versioning mechanism combined with a check-out/check-in approach. A key difference between this work and ours is that Mae supports only programmed reconfiguration (it achieves this by selecting architectural configurations from a 'version space'). It also lacks a formal approach with which to impose constraints to ensure consistency upon reconfiguration..

Frameworks that Support Reconfiguration. [18] focuses on evolution guided by the idea that architectures must react to events and perform architectural changes autonomously. 'Agents' receive external events, monitor the global architecture, and capture and manage changes in the architecture. Each agent maintains a knowledge base with information about the architecture and rules for programmed reconfiguration. The 'B' formalism is used to specify the architectural representation and constraints. This work has some similarities with Plastik in the sense they both use ADL and formal methods as a basis for implementing reconfiguration. Unlike Plastik, however, this work does not use reflection to implement dynamic reconfiguration and ad-hoc reconfiguration is restricted because it is based on a-priori defined rules.

FORMAware [19] is a reflective component-based framework that combines explicit architectural description and meta-information to constrain reconfiguration. To avoid inconsistency it checks architectural constraints according to style rules that restrict the types of architecture elements and possible configurations. A transaction service manages the reconfiguration. A fundamental difference between our work and FORMAware is that our proposal includes statements to improve ADL expressiveness for defining ad-hoc and programmed dynamic reconfiguration. In addition, unlike FORMAware, we adopt a formal approach to set constraints and ensure consistency upon reconfiguration.

Jadda (Java Adaptive component for Dynamic Distributed Architecture) [20] is another framework that relies on architecture specification to support dynamic reconfiguration. It uses xADL and again no formal support is provided for constraining dynamic reconfiguration. Jadda's support for ad-hoc reconfiguration is accomplished via a console that is used to submit a xADL file with the change specification. Although it handles dynamic architectural changes, Jadda is limited to ad-hoc reconfiguration with no formal support. Thus, it does not guarantee consistency.

Component Runtime Systems. Fractal is a hierarchically-structured component model [5] that provides reflective features to support dynamic architectural reconfiguration. It uses an XML-based ADL to specify the high level structure of an application. Although this work resembles our proposal in outline it does not support ad-hoc reconfiguration nor define expressive constructs at the ADL level to describe reconfiguration possibilities. In addition, the ADL has no formal support to ensure consistency. Moreover, the relationship between the architecture level and the component runtime is not clearly specified in the literature.

Finally, Koala [21] is a component model that uses an ADL based on Darwin to manage the complexity of software in electronics products. However, dynamic reconfiguration is restricted to switching between components based on statically defined conditions. Moreover, changes in component structure need administrator approval.

6 Conclusions

We have proposed a meta-framework that relies on a style-based ADL associated with a formal approach to describe the architecture and behavior of systems. It directly supports programmed reconfiguration and also provides invariants that constrain ad-hoc reconfiguration. The ADL level is supported by a flexible configurable component runtime which grounds the ADL level in a viable implementation environment. The paper focuses on extensions to ACME/Armani that express both programmed and ad-hoc reconfiguration. It also outlines the mapping from the ADL description to the OpenCOM component runtime entities and shows how ad-hoc changes can be initiated from either the ADL or the runtime level.

Currently, we are using the AcmeLIB tools to implement the compiler and runtime FSM engines discussed in section 3. At the time of writing we do not have a fully implemented system but rather have successfully trialed key aspects of the design.

Planned future work includes investigating further the issue of causality between changes made at the different architectural levels (see section 3.3), and carrying out experiments with more realistic application scenarios.

References

1. Shaw, M. and Garlan, D.: Software Architecture: Perspectives on an Emerging Discipline, Prentice Hall, (1996)
2. Allen, R. J. and Douence, R. and Garlan, D.: Specifying and Analyzing Dynamic Software Architecture In: Proceedings of the 1998 Conference on Fundamental Approaches to Software Engineering (FASE'98). March (1998).
3. van der Hoek, A., Heimbigner, D., Wolf, A.: Software Architecture, Configuration Management, and Configurable Distributed Systems: A Ménage a Trois. Technical Report CU-CS-849-98, University of Colorado, (1998).
4. Fassino, J., Stefani, J-B., Lawall, J. and Muller, G.: THINK: A Software Framework for Component-based Operating Systems Kernels. In USENIX'02, pages 73-86, Monterey, CA, USA, (2002).

5. Bruneton, E., Coupaye, T., Stefani, J-B.: Recursive and Dynamic Software Composition with Sharing. Seventh International Workshop on Component-Oriented Programming (WCOP02), Malaga, Spain, (2002).
6. Zachariadis, S., Mascolo, C., Emmerich, W.: Satin: A Component Model for Mobile Self Organisation. Distributed Objects and Applications (DOA), pages 1303-1321, (2004).
7. Coulson, G., Blair, G.S., Grace, P., Joolia, A., Lee, K., Ueyama, J.: OpenCOM v2: A Component Model for Building Systems Software, Proceedings of IASTED Software Engineering and Applications (SEA'04), Cambridge, MA, ESA, Nov (2004).
8. Yau, S., Karin. F.: An Adaptive Middleware for Context-Sensitive Communications for Real-Time Applications in Ubiquitous Computing Environments. Real-Time Systems, 26(1):29-61, January (2004)
9. Garlan, D. and Monroe, R. and Wile, D.: ACME: Architectural Description of Component-based Systems. Foundations of Component-based Systems. Leavens, G. T., and Sitaraman, M. (eds). Cambridge University Press, pp. 47-68, (2000).
10. Monroe, R. T.: Capturing Software Architecture Design Expertise with Armani. Technical Report CMU-CS-98-163, Carnegie Mellon University.
11. Coulson, G., Blair, G.S., Hutchison, D., Joolia, A., Lee, K., Ueyama, J., Gomes, A.T., Ye, Y.: NETKIT: A Software Component-Based Approach to Programmable Networking, *ACM SIGCOMM Computer Communications Review (CCR)*, Vol 33, No 5, pp 55-66, October (2003).
12. Coulson, G., Blair, G.S., Clarke, M., Parlavantzas, N.: The Design of a Highly Configurable and Reconfigurable Middleware Platform, ACM Distributed Computing Journal, Vol 15, No 2, pp 109-126, April (2002).
13. Ierusalimsky, R., Figueiredo, L. H., and Celes, W.: Lua – an extensible extension language. Software: Practice and Experience, 26(6):635-652, (1996).
14. Magee, J., Dulay, N., Eisenbach, S. and Kramer, J.: Specifying Distributed Software Architectures. In *Proceedings of 5th European Software Engineering Conference (ESEC 95)*, Sitges, Spain, pp. 137-153, September (1995).
15. Wile, D.: Using Dynamic Acme. In: Proceedings of a Working Conference on Complex and Dynamic Systems Architecture, Brisbane, Australia, December, (2001).
16. Morrison, R. et al.: Support for Evolving Software Architectures in the ArchWare ADL. In: *Proc. 4th Working IEEE/IFIP Conference on Software Architecture (WICSA), Oslo, Norway*. 2004.
17. Roshandel, R., van der Hoek, A., Mikic-Rakic, M. and Medvidovic, N.: Mae – A System Model and Environment for Managing Architectural Evolution. ACM Transactions on Software Engineering and Methodology (TOSEM), 3 (2):240-276, (2004).
18. Ramdane-Cherif, A. and Levy, N.: An Approach for Dynamic Reconfigurable Software Architectures. Integrated Design and Process Technology, IDPT-2002, June (2002).
19. Moreira, R., Blair, G., Carrapatoso, E.: FORMAware: Framework of Reflective Components for Managing Architecture Adaptation, 3rd. Int. Symposium DOA, Roma, 2001.
20. Falcarin, P. and Alonso, G.: Software Architecture Evolution through Dynamic AOP. European Workshop on Software Architecture (EWSA 2004), pp. 57-73, St. Andrews, UK, May (2004).
21. Ommering, R., Linden, F., Kramer, J. and Magee, J.: The Koala Component Model for Consumer Electronics Software. IEEE Computer, 33(3):78–85, March (2000).
22. ACME Home page, http://www-2.cs.cmu.edu/~acme/acme_downloads.html, (2005).

Architecting Global Automation Systems over a Distributed Multi-agent Infrastructure

Franco Guidi-Polanco[1], Claudio Cubillos[2], and Giuseppe Menga[2]

[1] Esc. de Ingeniería Industrial - Pontificia Universidad Católica de Valparaíso,
Av. Brasil 2241, Valparaíso, Chile
franco.guidi@ucv.cl
[2] Dip. Automatica e Informatica - Politecnico di Torino, Italy
C.so Duca degli Abruzzi 2241, Torino, Italy
{claudio.cubillos, menga}@polito.it

Abstract. In this work we present an agent-based architecture for Global Automation Systems. The architecture follows a layered abstract model that allows decoupling design responsibilities, promotes high cohesion within layers and clearly emphasizes the environment. A case of study is presented in the passenger transportation domain.

1 Introduction

In the era of Computer Integrated Manufacturing (CIM), an automation system was conceived as a strong and rigid hierarchy of control layers: Facility, Shop, Cell, Workstation, and Equipment. According to the USA-NBS CIM reference model [1], each layer is populated with a set of control modules (the device controller, the workcell controller, the cell controller, etc.) with precise responsibilities. In particular, a higher layer control module coordinates the control modules below it, and the flexibility of such systems is limited to the possibility of reconfiguring the production process off-line by re-programming each control module. A local area network or a hard-wired field-bus represents the communication medium between the different factories' sub-systems. The inter-factory communication is usually handled via telephone, fax, or e-mail. An example of this old style architecture is described in our past research [4].

In the era of the Internet, "global automation" is a new concept that transfers and extends classical process control and factory automation ideas to geographically distributed environments. It is supported by the current trends and technologies in the fields of information and telecommunication, in particular, embedding the Internet [7] in data acquisition and control devices. Global automation systems are conceived as flat interconnections of autonomous and decentralized decision making/control modules dominated by the two concepts of "heterarchy" and "proactivity": the former means that no hierarchy in decision making is enforced, the latter that each partner takes the initiative to reach a decision, and the global behavior of the system becomes an "emerging behavior" [3]. Control modules have decision-making capabilities and coordinate their activities by exchanging data and events according to a peer

R. Morrison and F. Oquendo (Eds.): EWSA 2005, LNCS 3527, pp. 18–29, 2005.

architectural model and common protocols. They can represent, for instance, autonomous mobile robotic systems, factory cell controllers, or on-board monitoring systems in transport vehicles.

Building global automation systems naturally poses new requirements and challenges in design. It means defining a new architectural model that is sufficiently flexible to be used at multiple levels of a global automation system, from the interfactory logistics of geographically distributed enterprises, to the coordination of production in a factory, down to monitoring and controlling production shops or coordination autonomous mobile robots inside a factory.

This work presents our framework for building global automation systems. This framework has been expressed as a reusable architecture made up by layers with specific design responsibilities.

The rest of the paper is structured as follows: Section 2 presents the related work. Section 3 describes our abstract architecture for multi-agent organizations. Section 4 introduces the agent platform we have developed for building multi-agent software. Section 5 describes the agent-based architecture for implementing global automation systems. Section 6 tackle the passenger transportation system as a concrete case of study. Finally, on section 7 some conclusions are drawn.

2 Related Work

The early literature offers several examples of multi-agent architectures and organizations created for domain-specific applications. These architectures focus in the identification of agent's roles and responsibilities, and the description of their interactions and communication mechanisms. As expected, due to their ad-hoc nature, they are hardly reusable outside their original domains.

As opposite to the former approach, the recent holonic paradigm [9] offers a organizational model highly reusable, which can be applied at diverse abstraction levels and replicable in different domains. However, it is just a conceptual model that does not specify what services can be required and reused when implementing such a system.

In terms of structure and services, the development of generic agent platforms (e.g. Jade [2], Zeus [10], etc.) presents concrete architectures with high degree of reusability, but made-up by low-granularity components (commonly, basic communication and directory services), that implement commonly agreed abstract models (e.g. FIPA). However, adopting them for the implementation of agent-based systems requires the development of new domain-specific agents.

In order to improve the design reuse, recent studies establish the convenience in identifying and separating domain-specific aspects from those generic aspects that are common in families of systems. One example is the orientation followed by Sims et al. [12], that proposes the reuse of organizational coordination mechanisms across different problem domains and environmental situations. Nevertheless, their work just emphasizes organization and distribution of tasks and goals, while the system's structure is not deeply treated.

On the other hand, even if the environment is an essential part in agent system's structure, in practice agent architectures fail to adequately identify and consider its role. As indicated in [13], popular frameworks minimize the environment reducing it just to a message transport system or to a brokering infrastructure.

Our approach innovates introducing a layered model, that identifies and classifies system's components and services with different granularities. Those components and services that share similar levels of reuse from both, the structural and the organizational point of view, are grouped together. The model is built recognizing at its basis the physical environment, which is virtualized in superior levels, making explicit the way in which agents will interact with it. As consequence, a new agent platform, aimed to fulfill specific requirements in global automation systems (communication, scalability, QoS metrics, access to the physical world, etc.) was developed. Over this platform a reusable set of services are implemented.

3 An Abstract Architecture for MAS

In general terms we envision the use of agents as a way of representing software architectures. This vision is constructed as the abstract model depicted in Figure 1. This model has three main characteristics:

- *Decouples design responsibilities*: the model presents the different aspects related to a multi-agent architecture in a separated way. Therefore, the design responsibilities can be clearly identified and assigned to different development projects or teams.
- *Promotes high cohesion within each layer*: components within each layer are closely related from the functional and communicational point of view, in such a way that their interactions are optimized.
- *Clearly emphasizes the environment*: traditional agent architectures consider the environment implicitly, in most cases just as a mere communication supplier. This model puts in evidence the complete environment, that is the physical and the virtual one.

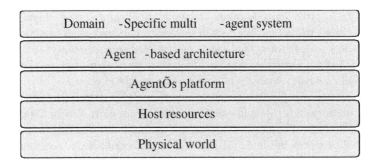

Fig. 1. The Abstract Architecture for MAS

The abstract model is composed by the following layers:

- *Domain-specific multi agent system (DSMAS)*: corresponds to a concrete instance of a multi-agent system, where domain-dependent agents are designed and interactions among them are well defined. In most cases agents at this level of abstraction are virtualizations of real entities pertaining to the application domain. DSMAS architectures can be reused within the scope of the context they were created for. A reusable DSMAS architecture constitutes an agent-based framework for the development of systems within its domain. DSMAS architectures are supported by the services offered by the agent-based architecture.
- *Agent-based architecture (ABA)*: represent a reusable architecture to support the development of different kind of DSMAS. An example of ABA is the FIPA architecture [7], which establishes common services and functionalities that FIPA-compliant agent systems must agree (e.g. the directory facilitator, ACL messages, etc.). This layer of the abstraction infrastructure is conceived to obtain interoperability between different and generic agent systems. The services offered at the ABA can be implemented as agent-based service (such as a yellow pages agent), or environment-dependent service (e.g access to some kind of physical device). The ABA for global automation systems is described in Section 5.
- *Agent platform (AP)*: corresponds to the software that offers the base classes to build agents, and to virtualize environment-dependent services (such as interfaces to measurement devices, motors, communication, etc.). It also offers the execution environment that controls the entire agent's life-cycle, and regulates its interactions with other agents, and other resources. In the case of global automation systems the G++ Agent platform (described in Section 4) is adopted at this level.
- *Host resources*: represents the computing environment, in terms of CPU, memory, data storage, data communication, operating system, connected devices (such as thermometers, valves, engines, etc.). Examples of common environments are desktop computers, vehicles' on-board units, and mobile robots.
- *Physical* world: represents objects and concepts that are present or that can be observed in the real world.

4   The G++ Agent Platform

The G++ Agent platform is a Java framework for the development of agent-based systems, focusing in architectural aspects related to components distribution and communication. The structure of this agent platform follows the abstract architecture of section 3, and can be appreciated in Figure 2.

It is important to notice that the G++ Agent Platform is a low-level agent infrastructure not committed to any standard agent architecture, e.g. FIPA, even if compatibility with standard specifications can be obtained. The FIPA standards represent the most complete specification (followed by the major producers of general-purpose platforms); however, it is oriented to achieve interoperation among agents, which is just one of the requirements of a global automation system. It does not suit very well facing other requirements, in particular related to security,

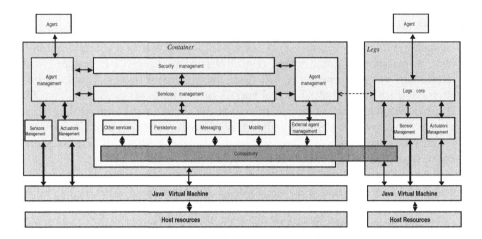

Fig. 2. The G++ platform's layered model

connectivity, and scalability when managing large-volume of communications (e.g. which in FIPA are delegated to single agents).

The layers are the following:

a) Host resources: the underlying layer is given by the host-dependent resources where the platform is in execution (such as network connectivity, resources of file system, etc.). The model does not make any special assumption about the characteristics of this layer other than be able to execute a Java virtual machine.

b) Java Virtual Machine (JVM): the second layer corresponds to the JVM, which is a runtime environment that offers independence of the programming language from the hosting machine. The JVM allows portability of the code of the platform among different hosts.

c) Agent's execution environment: the layer immediately above corresponds to the execution environment for agents. This layer is responsible for controlling the agents' lifecycle, and for offering the services that they require for their own activity (security, communication, mobility, data persistence, etc.).

d) Agents: agents are located in the model's top layer. They are autonomous components that manage their own thread of control, being capable to communicate between well-known interfaces, exchanging predefined data structures. Agents can exhibit reactive and a proactive behavior, accordingly with their assigned functionalities.

The platform also provides an API to interface non agent-based applications within the system. Such an API is available in Java and in C++.

4.1   Execution Environment Implementation

The execution environment of the G++ agent platform provides connectivity services, being responsible for the interactions among all agents. It is also responsible for the virtualization of the interactions among agents and the physical environment, through the implementation of sensors and actuators objects that agents can access. The platform offers two kinds of execution environment implementations, which are the Container and the Legs module as it is shown in Figure 2.

a) Container

It is the environment for the execution of contained agents. A container runs over a Java Runtime Environment, which allows the access to the resources offered by the host. The container offers to the contained agents common services such as messaging transport, local event communication, and support for access to external data repositories. Containers implement connectivity services among them for message interchange, and for agent and services migration. They also provide connectivity and state monitoring of external agents, and they instantiate proxies to make transparent the communication between external and internal agents. Message transport and event communication among containers are directed using routing tables managed by each container, accordingly with the topology of their network. These routing tables can be defined statically, or modified dynamically by certain agents.

b) Legs module

The platform can integrate agents running outside the container. These agents are called *external* agents or *stand-alone* agents.

The execution of external agents is allowed by Legs (Local External aGent Support) modules, which are limited execution environments able to host and execute one agent at time. They provide connectivity to a container, and then, to the entire platform. As contained agents, external agents can access all the services provided by the underlying JVM, and some of the communication services offered by the container, but they cannot access other services, such as the agent mobility. External agents can be useful, for example, for the implementation of control systems running on-board of mobile devices (e.g. mobile robots).

The implementation of external agents follows the same structure given for the implementation of contained agents. In fact, if a contained agent does not use resources restricted to contained agents, or host special resources, it can be transformed in an external agent just launching it from a LEGS module.

4.2   The Communication Infrastructure

Since early stages of the design, this agent platform has been envisioned as the cornerstone of the distributed architecture for global automation systems. In particular, under our conception this environment not only corresponds to the space where agents can perform their duties (as in all platforms), it is also aimed to provide a reliable communication infrastructure that agents can (and should) exploit to interact among themselves in a distributed application. As result, the G++ Agent Platform is able to offer an implementation of a global automation system that will delegate to the own agent's container the conduction of the major traffic.

The network of containers is the backbone infrastructure for message exchange in a global automation system, where communication among agents can be performed without awareness of the communicating parties' location. To achieve this, containers implement routing tables that define the path used to reach other containers, whose content is defined statically. As a restriction, in the current definition the platform is able to manage only acyclic network of containers.

In our platform, inter-container messaging is a regular service offered to agents. In this way, when an agent wants to send a message to another, the sender asks the container to use the *message transport service* to deliver the *message*, using the parameters indicated in the request.

The platform provides an agent-to-agent message exchange service. In such a service, the sender knows the name of the message's receiver, and the message is directly routed according to this information. It is an asynchronous communication mechanism in which a certain informative content is communicated from a source to a well-defined agent.

4.3 Global Time

The platform is not able to guarantee the exact sequence of messages delivered to a receiver, due to that the inter-container protocol does not provide such guarantee. In fact, the platform delivers messages following the best effort policy, that is, no unnecessary delays are introduced in their expedition. However, messages can arrive in wrong order due to two main reasons: 1) the latency of the Internet, plus costs incurred in retransmissions of packets naturally tends to increase the time required to transmit a message over long distances, and 2) the interconnections between containers define the paths that messages have to follow from the source to the target, each node acting as a router. The processing time on each container has to be added to the network delays described above.

However, the platform can guarantee the delivery of messages, detecting and informing the sender when they are not delivered within the pre-established time. A time window and a timestamp message field are used in the message for this scope. The time window value can also be infinite, which means no time window is specified. The message timestamp can also be useful to the message receiver, to determine the exact sequence of messages.

The timestamp is a key data to support the quality of the messaging service, but its generation is not easy because requires the adoption of a global time, shared among containers.

5 The Agent-Based Architecture for Global Automation Systems

In this section is described the agent-based software architecture for Global Automation Systems. The architecture follows the abstract model described in Section 3. It provides a set of agent-based meta-services to support advanced communication of the domain-specific systems built on top of it.

This framework is sufficiently flexible to be used at multiple levels, from the monitoring and control system for a single production cell (the virtual SCADA), to the supply chain integration of a multi-national corporation (the virtual factory), up to the construction of a global virtual organization.

Conceptually GAP is similar to the open platforms in the network operating systems, but it has other scopes, contents and different goals. It is designed to addresses four main aspects related to (1) the innovative adoption of Internet in automation systems, (2) the logical structure of enterprise information systems; (3) the virtual interconnection of manufacturing centers; and (4) the seamless integration of wireless technologies.

5.1 The GAP Services

This agent-based architecture introduces a communication standard and a set of services to build global automation systems in different domains. The former defines the languages that will be used for exchange of information between entities participating in global automation systems. The latter, the set of services that are available for supporting their activity. Three services are offered at this level:

a) *Messaging*: it provides persistence and reliability in direct messaging between senders and well-defined receivers. It is based on based on persistent messages queues, which allows time-decoupled communications among participants

b) *Event distribution*: it implements the asynchronous publish/subscribe communication model. Each container provides local event publication and notification services. The architecture for global automation systems includes agents for the management of distributed subscriptions and notifications (that is, among different service points).

c) *Service brokering*: it supports dynamic reconfiguration of the relationships between service providers and consumers. Each container provides local event publication and notification services. The architecture for global automation systems includes agents for the management of distributed subscriptions and notifications (that is, among different service points).

The design of the GAP services has explicitly considered the problem of distribution, particularly the unreliability of network connections, which makes indistinguishable crashed components from slow components. This problem, common to all implemented GAP services, was addresses through a mechanism of registration and renewal of the registration with the service provider, that interested users must perform during their lifecycle (this approach is similar to the "leasing" in the Jini technology [6].

The topology of the distributed system also requires being addressed at this level, because it defines the management of the relationship among the network. In our implementation, we suppose an acyclic peer-to-peer architecture of containers. This architecture allows bi-directional communication between containers, and it can be represented by an undirected graph. We have adopted this model because no hierarchy of responsibility is enforced, and because is simpler to manage than more general peer-to-peer architecture. In the other hand, a general peer-to-peer model can be traduced into an acyclic one eliminating the possible existence of multiple paths between containers. The selected architecture is less robust than the general acyclic architecture, but it was considered adequate for our initial laboratory tests.

6   Case of Study: A Passenger Transportation Planning System

In the following, the passenger transportation concept is explained for then detailing the concrete MAS for this specific domain.

Changes in transport requirements in European citizens have brought the opportunity to create new services aimed to fulfill special transportation demand, in addition to regular population mobility services. Those systems are known as demand-responsive transport (DRT) services, and their objective is to satisfy personal transportation requests at relatively low costs, thanks to an integrated planification in the use of the different available resources on transport networks. Traditional approaches in DRT service planning are focused on an isolated view of the whole system, in which categories of services are well defined, and separated solutions are provided for each category (e.g. advance request, immediate request, etc.) [11]. These systems are usually implemented as heuristic procedures that extend basics graph search algorithms, acting over large collections of data that describe the entities of the problem domain (vehicles, service requests, schedules). An example can be found in the research with the *Advanced Dial-A-Ride with Time Windows* (ADARTW) algorithm described in [5].

In this work is defined the system architecture that can be used for the implementation of DRT services for a single operator that manages a heterogeneous fleet (e.g. composed by busses, minivans, vehicles for disabled people, etc.), without enforcing the division of the service in predefined categories. In the model, the operator receives service requirements coming from clients (pick-up place and time, delivery place and time, etc.), through a Web interface provided by an interface agent or directly by an external client agent. The model processes the requirement by interacting with internal agents that represent different vehicles of the fleet, to finally propose a feasible trip solution. The architecture considers the integration of a broker agent, responsible for the dynamic registration of new vehicle profiles. This agent, together with the definition of a shared ontology for describing services, makes it possible to manage a variable set of services that can be supplied along the time. As result is obtained a scalable and flexible architecture, able to support interoperability without loosing neither performance nor quality of the solutions, and with easy integration of Web resources. In this case is proposed the application of a distributed version of the ADARTW algorithm to perform service planning in DRT services. It takes into consideration a global utility function for the fleet operator, and specific utility functions for each single vehicle and customer.

6.1   The DRT System

The DRT system that is being treated consists of transport requests coming from a set of clients, which should be satisfied by the vehicle fleet pertaining to a single operator. Vehicles are characterized by different *properties*, but in general they have a limited capacity, periods of time during the day in which they are available, and area of geographic coverage. Transport requests commonly specify a pick-up and delivery place and time, and can include other descriptions, e.g. wheel-chair places, number of

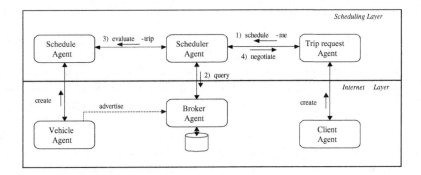

Fig. 3. The general architecture of the DRT system

seats, shared or exclusive use of the vehicle, etc. Properties required by clients can be classified in *constraint-properties*, i.e. characteristics that the service must ensure in order to be accepted, and *weighted-properties*, i.e. not mandatory characteristics having a positive contribution in the utility function of the client.

Facing each request, the operator has to solve an assignment and scheduling problem, according to his objective function that evaluates the global utility and the service level given to his clients (an estimation of their utility function). As response the operator should return to the client a (possible not empty) set of feasible alternatives with relative costs that fit the constraint-properties and hold a high-level value for the weighted-properties. From this set, the client should select the better option in function of his own interests, or reject all the solutions and ask for a counterproposal.

Earlier planning methodologies developed for DRT systems adopted *centralized* approaches, where the control and decision-making was done by only one entity that maximizes the global utility of the whole system (i.e. the utility for the operator and for his clients). In general, these approaches are able to produce better solutions if good estimators of the client utility can be identified, which is not always feasible (not all the clients share the same desires, nor appreciate them with the same importance). Recent *decentralized* or *market-based* approaches, in the other hand, exploit cooperative relationships in communities of agents that perform low-level planning, scheduling, execution, and control tasks, and where negotiation processes among them (e.g. contract-net, auctions, bargain, etc.) tend to maximize the utility of individual agents, leading to Pareto-optimal solutions. As opposite to centralized evaluations, optimization is done with less information and, as consequence, the solution could be far from the best for the whole system.

In this implementation has been adopted a *mixed* approach, where a global optimization is done from the operator's point of view, and a negotiation process is carried out between the clients and the operator, by means of ranked alternatives. In this case the operator tries to maximize the same objective that a centralized approach, but considering a service level evaluation personalized for each client. This allows producing a set of solutions closer to real client desires.

6.2 The Transportation Agents

We have grouped these specific agents in two layers. The *Internet layer* is in charge of the communication with the external world (vehicles, clients, other systems). In the other hand, the Scheduling layer encapsulates the scheduling and assignment services.

In this work we have adapted the ADARTW algorithm to a multi-agent collaborative execution, delegating algorithm's tasks to different agents. The main agents we identify are shown in Figure 4, and its roles are described as follows.

The *Internet layer* of the architecture consists of: 1) *Vehicle* agents, that wrap real world transportation vehicles; 2) the *Broker* agent, that register available vehicles and its profiles; and 3) *Client* agents, that interfaces users with the system.

Each Vehicle agent holds its own properties that define the kind of transport service offered, and its utility function. The *Broker* receives advertisement messages from Vehicles, describing their service characteristics, and registers them in its internal database.

Clients agents are in charge of capturing the final user's requirements and translating them into a suitable specification according to a specific ontology that we call *Service ontology*. Client agents should ask the corresponding human user for the constraint and weighted-properties of the desired service together with the preferences and level of importance given to each one. Client agents can also be developed externally to the platform but, independently of its origin, they act as factories of the Trip-Request agents.

The *Scheduling layer* of the architecture provides three kinds of agents that interact directly in the evaluation and creation of the routing plan: 1) *Schedule* agents, representing route plans of single vehicles, 2) *Trip-Request* agents, modeling single client request specifications, and 3) the *Scheduler* agent, implementing the assignment and scheduling policy.

Schedule Agents are created by Vehicle agents when they advertise their availability to the Broker. Trip-Request agents, instead, are created by Clients agents every time a new service request has to be included in the system. The Trip-request agent performs a *schedule-me* request to the Scheduler agent, sending his service specification (constraint/utility-properties). With that information the Scheduler performs a query to the Broker, asking for all the vehicles that match the constraint-properties indicated in the request. Afterwards the Broker returns a list of vehicles that fulfill the received profile and then the Scheduler performs an *evaluate-trip* request to each Schedule agent that corresponds to a vehicle in the list. In the evaluate-trip requests are sent the utility-properties specified by the Client through the Trip-Request.

Each Schedule agent evaluates the insertion of a trip request (that means, the client) in his route, according to the weighted-properties received and his own ones. The Schedule agent returns to the Scheduler the trip's feasibility and utility value, considering both client and vehicle utilities.

Once the Scheduler has collected all the answers from the Schedule agents, it drops the solutions that not fulfill its policies of global utility (e.g. minimize total number of vehicles), and sends the remaining ones to the Trip-Request agent for its selection.

Depending on the level of autonomy of the Trip-Request agent, it can select according to the preferences specified by the client or can contact him to make the final selection.

The multi-agent architecture allows the planning process execution in a heterogeneous network of computer systems. Flexibility is given in this architecture by the possibility of dynamically adding new typologies of services and requests according to our *service specification ontology*, which is used to describe the transport services.

7 Conclusions

In this work we have described the agent architecture that follows an abstract model for the implementation of MAS. Its design was driven by the interest to obtain a decoupled and scalable system that supports the integration of agents with their environment. This is a differentiating point when comparing it with other architectures whose functionalities are more focused in distributed artificial intelligence or in agent mobility.

The architecture was applied to a case of study in the passenger transportation domain, where the specific agents were identified for a distributed planification of trip requests.

References

1. Mclean C. et al.: "A Computer Architecture for Small-Batch Manufacturing". *IEEE Spectrum,* vol. 20, n. 5 (1983)
2. Bellifemmine F. et al.: "Jade, A FIPA-compliant Agent Framework. 4th Int. Conference on Practical Application of Intelligent Agents and Multi-Agent Technology (1999)
3. Brugali D., Menga G.: "Architectural Models for Global Automation Systems". IEEE Transactions on Robotics and Automation, vol. 18, n. 4 (2002)
4. Brugali D., Menga G., and Aarsten A.: "A Case Study for Flexible Manufacturing System". *Domain-Specific Application Frameworks.* John Wiley & Co. (1999)
5. Cubillos C. et al.: "On user requirements and operator purposes in Dial-a-Ride services". *Proceedings of the 9th Meeting of the EURO Working Group on Transportation* (2002)
6. Edwards W.K.: "Core Jini". *Prentice-Hall, Inc.* Upper Saddle River, New Jersey (2001)
7. Estrin D.E. et al. "Embedding the Internet" Communications of the ACM, vol. 43 n. 5 (2000)
8. Foundation of Intelligent Physical Agents (FIPA). FIPA Abstract Architecture Specification 2002. Available at http://www.fipa.org/, last visited: January/2004
9. Koestler A.: The Ghost in the Machine. Arkana Books, London 1989
10. Nwana S. et al.: Zeus: A toolkit for Building Distributed Multi-Agent Systems. 3rd Int. Conference on Autonomous Agents, Seattle (1999)
11. Psaraftis N.H.: "Dynamic vehicle routing: Status and prospects". *Annals of Operation Research.* No 61 (1995), pp. 143-164
12. Sims M. et al.: Separating Domain and Coordination in Multi-Agent Organizational Design and Instantiation. Proc. Int. Conf. on Intelligent Agent Technology, Beijing, China (2004)
13. Weyns et al.: Environments for Multiagent Systems: State-of-the-Art and Research Challenges. Lecture Notes in Artificial Intelligence volume 3374 (2005)

The ArchWare Tower: The Implementation of an Active Software Engineering Environment Using a π-Calculus Based Architecture Description Language

Brian Warboys[1], Mark Greenwood[1], Ian Robertson[1], Ron Morrison[2],
Dharini Balasubramaniam[2], Graham Kirby[2], and Kath Mickan[2]

[1] School of Computer Science, The University of Manchester,
Manchester, M13 9PL, UK
{brian, markg, robertsi}@cs.man.ac.uk
[2] School of Computer Science, The University of St Andrews,
St Andrews, Fife, KY16 9SX, UK
{ron, dharini, graham, kath}@dcs.st-and.ac.uk

Abstract. This paper outlines our experience of using a reflective π-calculus based Architecture Description Language (ADL) to create an 'Active' Software Engineering Environment (SEE). It describes the concept of an 'Active' SEE developed as part of the, EU supported, project ArchWare. It analyses a small fragment of that implementation to illustrate the suitability, of the ADL language and environment, for the task of implementing such 'Active' systems.

1 Introduction

We define a Software Engineering Environment (SEE) as a software environment tailored to the production of software systems. We define an 'active' SEE as an SEE where a user (typically a Software Developer) can redefine, with immediate effect, any software engineering process supported by that environment and to which the appropriate change permissions have been given. In order for this to be possible, an 'active' SEE contains a definition of the environment's software processes as an 'active' model.

We define an active model [1] as being a model in which the specification and the execution of that model remain in lock-step with each other. In other words changes to either the specification or the actual execution are reflected in the other.

The advantages of building such an 'active' SEE are that the various steps, or phases, used in the development of a software artifact, can be evolved to suit the contexts which apply following any previous step(s). In particular we note that the development of large software systems requires complex engineering processes that are often tactical and cannot be completely preplanned at the start of a project. For example, development of some complex software definition is usually more complex than a series of strict refinement steps. Thus, in an active SEE, refinement steps can be changed to reflect the conditions that apply following some previous step(s). This yields a software process akin to the concept of retrenchment [14] and provides a far more flexible software development process than one that is defined by a, more traditional, strict refinement approach.

R. Morrison and F. Oquendo (Eds.): EWSA 2005, LNCS 3527, pp. 30–40, 2005.

2   The Design of the Active SEE

Given that the objective is to build an SEE in which a software developer remains in control of the various software construction processes, then the design of the SEE needs to constrain such a developer only when it is helpful to do so. The design of the framework for the environment should thus be made as simple and unconstraining as possible. Essentially the requirement is to define an abstract architecture with a set of minimal but extensible capabilities. This notion of starting with an abstract, yet executable, architecture specification and then continually evolving this specification in lock-step with its execution is fundamental to our 'active' model paradigm.

In the case of an SEE, the core idea for such an architecture derives from the, rather obvious, observation that, at every step of a software development process, a developer is creating some artifact. Such an artifact will be used in some subsequent step; typically by a software process tailored to this input. This observation, of course, yields a concise recursive definition of an SEE. An SEE is an environment which yields an artifact, in fact a software or a software related artifact. It consists of a set of steps in which each step yields an artifact. Thus we can consider an SEE as a set of smaller SEEs, each SEE being tailored to producing a specific type of artifact. Thus a specification type SEE yields a specification and so on. In our example active SEE, this set of artifact producing steps is represented as a graph. The nodes of the graph represent SEEs and the arcs the relationships between these SEEs.

We can now set about implementing an instance of this active SEE. In this example the graph of SEEs is implemented as a structure which we term a 'Tower'. It is so called because it consists of a multi-dimensional set of hierarchical graphs. The faces of the 'Tower' represent the different views that might be taken of this SEE.

The 'Tower' is built as a set of Nodes joined by a set of relationships. The relationships represent the derivative process used to develop one Node from another.

Through an analysis of software engineering processes, we identified three types of generic processes that occurred when software related artifacts were manipulated. Thus a step in a software development process could then be classified as being one of these three generic step types. These are:

- A Refine process - develops a more detailed definition of the original component. The child is thus a more concrete refinement of its parent.
- A Partition process - develops a child of the original component. The child is a part explosion of its parent by decomposition.
- A Satisfy process – creates a set of constraints that need to be satisfied by the parent.

Each Node is essentially the reference to an SEE, whose purpose is to produce an artifact referenced from the Node, and also contains references to the software processes available from that Node. These processes are divided into two sets. One set of processes are to support the definition of further Nodes (SEEs) as outlined above and another set are to support the development of the required artifact. The Do process in the Fig. 1 represents the process that will support the development of the relevant artifact.

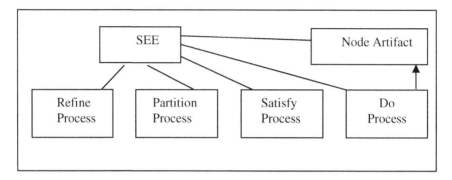

Fig. 1. The Initial Tower NODE

3 Implementation of the SEE

The system was implemented as a contribution to the EU Framework V project ArchWare [4]. ArchWare provides support for a reflective π-calculus based Architecture Definition Language (ADL) [2,15]. It is reflective in the sense that it supports the notion that a running program can generate new fragments and integrate these into its own execution [17]. In order to support dynamic evolution the system also supports the notion of reification; that is the ability of the system to provide a concrete representation of its internal state. It is worth noting that such an ADL also satisfies our requirements for a Process Modelling Language, an important ingredient of an SEE. This is hardly surprising as software architecture and process models are both descriptions of software structures and behaviours. In particular a Process Modelling Language is basically concerned with the specification of behaviours and the possible

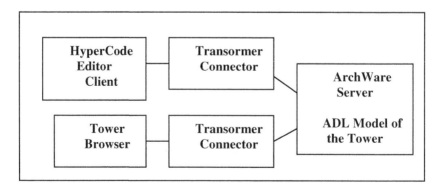

Fig. 2. An Initial ArchWare System

interactions between these behaviours. However, and significantly, since processes in the real world are subject to constant adaptation, it is imperative that this network of behaviours can be dynamically reconfigured. The π-calculus notions of mobility and renaming gives us such capabilities.

The Tower is implemented as an ADL model executing on an ArchWare server. A Tower Browser, for browsing and interacting with the Tower model, and a Hypercode Editor [8], for browsing and editing the ADL, run as clients and are implemented in Java. The clients are each connected to the server via a Transformer/Connector. This network is provided as part of basic pre-configured ArchWare system, allowing the ArchWare system itself to be evolved using this SEE. The arrangement is shown in figure 2.

4 Using the Active SEE

An initial user interface to the Tower is provided by the Tower Browser and a user begins his interaction with the SEE through this Tower Browser. The Tower Browser displays the graph of Nodes available to a specific user and provides the capability to select Nodes. The act of selecting a Node connects the user to the processes, already enacting in the server, available via that Node. A user may thus utilise the Refine, Partition and Satisfy processes that enlarge the Node graph as detailed above.

The user may also communicate with the process that will 'explode' a Node. The explosion results in the display of the internal structure of the Node processes. All Nodes, initially, consist of a software component termed an 'ArchWare Tower Component' and an empty artifact. The Tower Component consists of two processes. Firstly a Produce Process (P) which is responsible for the reproduction of Nodes from that Node and the artifact attached to that Node. Secondly an Evolve Process (E) which is responsible for the 'fitness for purpose' of the associated Produce Process (P). P is installed by E and generates feedback that is processed by E.

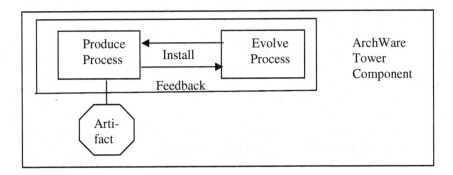

Fig. 3. Initial NODE Showing the ArchWare Tower Component

Further explosion of the Produce Process results in the display of the various processes available i.e Refine, Partition, Satisfy and Do (the process which produces the artifact referenced by the relevant Node). Further explosion of the Evolve Process displays its sub-processes, essentially forming an evolution step. All these processes are themselves ArchWare Tower Components and hence consist of P/E pairs with steps to enact the relevant process (P) and steps to ensure the fitness for purpose of these steps (E). This Evolve process is the means by which the Refine, Partition and Satisfy processes are customised by evolution.

Thus the environment has the capability to extend itself by creating more SEEs (Nodes) and evolving all the processes (Ps) associated with these Nodes. The default action, associated with creating a new Node, is to link the Node to its parent with the appropriate relationship (Refine, Partition, Satisfy) and install the parent processes in the new child i.e the child inherits the process steps of its parent. These process steps can be dynamically evolved using the capabilities of the reflective ADL system.

The initial Partition Process thus produces a new child Node with a Partition relationship to its parent. The initial Refine Process invokes the Hypercode Editor which allows users to browse and edit ADL text presented in the form of Hypercode ADL text. Thus the initial Tower consists of a single Node with these initial processes enacting. The Tower is executing in an persistent reflective environment and then 'evolves' into the required development structure as a software project proceeds. This is a rather interesting example of an architecture that grows as it is used. As noted previously such architectures are the basis for 'active' software systems.

5 Context for the Work

The SEE Tower was first implemented using the ProcessWeb system [5], a system supporting a process language called the Process Management Language (PML). This system was constructed using the persistent language PS-algol [13] from the University of St Andrews. The system has many of the same properties as the new ArchWare system in that it was possible, using the facilities of the PS-algol system, to implement a reflective system allowing for the creation of an 'active' SEE. The PML language is an Object Oriented language with built-in Objects to represent Roles and the Interactions between Roles. Roles are objects with their own single thread of computation and communicate by sending messages through Interactions.

After some 20 years of usage of this language by the IPG at Manchester, it was timely to construct a new system reflecting our experiences of the ProcessWeb system. The new system was constructed as a contribution to the ArchWare project.

ArchWare adopted the same basic architecture as ProcessWeb, since this had worked so well for the last 20 years. However this time, the persistent language was ProcessBase (PBase) [10] a language developed at St Andrews as part of the Compliant System Architecture projects; EPSRC funded collaborations between IPG in Manchester and the Persistent Programming Group at St Andrews [16]. In fact this PBase language was used to implement an early prototype of the Tower environment and this demonstrated that the underlying facilities provided by the PBase Abstract Machine (PBAM) were sufficient to support the implementation strategy.

As a Process Modelling language, the ArchWare ADL language was a clear advance on ProcessWeb PML in two main respects. Firstly the language adopted the semantics of the π-calculus [3] giving formal semantics to the machine, in contrast to PML which had only been defined by its implementation. This ensures that we are able to reason about designs and also have some chance of developing the formal techniques needed to demonstrate the safety of user defined evolutions of such designs. Secondly the notion of Roles and Interactions was replaced by the much finer grain notions of Behaviours and Connections (equivalent to the processes and channels of the π-calculus). Our experience with PML, and in particular the production of a book on Process Modelling [6], defining a development approach based on PML, had shown that the notions of Roles and Interactions, although extremely powerful, were too course grained for many types of models. These notions, as a result of their granularity, also imposed a very strong style on all the process models. In particular we felt the need to be able to define many different types of interactions between objects reflecting the rich array of communication mechanisms that are used in real life process situations. The primitive concepts of Behaviours and Connections allow these to be flexibly modelled. Indeed the PML notions of Roles and Interactions can clearly be constructed using these ADL concepts.

6   The Mechanisms Supporting Evolution in the ArchWare System

The ADL environment supports the notion of HyperCode [8,9]. HyperCode supports incremental change in long-lived systems, where internal system state and data are preserved over the change. This is referred to as dynamic evolution. In contradistinction, static evolution implies no dependency between states of the system before and after the implementation of change.

We construct a simplified example supporting the basic operation of a P/E pair of ADL processes. The example is simplified for the benefit of the user and paper brevity but it illustrates the approach taken to construct the entire Tower, some 4,000 lines of ADL code. This example demonstrates both static and dynamic evolution, two essential properties of 'active' environments. An operational process, a Produce process (P) is instantiated, and the user decides to evolve it using an Evolve process (E). A Hypercode Editor is launched, the user makes the necessary changes, and evaluates the new definition (during this activity the Producer is performing its normal operational functions). A reference to the compiled behaviour is returned to the model where it replaces the previous instance.

The ArchWare environment incorporates two modes of evolution – programmatic and HyperCode. They both make use of a Callable Compiler, provided as a built-in function in the ADL system, however the former handles source and object code in the conventional manner (the association between source and object is maintained manually), and the latter manipulates only hyperlinked source code that maintains the correspondence with the current executing object code.

As mentioned previously ADL provides a basic type, termed a behaviour, and structures can be defined on behaviours in an analogous way to types in expression based languages; these structures are defined using the concept of abstractions. Application of such an abstraction yields the execution of its constituent behaviours.

7   The Evolution Cycle Example

There follows a simple example of the implementation of a possible evolution cycle based on the concepts of the producer/evolver pairs (P/E) outlined earlier. This simple cycle is the important element in the construction of the active SEE. It is also typical of the structures used to develop the Tower model. The implementation in both ADL and its predecessor ProcessWeb PML are given.

Producer

This is an abstraction that contains two operational behaviours, one for periodically sending incremented messages and one for receiving them. There is also a primitive infrastructure that listens for messages from the Evolver indicating impending evolution and reacts to them. When an evolution is imminent, the Producer's messaging behaviours are shut down in an orderly manner and this concludes with a signal to the Evolver process to proceed with the evolution. The life cycle of the Producer is simply start up, run and quit.

The preservation of internal state and data, during dynamic evolution, is handled by the Hypercode System. The Hypercode system displays a textual representation of the executing ADL script including references to current stored values through the notion of Hyperlinks. Only hyperlinked values are preserved over system change.

Evolver

This behaviour has a connection to the user and loads and launches the Producer. It ensures that the Producer is always 'fit for purpose'. In this example we assume that the feedback from the Producer is via the user, i.e. the user observes the Producer's behaviour, detects that a change is needed, decides what this change will be and initiates the change. When the user signals an evolution, the Evolver launches the Hypercode Server, waits for the user to complete, and handles the modified behaviour. It is comprised of the simple Loader with an additional Evolution Cycle. The loader merely reads a file of ArchWare ADL. It is compiled using the ArchWare ADL Callable Compiler, and is executed. The user interacts with this model to load the desired Evolver. This ArchWare ADL, compiled using the Callable Compiler, possesses the necessary Hypercode tags for the operation of the Hypercode Editor.

The Evolution Cycle

- The user sends an evolve message to the Evolver.
- The user launches the client Hypercode Editor. It is populated by a link to the executing producer.
- Exploding the link displays a snapshot of the value of the Producer (this value is text plus hyperlinks - the Producer's abstraction definition). The Producer continues to execute normally.
- The Producer's abstraction definition is now modified by the user.
- The resulting hyperlink is sent back to the model (it is a link to a compiled abstraction).
- The executing instance of Producer is shut down and the abstraction of the modified producer is applied and the system is now ready for a new evolution cycle.

The ADL implementation

The ADL implementation is shown in fig 4. We do not describe the implementation in detail as this would require a deviation into the nature of ADL. This is not relevant to this particular paper and the important point to note is that this represents a highly abstract definition of the evolution cycle. It essentially merely defines the structure of the cycle in terms of connections and behaviours. The Hypercode Editor essentially provides the full environment for browsing, editing, compiling and linking the required change.

```
recursive value evolCycle=abstraction()

    {via userConn send "Ready for next Evolution>'n"
    via userConn receive trigger
    via userConn send "Sending the operational behaviour (applied
abstraction) to the HCE'n"
    value zzz = 'operationalBehaviour
    value newProducerAbs = edit(any(zzz),"Producer-2")
    via evolConn send "I want to evolve you"
    via evolConn receive proceed
    value projectString = location("")
    projectString :=  project newProducerAbs as Z onto
            abstraction[params:any]  :
                {locAbs:= Z; "abstraction[params:any]"}
            default       : "default"
    via userConn send "Applying modified ProducerAbs'n"
    value anotherparam = any(evolConn)
    value thisAbs =  'locAbs
    operationalBehaviour := thisAbs(params=anotherparam)
    evolCycle() !applies the abstraction evolveCycle

} !end evolCycle
```

Fig. 4. The ADL Implementation

The PML implementation
The equivalent, well as equivalent as possible, implementation in PML is shown in fig 5. Again there is neither relevance nor space to explain the intricacies of the PML text. However note that here the equivalent action to the Hypercode Editor behaviour has to be explicitly programmed into the PML (The Edit, Compile sequence and the FreezeRole,GetRoleData sequence).

As with ADL, the main PML logic is concerned with the structure of the evolution cycle, this time expressed in terms of Roles and Interactions.

8 Discussion

Active Models
The example illustrates the tight link that needs to exist in active systems between the object and source representations, a mapping that the HyperCode maintains,

thus providing a single computational model of a system. The 'Evolution Cycle' is in effect a software development process closely bound to an executing system, i.e. specially tailored for maintenance and evolution of the Producer. The activities that typically occur in practice – handling change, specifying and aggregating changes,

```
EvolRole isa Role with
parts
  zzz : String  ! source PML for Producer
  newClasses : Classes
  producerRole : Role
  roleData : tableof ( String -> Any )
  initData : tableof ( String -> Any )
...
actions
evolCycle :
 Give( interaction = toUser, gram = "Ready..." )
 Take( interaction = fromUser, gram = msg )
 ! Edit and compile a new Producer based in the old source
 Give( interaction = toUser, gram = "About to edit source ..." )
 Edit ( oldSource = zzz, newSource = newProducerSource )
 Compile ( currentClasses = classes, source = newProducerSource,
              newClasses = newClasses, errors = compErrors )
 ! Stop the current P and extract relevant current state
 Give( interaction = evolConnSending, gram = "I want ..." )
 Take( interaction = evolConnReceiving, gram = proceedMsg )
 Give ( interaction = toUser, gram = "Modifying producerRole ..." )
  FreezeRole( roleInst = producerRole)
 GetRoleData( roleInst = producerRole, currentData = roleData )
 initData( 'evolConnGetMsg' ) := roleData( 'evolConnGetMsg' )
 initData( 'evolConnGiveMsg' ) := roleData( 'evolConnGiveMsg' )
 ! Start revised P initialised with the relevant state
 StartRole ( classes = newClasses, className = "Producer",
             roleInst = producerRole,
             initalData = initData )
when
    true  ! run this action repeatedly - it will wait for user input

end with ! end EvolRole
```

Fig. 5. The PML Implementation

design, implementation analysis and test – could all be defined and embedded in this process. Clearly safeguards are required to guarantee that the evolved system will behave as predicted and this is the subject of ongoing research into formal reasoning support for this notion of evolution.

This example also illustrates that the actual installation of the change must be carefully choreographed to ensure an orderly shut down of the old system and its replacement with the new one. Key to this is the set of behaviours in the Producer that only come into play when a change is about to be installed. They take no part in the operational functioning of the Producer.

The software process briefly illustrated here consists of an enacting definition of a number of associated tasks. Clearly there is no guarantee that this process will be correct forever thus it will be wise to associate with it another E, i.e. our E will, on closer inspection, reveal an E_e/P_e pair where P_e undertakes the evolution of P, and which itself can be evolved by E_e.

Architectural Simplicity

The model also illustrates that by describing and building systems using such an evolutionary approach (the active model) the structure of the system can be defined as a highly abstract model, essentially concentrating on the basic components and their interconnections. However, and significantly, this specification of the abstract system also acts as the initial implementation in our 'single computational model' approach. The π-calculus [3] giving us both the necessary tools for flexibility and mobility as well as a language in which to describe and indeed execute abstract specifications of systems.

The evolvable nature of the resulting environment allows for the development of more concrete process steps at every stage of the software development process. Of course the model recurses and so such development of the SEE is under the same controls, or indeed lack of them, as the SEE itself provides.

9   Conclusions

This type of approach to software development and software evolution will, in the long run, enable software development environments to be far more responsive to the needs of business. Indeed applying the approach to business systems in general means that such environments will thus enable, rather than constrain, business evolution.

The active architecture paradigm, illustrated here with the construction of an SEE, has two clear advantages. Firstly architectures may be developed by evolving abstract specifications of their structures whilst at the same time using the abstract specification as a prototype of the final system. Secondly the resulting final concrete system retains the evolutionary power of the development system and thus is able to react to new requirements. In particular it has the ability to deal with emergent behaviour, perhaps the most important requirement of new systems developed for the future world of autonomic and ambient computing systems [7,11,12].

Acknowledgements

This work is supported by the EC Framework V project ArchWare (IST-2001-32360). It builds on earlier UK research council EPSRC-funded work in compliant systems architectures (GR/M88938 & GR/M88945).

References

1. Morrison, R, Kirby, GNC, Balasubramaniam, D, Mickan, K, Oquendo, F, Cimpan, S, Warboys, BC, Greenwood, RM.: Support for Evolving Active Architectures in the Arch-Ware ADL. In: Proc.4th Working IEEE/IFIP Conference on Software Architecture (WICSA 2004). 2004. Oslo, Norway. IEEE Computer Society. pp 69-78

2. Balasubramaniam, D, Morrison, R, Kirby, GNC, Mickan, K, Norcross, S.: ArchWare ADL - A User Reference Manual. 2004. ArchWare Project Report

3. Milner, R.: Communicating and Mobile Systems: The Pi-Calculus. 1999: Cambridge University Press

4. Oquendo, F, Warboys, BC, Morrison, R, Dindeleux, R, Gallo, F, Occhipinti, C.: Arch-Ware: Architecting Evolvable Software. In: Proc. First European Workshop on Software Architecture (EWSA'04). 2004. St Andrews, UK. Springer-Verlag. pp 257-271

5. Yeomans, B.S.: A Process-Based Environment for the Evolutionary Development of Large Software Systems. 1997 M.Res Thesis University of Manchester UK

6. Warboys, BC, Kawalek, P, Robertson, I, Greenwood, RM.: Business Information Systems: A Process Approach. 1999. McGraw-Hill

7. Cheng, S, Huang, A, Garlan, D, Schmerl, B, Steenkiste, P.: Rainbow: Architecture-based Self-adaptation with Reusable Infrastructure. In: Proc. First International Conference on Autonomic Computing (ICAC'04). 2004. New York, USA. IEEE Computer Society. pp 276-277

8. Zirintsis, E, Kirby, GNC, Morrison, R.: Hyper-code Revisited: Unifying Program Source, Executable and Data. In: Proc. 9th International Workshop on Persistent Object Systems. 2001. Lillehammer, Norway. Springer-Verlag. pp 232-246

9. Mickan, K, Morrison, R, Kirby, GNC, Balasubramaniam, D, Zirintsis, E.: Using Generative Programming to Visualise Hyper-code in Complex and Dynamic Systems. In: Proc. 27th Australasian Computer Science Conference (ACSC2004). 2004. Dunedin, New Zealand. Australian Computer Society. pp 377-386

10. Morrison, R, Balasubramaniam, D, Greenwood, M, Kirby, GNC, Mayes, K, Munro, DS, Warboys, BC.: ProcessBase Reference Manual (Version 1.0.6). Universities of St Andrews and Manchester Report 1999

11. Kephart, J, Chess, DM.: The Vision of Autonomic Computing. In: IEEE Computer Journal, Vol. 36, No.1. 2003. pp 41-50

12. IBM Autonomic Computing. http://www-306.ibm.com/autonomic/index.shtml

13. Atkinson, MP, Bailey, PJ, Chisholm, KJ, Cockshott, WP, Morrison, R.: PS-algol: A Language for Persistent Programming. In: Proc. 10th Australian National Computer Conference, Melbourne, Australia, pp 70-79. 1983

14. Banach R., Poppleton M.: Retrenchment: An Engineering Variation on Refinement. in: Proc. B-98, Bert (ed.), LNCS 1393, 129-147, Springer. 1998

15. Oquendo, F, Cîmpan, S, Balasubramaniam, D, Kirby, GNC, Morrison, R.: "The ArchWare ADL: Definition of the Textual Concrete Syntax", ArchWare Technical Report D1.2b

16. Morrison R, Balasubramaniam D, Greenwood R.M, Kirby G.N.C, Mayes K, Munro D.S, Warboys B.C.: A Compliant Persistent Architecture, in Software Practice and Experience vol. 30, no. 4, 2000, 363 – 386

17. Kirby, G.N.C.: Persistent Programming with Strongly Typed Linguistic Reflection, in Procs 25th International Conference on Systems sciences, Hawaii (1992) 820 – 83

Aspect Modelling at Architecture Design[*]

Amparo Navasa, Miguel Angel Pérez, and Juan Manuel Murillo

Departament of Computer Science,
Escuela Politécnica. Universidad de Extremadura,
Avda. Universidad s/n. Cáceres España
{amparonm, toledano, juanmamu}@unex.es
http://quercusseg.unex.es/QuercusProy/

Abstract. The increment of the complexity of systems requires new techniques that allow manipulating it adequately. Software architecture is becoming an important part of software design, which helps developers to handle the complexity of large systems. In addition, the management of the evolution as well as the maintenance of complex systems are two of most important problems to be solved by software engineering. Several solutions have been considered, one of them being the separation of concerns. These concepts have been extended along the life cycle and thus, Aspect Oriented Software Development (AOSD) arose. In this paper the architectural design phase and Aspect Oriented concepts are considered jointly. A proposal introducing aspects modelling in the architecture design phase is presented. The research is based on the combined use of a conventional architecture description language and an exogenous co-ordination model. When new requirements are going to be included in the system, the proposal provides the required steps to allow its evolution and maintenance by specifying an Aspect Oriented Architecture, which will permit us to change the system easily.

1 Introduction

More and more the complexity of systems to be developed increases and new design techniques are necessary. In addition, the structure of the systems changes throughout their life cycle and evolves to adapt it to new situations, making it necessary to develop the systems keeping an easy maintenance.

On the one hand, new approaches propose the Software Architecture as an important part of the design phase helping to manage the systems complexity as well as to define the system structure in such a way that its maintenance and evolution are easy.

On the other hand, AOSD, which extends aspect oriented (AO) programming concepts to the early stages, gives approaches to allow for the early identification of the aspects; their extraction, representation, and composition are their main goals (*early aspects* [1]). It recommends considering crosscutting concerns throughout the life cycle to obtain a clear designs and untangled code. Crosscutting concerns can be

---

[*] This research work is partially supported by CICYT under the TIC2002-04309-C02-01 project.

R. Morrison and F. Oquendo (Eds.): EWSA 2005, LNCS 3527, pp. 41–58, 2005.

encapsulated into so-called aspects. AOSD provides techniques for modularising and composing concerns which are difficult to untangle using the traditional ones.

Software Architecture is an appropriate moment in the life cycle to consider aspects, because it is when the structural definition of the systems is done. The suitability of the definition of an AO architecture design appears when it is observed that crosscutting concerns cross the architectural components, contaminating components and connectors, and the final design become complex.

The aspects can be considered as first class elements of architectural development. For this, having mechanisms to identify and specify them during the architectural design is needed; as well, its interaction with other architectural elements must be defined. Recently, a great number of research whose results show the benefits of an architectural approach have been presented [1], [2]. Therefore, the complex systems design is easier.

Systems, throughout their life, need to be maintained due to the changes in the world that they represent. This means that the requirements defining the changes of the system need to be considered. The design of systems can be redefined by adding, eliminating or changing elements of the current design structure.

In this paper a proposal to model aspects at architectural design phase is shown. Some methodological considerations about how to deal with the integration of the aspect separation at the architectural level are made. This allows us to manage the evolution of systems by considering the changes as aspects. To achieve it, the aspects are extracted during the architectural design stage. The model, which proposes to give a structural specification of an AO system, is based on the combined use of a conventional architecture description language (ADL) and an exogenous co-ordination model. In particular, LEDA [3] has been chosen as ADL and Coordinated Roles [4] as co-ordination model. The formal basis of the language will allow us to reason about the properties of the software architecture as well as to execute a prototype of the system from its architecture design. The generated systems have a clear design, easy evolution and maintainability. In addition, the language needs to be extended to express the AO concepts.

The proposal is a contribution to obtain an AO life cycle: a methodology is defined to evolve architectures, based on Aspect orientation. An *ad-hoc* architectural reconfiguration is obtained when a new requirement is added by a software architect, who can obtain a "new design" from the current system by applying the proposal. In others words, it is possible to apply aspectual concepts to a system, which need to evolve due to new requirements or unanticipated changes. It is assumed that the new requirements that will be modelled as aspects[1] at the software architecture phase have been identified in earlier steps. So, from an initial system, a tool allows us to obtain the design of the extended one with new requirements (considering them as aspects). The definition of an AO-ADL gives the necessary support to do it.

The article is structured as follows: in section 2, the proposal is presented, considering the development process of the AO systems during the architectural stage. The proposal includes the definition of an architectural structure with two levels, the component level and the aspect level. Also, how to manage the aspect

---

[1] New requirements considered as aspects can crosscut or not the architectural modules of current system.

separation at the architectural design as a co-ordination problem is shown. In section 3 related works are presented and section 4 presents some future works and conclusions.

2   A Proposal to Develop AO Systems at Architectural Level

In this section a proposal to carry out the design of AO systems from an architectural point of view is presented, considering the aspects as first class entities. So, the problem of developing AO Systems can be considered as a special way of maintaining and evolving the systems. In the software architecture phase, they are defined as a set of components, describing their high level functionality, which are connected through a set of architectural connectors. The aim of the proposal is to show how the evolution of systems (addition and change of requirements) can be managed using aspect. The system extension is obtained by applying aspect restrictions (new requirements) without modifying the existent components and connecting the new elements to the existent ones. The following is considered:

1. The systems are built from independent components.
2. To build complex systems, taking into account AOSD concepts, aspects will be considered as design artefacts [5]. So, it is possible to manipulate them through the whole development process. Moreover, these artefacts must be connected to the other components of the system. By using this aspectual feature, new requirements can be added to a designed system.
3. In the architectural design, the systems must be described with an ADL.

Before an aspect can be considered as a design component and then incorporated into a system, it is necessary to identify and specify it by describing its interfaces as well as its conditions of application. Then the interactions (architectural connectors) between the aspects and the components of the system can be defined taking that information into account.

In previous works [5], [6] we propose that in software architecture, the aspects separation in a system can be treated as a co-ordination problem. For this purpose, exogenous co-ordination control driven models can be applied to add new requirements.

In the proposal, the system is initially designed without considering the crosscutting concerns but adding them later. The final goal is to obtain the execution of a prototype of the extended system (including the new requirements as aspects).

The steps of the proposal are the following (Figure 1): a) to consider the detailed specification of the system; b) to create a design model and to define the system architecture, by using an ADL to obtain its high level design specification (note that in these steps the crosscutting concerns are ignored); c) to make the system evolve by adding new requirements like aspects in order to get the extended one in an oblivious way [7]; and finally, d) to define the architecture of the extended system as an AO architecture. A co-ordination model is used to manage the interaction between aspects and components. An architectural structure with two levels is defined, the first one

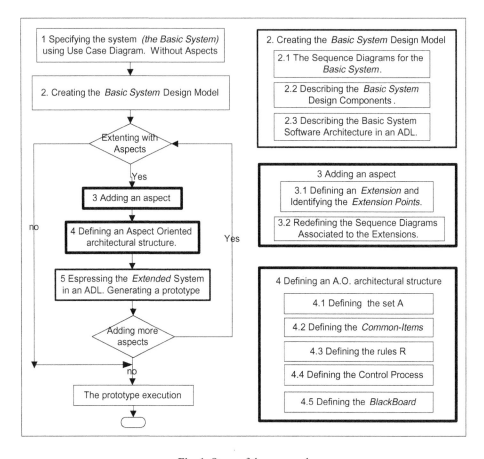

Fig. 1. Steps of the proposal

defines the basic system structure and the second (aspect level) defines a structure supporting the added aspects.

To clarify the concepts, a simple example is presented:

"A bank system manages the accounts of its clients who deposit and withdraw money from their bank account, and consult their balance from an ATM service. The client begins his interaction with the system when he introduces his credit card. After that, the ATM reads it, and then it can go on carrying out the requested operation, abort it by holding the card, or return it without doing any operation. If the operation is going on, the ATM system checks the current situation of the client's account on which the requested operation is being done. Besides, it is also necessary to consider an *audit operation,* which controls some functions of the system. The *audit operation* has been identified as a crosscutting concern during the requirement specifications. Here it will be considered as an aspect. The *audit aspect* is a new requirement modifying the server (*B_manager*) behaviour without modifying the design components in the initial system".

The following sections describe the steps to be taken with our proposal to solve the problem.

2.1 Specifying the System

In this step the system is specified without considering aspects; they will be included later (step 3). The system (*basic system*) specifications are firstly expressed by using UML diagrams. Figure 2(a) shows the use cases diagram for the example *basic system*. A full description of each use case needs to be done to express its documentation. The template proposed by Coleman [8], including some modifications is used.

The use case "modifying account" documentation is expressed partially in Table 1.

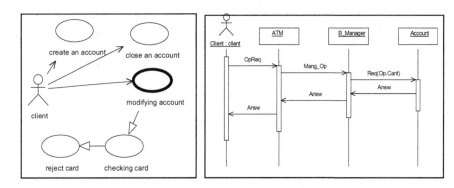

Fig. 2. (a)UC Diagram for the *Basic System* **(b)** Sequence Diagram for Modifying Account UC

Table 1. Extracted Documentation for "Modifying Account" UC

Use Case name	Modifying account
Description	Changes a bank account state
Comment	Client requests an operation

2.2 Creating the Basic System Design Model

In this section the system architectural description is shown. The different steps to be taken are developed in the following subsections:

The Sequence Diagrams for the Basic System. A sequence diagram is obtained from each use case, containing the design components of the system. The interactions are represented as well.

Figure 2(b) represents the associated sequence diagram to "modifying account" use case showing the design components and their interactions.

The Decomposition of the System in Design Components. After the detailed specification of the system has been done, its architecture is defined. The designcomponents are specified by describing their interfaces and the interactions by considering the relationships between components. They are established during the system specification and expressed in the sequence diagram.

Describing the System Architecture. To formalise the obtained design model (as a set of components and their interactions), an ADL is used. The selected one is LEDA in whose architecture two levels can be distinguished: the component level representing the system functionality, and the role level. The control of the system is due to the roles because they manage the interactions among the components (these being passive elements and doing only the computations). It would be possible to use other languages as ArchJava or Acme [9], [10].

```
component atm {
        interface none;
        composition
                atm : Client;
                b_manager: Server;
attachments
atm.requireM(executeopman,typeop,cant,balance)<>
b_manager.provideM(executeopman,typeop,cant,balance);
}
component Client{
        interface
            requireM:RequireM;
        }
component Server{
        interface
            provideM:ProvideM;
        }
role ProvideM(executeopman,typeop,cant,balance){
   spec is
executeopman?(answer).(value)answer!(value).
ProvideM(executeopman,typeop,cant,balance);
        }
 role RequireM(executeopman,typeop,cant,balance) {
   spec is
(answer)executeopman!(answer).answer?(value).
RequireM(executeopman,typeop,cant,balance);
        }

instance atm:Atm;
```

Fig. 3. The *Basic System* Description in LEDA

The architectural description of the example in LEDA is in Figure 3. There, the components of the system are defined in the *composition* section (the *atm* component as a client and the *b_manager* as a server). The roles *ProvideM* and *RequireM* define the characteristics of the interactions. The *attachment* section represents the glue defining the system associations between components and roles.

2.3   Adding a New Requirement as an Aspect

After defining the *basic system*, aspects are added to introduce new requirements obtaining the *extended system*. This is either to complete the system specification with the identified crosscutting concerns, or to evolve the system. The *extended system* is defined keeping up the obliviousness principle [7], according to the following steps. (In the example, *B_manager* behaviour is modified when the *audit aspect* is applied).

Adding an Aspect by Defining an Extension and Identifying the Extension Points. The aspect to be added is considered as a special kind of use case [11]: a Use Case Extension (*Audit aspect* in Figure 4). The points where the added aspect interacts with the *basic system* use cases must be determined. They are the extension points [12]. Besides, how each aspect interacts with the system must be defined (its application conditions). For each extension point the following must be indicated: the events triggering the aspects execution; the preconditions (conditions of execution) to be satisfied; and when they will be executed (before or after the action triggering the event). All this information will be expressed in the *extended use cases* diagram, and then transcribed to a template (extending Coleman's). For each use case and aspect to create a table is proposed. This is obtained from the above (Table 1) and extended with the information aforementioned. Table 2 shows the associated information with the use case and the aspect in the study case.

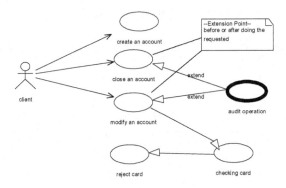

Fig. 4. UC Diagram for the *Extended System*

Table 2. Documentation for the "Modifying Account" UC and the *Audit Aspect*

Use Case name	Modifying Account
Description.	Changes a bank account state ....
Extending Use Case	**Audit. UC**
Extension Points List	Call to Manage_op operation.
Event	Receive Message.
Application Condition	None
When Clause	None (after is the default value)

Redefining the Sequence Diagrams Associated to the Extension. For each *use case extended* with an aspect, the sequence diagram is redefined. This new diagram contains the components in the initial use case to be extended and the aspect component to be added. New interactions are not defined yet.

Before specifying the nature of the new interactions it is necessary to define a new element, which contains the aspect component and manages its interaction, which we call *Aspect-Manager* (Figure 5). This new element is considered now as an abstract component but later it will be the *Aspect Level* in the model (2.4 section).

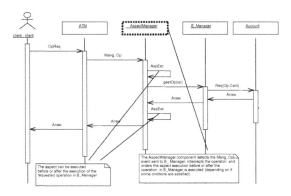

Fig. 5. Sequence Diag for Modifying Account UC with an Aspect

Table 3. "Modifying Account" UC Documentation for each extension point, aspect and component

Insertion Point	Manage_op
Extension Point	Call to Manage_op.
Aspect	Audit
Component	B_manager
Event	Receiving Message
Application Condition	None.
When Clause	None.

The *Aspect-Manager* function is to co-ordinate and manage the interaction between the aspect and the other components in this scenario. The description of the *Aspect-Manager* behaviour is the following:

- *Aspect-Manager* is waiting for an event occurrence.
- When one is detected, it is intercepted and analysed.
- If the operation triggering the event is not associated to the aspect managed by *Aspect-Manager*, the operation continues its normal sequence.
- On the contrary, *Aspect-Manager* studies whether the conditions for the aspect application are satisfied, and if the aspect must be applied before or after the requested operation.
- The associated information to the *extension points* identified in the use cases diagram should be propagated to the sequence diagrams: a table is defined for **each extension point, aspect,** and **the corresponding design component**. For the case study the Table 3 is obtained.

These three elements jointly define one point on a design component in which an extension point is detected. It is called **Insertion Point**. This concept is near the *join point* concept, but at a higher level. For each *extension point, aspect* and *design component* one or more **insertion points** can be defined.

2.4   Defining an Architectural Structure to Support the System Changes by Adding Aspects

The *Aspect-Manager* definition allows that, when new requirements (aspects) are added, the design components are not changed. To manage this during the architectural design, a two level architecture is proposed: The Component Level, to define the *basic system* and the Aspect Level[2] to include the new components supporting the added aspect and the management of its interaction. This makes it possible to define a new workspace but independent of the *basic system* architecture.

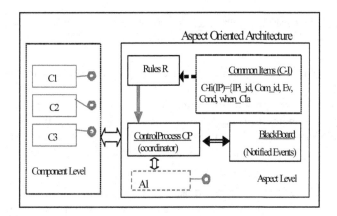

Fig. 6. *Extended System* Arch., Component and Aspect Levels

The *Aspect Level* is constituted by (Figure 6): a set of aspect components (**A**), a static structure that we call **Common-Items** (C-I), a set of rules (**R**) specifying interactions between the first level and the second one, a **Control Process** (**CP**) and a dynamic structure, the **BlackBoard** (**BB**). Each element is defined bellow.

The Set A. A is the set of aspects. Each is defined as a design component, having an interface providing the operations that determine its operability. In the case study, the Audit operation is the considered aspect.

Common Items (C-I). All information from previous steps is contained in this structure, in which the associations between the components and the aspect are considered, as well as the conditions for their application.

The **C-I** table is generated from the previous ones having the following columns:

-   **Insertion Point -IP-.** It is each cutting point identified in the sequence diagram. **IP** must be in the component interface.

---

[2] *Aspect-Manager* component aforementioned is from now the Aspect Level in the model.

- **Component**: The name of the component affected by the above **IP**.
- **Aspect**: The name of the aspect to be applied.
- **Event**: The event type triggering the aspect application. It can be "received message (synchronous or asynchronous)" or "reached state".
- **Condition/s**: They are the conditions that must be satisfied allowing the aspect functionality to be executed.
- **When Clause**: It indicates when the aspect can/must be applied (after or before).

In table **C-I** there is a row for each *insertion point*. So, the detailed specification of the system lets us obtain this structure completely defined. In the case study, the **C-I** structure is in Table 4.

Table 4. C-I values for the case study

IP	Component	Aspect	Event	Condition	WhenClause
Manage_op	B_manager	Audit	Receive Message	None	None (after)

Rules. The set of rules is defined to describe the characteristics of the interaction between the aspect component (at the aspect level) and the components in the underlying level. They provide the actions to be executed when applying the aspects, considering the conditions to be satisfied. The left side specifies the list of conditions to be satisfied (deduced from the information in the C-I structure) to execute the actions on the right side (deduced from the set A of aspects). For each C-I row, a rule is defined. Its general syntax in pseudocode is:

```
IF  (event)   and   (IP OF Comp)   and   (cond)   THEN
              DO  [Aspect_Op_Name(param)]   WHEN   when_condition

              being  Aspect_Op_Name (param)  the  name  of  one  operation
              provided by an aspect component.
```

An **IP** can be affected by more than one aspect. In this case it is necessary to consider the *event* and *cond* items in the associated column of **C-I** to solve the conflict. As a result of this, two rules or one complex rule (considering priority) can be generated. In the example, the associated rule to our aspect extension is:

```
IF  (RM³)   and   (Manage_op OF B_manager)   and   (null) THEN
     DO  Audit_op  WHEN   after
```

Control Process CP. The Control Process manages the o-ordinated execution of t he *extended system* considering the rules information. It co-ordinates the execution of the components affected by the triggered events and each aspect associated to them. After executing an aspect the *basic system* behaviour can change.

---

³ RM : Receive Message.

To solve the problem of co-ordinating the aspects and the components execution an exogenous control-driven co-ordination model [13] is considered [5], [6]. The selected one has been Coordinated Roles (CR) [4], based on event notification protocols. In CR, each co-ordinator is monitoring the system in a transparent way to the components. When an event is detected by a CR co-ordinator, it executes the co-ordination actions associated to the events. The events can be treated in a synchronous way (the component affected by the triggered event is blocked until the event is treated) or an asynchronous way (the component affected by the triggered event continues its execution while the event is been treated).

As the *extended system* can become complex because of the number of aspects to be included, **CP** is constituted by:

- Several co-ordinators (in CR sense): Each is defined for each design component having one *insertion point*. A co-ordinator can manage several aspects associated to the same **IP**.
- A co-ordinator of co-ordinators named *SuperCoordinator*. Its definition is necessary when several aspects are being included (section 2.8.3).

The detailed **CP** execution is described in section 2.8.4.

Blackboard. The Blackboard is a dynamic structure, which stores the triggered events (waiting to be treated) during the system execution. The information stored for each event is: the Event type; the insertion point name (IP); the name of the component affected by the IP; and the values of the conditions on the left side of the rules. This information will be compared with those in the C-I structure.

The events and their associated information are written by the co-ordinator when they are detected, then read by the *SuperCoordinator* who makes the comparisons with the information in **C-I**. The treated event is eliminated from the blackboard by the same co-ordinator causing its insertion.

2.5   Expressing the Extended System in an ADL

The next step is to describe the *extended system* in terms of the ADL. This implies enlarging the *basic system* description by adding the aspect level elements. This is the *Aspect-Manager* information. As it was shown, this design component is mainly constituted by two elements: the aspects establishing the extension of the system; and the *Control Process* managing the complex interaction between the aspect and the *basic system* components by co-ordinating both executions.

The *Aspect Level* definition in LEDA (the selected language) is as follows:

- Each aspect will be a LEDA component.
- The co-ordinators and the *SuperCoordinator* will be LEDA components, too.
- We will define as LEDA roles the interactions between:
  - Each server component triggering an event and its associated co-ordinator.
  - Each co-ordinator and the *SuperCoordinator*.
  - Each co-ordinator and its associated aspect.

```
component atm {
interface none;
composition
        atm : Client;
        bmanager: Server;
        audit :Aspect;
        coor : Coordinator;
        sc : Supercoordinator;
attachments
     atm.requireM(executeopman,typeop,amount,
balance) <> coor.intercept(executeopman,typeop,
amount,balance);
     coor.calltosc(scoperation,a,b) <>
sc.replytoco(scoperation,a,b);
     coor.act(aspectop,typeop, amount,balance,
executeopman,x) <> bmanager.provideM(aspectop,
typeop,amount,balance,executeopman,x) <>
audit.modify(aspectop,typeop,amount,balance,execu
teopman,x);
}
component Client{
interface
   requireM:RequireM;
}
component Server{
interface
   provideM:ProvideM;
}
component Aspect {
interface
   modify:Modify;
}
component Coordinator {
var
   match : Boolean;
   after : Boolean := true;
interface
        act:Act;
        calltosc:Calltosc;
        intercept:Intercept;
}
component Supercoordinator {
interface
        replytoco:Replytoco;
}
role ProvideM(aspectop,typeop,amount,balance,
executeopman,x) {
spec is
executeopman?(answer).t.(val)answer!(val).Provide
M(aspectop,typeop,amount,balance,executeopman,x);
}
```

```
role RequireM(aspectop,typeop,amount,balance) {
spec is
(answer)executeopman!(answer).answer?(val).t.Requ
ireM(aspectop,typeop, amount, balance);
}
role Modify(aspectop,typeop, amount,balance,
executeopman,x){
spec is
aspectop?(reply).t.(val)reply!(val).Modify(aspect
op,typeop,amount,balance,executeopman,x);
}
role
Act(aspectop,typeop,amount,balance,executeopman,x
){
spec is
[match=FALSE](answer)executeopman!(answer).answer
?(val).t.Act(aspectop,typeop,amount,balance,execu
teopman,x)
+[match=TRUE and
after=FALSE](reply)aspectop!(reply).reply?(val).(
answer)executeopman!(answer).answer?(value).t.Act
(aspectop,typeop,amount,balance,executeopman,x)
+[match=TRUE and after=TRUE](answer)executeop
man!(answer).answer?(val).(reply)aspectop!(reply)
.reply?(value).t.Act(aspectop,typeop,amount,balan
ce,executeopman,x)    ;
}
role
Intercept(executeopman,typeop,amount,balance){
spec is
(val)answer!(val).Intercept(executeopman,typeop,a
mount,balance)
+ executeopman?(answer).t.Intercept(executeopman,
typeop,amount,balance);
}
role Replytoco(scoperation,a,b){
spec is
scoperation?(answer).t.(val)answer!(val).Replytoc
o(scoperation,a,b);
}
role Calltosc(scoperation,a,b){
spec is
(answer)scoperation!(answer).answer?(val).Caltosc
(scoperation,a,b);
}

instance atm:ATM;
```

Fig. 7. *Extended Syhjfhgd* rchitecture in LEDA

These new elements lead us to consider a new set of high order instructions. In this way, an aspect oriented architecture description language (AO-ADL) is obtained. The *extended system* description in this AO-ADL can be generated automatically from the *basic system* description in a partial way. This is possible because at the design level, aspects, co-ordinators and *SuperCoordinator* have a known behaviour. Roles in LEDA which define associations between components (new and old) can be generated partially too. Figure 7 shows the *extended system* in LEDA for the case study. The *basic system* architecture (Figure 3) has been enlarged with new instructions to obtain the *extended system* description. (marked in bold).

2.6 Generating a Prototype

After the *extended system* description in the ADL is done, the system behaviour can be known at design time by executing a prototype of an AO system from the architectural design phase (if the ADL makes it possible). In addition, due to the LEDA formal basis (Π–calculus), it is possible to demonstrate the properties of the *extended system* architecture. So, it is possible to see how a system evolves by enlarging in this way the current one with new requirements.

2.7 Eliminating Aspects or Requirements

Adding aspects or new requirements to make the system evolve supposes following steps 3 to 6 of the proposal. To remove aspects, the corresponding elements and the associated information to them must be extracted from the aspect level. In both cases it is necessary to study how the rules need to be modified.

2.8 Detailed Description of the Aspect Level Components

In this section, the design components in the aspect level are described but only its high level description is presented.

Describing the Client and Server Components. The proposal follows the client-server philosophy to make it possible to introduce new elements in an existent system. A client is a design component, which requires services provided by another, the server.

Two related components in the *basic system* can be represented as in Figure 8a. They are a part of the component level. When the *extended system* is defined, the client-server association is intercepted for a new "co-ordinator" component, which will determine (following the proposal) if an aspect will be applied or not (Figure 8b[4]). The client and server components ignore the co-ordinator existence.

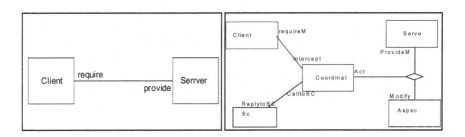

Fig. 8. (a) *Basic System.* Client-Server relation   **(b).** *Extended System.* Client-Server relation

Describing the Co-ordinator. A co-ordinator is defined associated with both an aspect and a server component. A co-ordinator is considered in association with an event required to a server component (for instance, to receive the request of executing one operation of the server interface). The triggered event makes the aspect execution possible, depending on if some conditions are satisfied. The Co-ordinator only acts if the detected event has been associated to the aspect co-ordinated by it[5].

After the *extended system* design specification has been completed, the co-ordinator behaviour is defined by the information kept in **Common-Items** and the set

---

[4] The LEDA representation is followed in the figure expressing this ternary association.

[5] In especial cases, a coordinator can coordinate the execution of several aspects.

of rules (allowing their right side to be executed). A co-ordinator is defined for each rule.[6]

Description of the Co-ordinator's Operation. When a triggered event is detected by the co-ordinator, it determines if this event is associated to the aspect, which it co-ordinates. In this case, the co-ordinator writes on the blackboard the associated information to the detected event. Then, it notifies this occurrence to SuperCoordinator, (see 2.8.3), and it waits for the reply. This reply depends on the value of the conditions when the event is triggered. Three situations can be considered: no rule is satisfied; some rule is satisfied and **when clause** = before; some rule is satisfied and **when clause** = after. Due to lack of space this is not presented in this paper.

Describing the SuperCoordinator (SC). The goal of this component is to determine if the conditions in the rules associated to an event are being satisfied when it is triggered (at run-time, their values are written in the blackboard by a co-ordinator). SC analyses the run-time information associated with the triggered events by looking for a match with the value of the conditions defining the co-ordination policies (rules).

The **SC** component has been introduced to reduce the co-ordinator workload. This is because in complex systems, the information associated to several triggered events can be written in the blackboard by a co-ordinator before **SC** considers those previously written. In this case, the events would be awaiting their study by **SC**.

To solve this situation, a dynamic re-definition of **SC** is proposed. A new component named **SC_Generator** is created. When the **SC** is invoked by a co-ordinator, the **SC_Generator** dynamically creates a new **SC** instance, which only pays attention to the co-ordinator request for whose service it was created. In this way, having a request queue is avoided, because each **SC** instance pays attention to a request at the same time as any other. When its execution is finished, the instance is destroyed[7]. When each **SC** instance is created, it acts as follows (Figure 9):

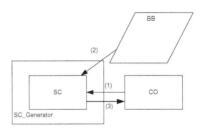

Fig. 9. The *SuperCoordinator* Description

It receives from its associated co-ordinator the notification of a triggered event (1). Then, it reads the information on the blackboard (2), and checks if this matches with

---

[6] In special cases, it is possible that the coordinator behaviour was defined by more than one.
[7] The events are considered according to the order in that they arrive.

the left side of any rule. After that, **SC** returns the control to the co-ordinator, which invoked it by notifying the result of its execution (3). If there is a match, the co-ordinator will execute the rule (that is, the aspect). In any other case, it doesn't. Finally, the **SC** instance is destroyed.

Detailed Description of the Control Process Execution. Once the elements of the Control Process have been described, it is easier to explain its detailed execution. We can distinguish between the Control Process execution for a received message synchronous event and for an asynchronous one.

The Control Process Description for Received Synchronous Messages. When a component (client) requests an operation to another (server) the Control Process functionality can be described as follows (Figure 10):

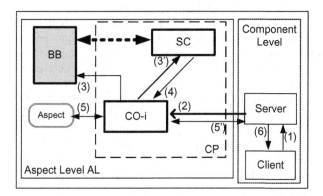

Fig. 10. CP Behavior Description to Sync Messages

- The associated co-ordinator component detects the triggered event (1, 2), then it stores in the Blackboard the following information (3): the triggered event, the insertion point name and the name of the component triggering the event (section 2.4.5). After that, the co-ordinator (3') notifies the SuperCoordinator and remains waiting for the reply.
- SuperCoordinator receives the co-ordinator notification (3') and analyses the associated events information (in the blackboard) looking for a match with one of the rules defining its behaviour – checking the value of their conditions- (co-ordination policy). The results of the search are notified to the co-ordinator (4), so that it knows what actions to take.
- When the co-ordinator receives this notification, it acts as follows:
  - If no rule matches, the co-ordinator deletes from the blackboard the information of the considered event and returns the control to the server component without executing the aspect.
  - If a rule matches, the co-ordinator has to co-ordinate both the execution of the aspect and the server component, considering the *when-clause* value - before (5) or after (5')-. This co-ordinator executes the right part of the

matching rule (the aspect) and deletes from the blackboard the information of the considered event.
-     For its part, server and/or aspect components notify the co-ordinator when the operation is finished. Then, the co-ordinator acts in consequence (6) and finishes its activity.

The CP definition for *received asynchronous messages* is similar to the before. It is not presented here due to lack of space.

3   Related Works

Extracting aspects at the early phases in the life cycle is the aim of several works. In general, each one deals with the problem from different perspectives. Some of them have been selected to be compared with our proposal.

The aim of ASAAM, into AOSD project [14], is to specify architectural aspects by using rules allowing them to be deduced. To identify the components which crosscut the design by using scenarios is another goal. In [15] the aspects in CBSD are studied. There, identifying the requirements of the AO components is delayed until the design level. MDSoC [16] introduces the *hyperslice* concept, which lets us encapsulate and manage the interaction among aspects and its integration into the system by using *HiperJ* as a tool. We think this model is too near to the implementation phase. Other remarkable researches are [17], [18], [19].

[20], [21], [22] refer to the early identification of aspects. They work around requirement engineering and, perhaps for this reason, the way the systems defined under these proposals can be executed is not defined. [23], [24] consider AOSD from a structural perspective. None of them proposes using an ADL to describe the AO systems at the design level, neither to use co-ordination models to express the aspects interaction with the functional components.

In [25] an ADL to design the AO systems is described. This language is based on XML schemes, which gives several advantages. However, at this moment, XML lacks a strong formal base. In [26], an ADL to design AO systems is described too. In this case the selected and extended language is Rapide [27] obtaining AO-Rapide, and the Reo [13] co-ordination model is used to define architectural connectors between functional components and the aspectual ones.

4   Conclusions and Future Works

In this paper a methodological approach to design AO system is presented. Aspect separation is managed at the architectural level by defining a special architectural structure and treating the aspect separation as a co-ordination problem. An exogenous co-ordination model (Coordinated Roles) is considered to realise co-ordination tasks observing the obliviousness principle. The proposal makes it possible to give an architectural definition of systems by changing their behaviour at design time, by adding or eliminating logical restrictions, without changing the components constituting it. The defined architecture gives us an architectural dynamism by adding and removing components and interactions.

So, the systems are built from design components describing their functional behaviour, and a set of design components doing the aspect policies. Defining the interactions between new and old components is necessary as well. The designed systems considering the proposal have a clear design and highly cohesive components because the functional and aspectual components remain separated. These systems will also have easy maintenance, evolution and adaptation to unanticipated changes.

The incremental development process proposed to design extended systems from initial ones allows us to enlarge them with new requirements by considering them as aspects. Including the new requirements is done having a minimum impact on the architecture of the existent system and with no changes over the design components of the current system.

It is necessary to adequately express the system characteristics and using an ADL does this. The selected ADL and the co-ordination model have a strong formal base, which makes possible to analyse and verify the system properties. Besides it is possible to simulate the system execution during the design phase.

The way to extend the language in order to adapt it to develop AO systems was shown. The extensions will allow us to execute the aspects (considered as design components) and the functional components over which they are applied, in a co-ordinated way. Finally, the model is platform independent.

The proposal presented refers to an aspect oriented architectural model. Our current task is, on the one hand, to obtain an aspect independent model, and on the other, to generalize the AO-ADL to obtain a new aspect independent ADL with an improved language infrastructure where the AO elements will be considered as real notions in the language.

The ongoing research has the following tasks, as well: to create a tool to generate the new system in the most automatic way and to formalise the LEDA extensions and the other architectural elements. Finally, other languages like ArchJava and Acme are being studied to express the proposal.

Acknowledgements

We would like to thank to the anonymous referees for the useful comments on this paper and the suggestions given by them.

References

1. Early Aspects homepage http://www.early-aspects.net/
2. Aspect Oriented Software Development homepage http://aosd.net
3. Canal,C, Pimentel,E., Troya,M.: Compatibility and Inheritance in Software Architcture. Review Scene and Computing Programming. vol 41 nº2, pp 105-130. 2001
4. Murillo,J.M., Hernandez,J., Sánchez,F., Alverez,L.: Coordinated Roles: Promoting Re-Usability of Coordinated Active Objects Using Event Notification Protocol. Coordination Proceeding, pp53-68, 1999
5. Navasa,A., Pérez,M.A., Murillo,J M., Hernández,J.: Aspect Oriented Software Archi-tecture: A structural Perspective. WS on Early Aspect. AOSD Conference 2002. Enschede Holanda. http://trese.cs.utwente.nl/AOSDEarlyAspectsWS/works hop_papers.htm

6. Navasa,A. Pérez,M.A., Murillo,J.M.: Una arquitectura software para DSOA. IX Jornadas de Ingeniería del software y Bases de Datos.JISBD'04. Nov 2004. Málaga. Spain
7. Filman,R.E., Friedman,D.P.: Aspect-Oriented Programming is Quantification and Obliviousness Workshop on Advanced Separation of Concerns. OOPSLA 2000, USA
8. Colman,D. A.: Use Case Template: Draft for discussion. Fusion Newsleter, April 1998. http://www.npl.hp.com/fusion/md-newsletters.html
9. Aldrich,J., Chambers,C., Notkin,D.: Architectural reasoning in ArchJava. ECOOP'02, June 2002 Malaga, Spain
10. Garlan,D., Monrie,R.T., Wie,D.: Acme: An Architecture Description Interchange Language. Proceeding of CASCON'97. Ontario, Canada 1997
11. Jacobson,I.: The case for aspects y aspects: the missing link. Journal of Object Technology. October and November 2003. http://www.sdmagazine.com
12. Jacobson,I.: Use Cases and aspects – working seamlessly together. Journal of Object Technology, vol 2 n°4, July-August 2003, pp7-28 http://www.jot.fm/ issues/issue_2003_ 07/column1
13. Arbab,F.: What Do You Mean Coordination?. Bulletin of the Duth Association'96. LNCS 1061. Springer-Verlag. Cesena. April 1996
14. Aspect-Oriented Software Architect Design Portal http://trese.cd.utwente.nl/taosad
15. Grundy,J.: Aspect-Oriented Requirements Engineering for Components-based Software Systems. 4th Int. Sym. on RE. IEEE Computer Society, Limerick, Ireland, 1999, pp.84-91
16. Tarr,P. ,Ossher,H.: Multidemensional Separation of Concern and Hyperslices Approach. Proceeding of Symposium on Software Architecture and Component Technology: the State of the Art in Software Development. Kluwer. Jan 2000
17. Wagelaar,D.: A Concept-Based Approach for Early Aspect Modelling. Workshop on Early Aspect. AOSD Conference, Boston, USA, 2003
18. Clarke,S., Walker,R.: Towards a Standard Design Language for Aspect Oriented Development. AOSD Conference Enschede, Holand, 2002
19. Sureé,D., Vanderperren,W., Jonkers,V.: JasCo: an Aspect Oriented Approach Taylored for CBSD. AOSD Conference. Boston, USA, 2003
20. Sutton,S.M.,Rouvellow,I.: Modeling software concerns in Comos. AOSD Conf. 2002
21. Rashid,A., Moreira,A. Araujo,J.: Modularisation and Composition of Aspect Requirements. AOSD Conference. Boston USA, 2003
22. Brito,I., Moreira.A.: Towards a Composition Process for Aspect-Oriented Requirements. Workshop on Early Aspects 2003. AOSD conference. Boston USA
23. Katara,M., Katz,S.: Architecture Views of Aspects. AOSD Conference, USA, 2003
24. Kande,M.M.: A Concern-Oriented Approach to Software Architecture. Doctoral Thesis n°2796 Lausane, EPFL, 2003
25. Pinto,M., Fuentes,L., Troya,J.M.: "DAOP-ADL: an Architecture Description Language for Dynamic Component and Aspect-Based Development". Proc. of 2nd Int. Conf. on GPCE, vol. 2830 LNCS ,pp.118-137, Germany. Springer-Verlag. 2003
26. Palma,K.M.: Using a coordination model to specify Aspect-Oriented Software Architectures. Santiago de Chile. Chile Diciembre 2004
27. Luckman,D.C., Kenney,J.J., AugustinL.M., Vera,J., Bryan,D., Mann,W.: Specification and Analysis of Systems Architecture Using Rapide. IEEE transaction on SE. Special Issue on Software Architecture, vol 21, n°4, April 1995

Dynamic Evolution in Aspect-Oriented Architectural Models[*]

Jennifer Pérez, Nour Ali, Jose Ángel Carsí, and Isidro Ramos

Department of Information Systems and Computation,
Polytechnic University of Valencia, Camino de Vera s/n,
E-46022 Valencia, Spain
{jeperez, nourali, pcarsi, iramos}@dsic.upv.es

Abstract. This paper presents a solution to the evolution problem of software architectures. This solution is provided by PRISMA. PRISMA is an architecture modeling approach that integrates the advantages of Component-Based Software Development (CBSD) and Aspect-Oriented Software Development (AOSD). This integration is reflected in its model and in its Architecture Description Language (ADL). In this paper, PRISMA is presented as a framework to evolve aspect-oriented and component-based architectures by requirements-driven evolution. The evolution is supported by means of a meta-level and the reflexive properties of PRISMA ADL which have been implemented as a middleware. In addition, it is demonstrated how the evolution services of the PRISMA meta-level permit the run-time evolution of software architectures using an industrial case study, the *TeachMover* Robot.

1 Introduction

Complex information systems frequently undergo changes in their functional and non-functional requirements. This is due to the fact that they are exposed to a high set of variability sources and they have a dynamic nature. In these software systems, the reconfiguration of the architecture topology at run-time is one of the most important requirements, especially in real-time systems. The relevance of this dynamic reconfiguration is due to the fact that complex systems usually cannot stop their activity.

In the last few years, there has been greater interest in evolution research in order to reduce the time and the cost of the maintenance process and to provide a solution for dynamic evolution. Thus, dynamic evolution appears as one of the main challenges of software.

Software architectures [4] have emerged as a solution for the design and the development processes of complex information systems. There is a wide variety of architectural models, but there is no consensus about the different concepts and

---

[*] This work has been funded by the Department of Science and Technology (Spain) under the National Program for Research, Development and Innovation, DYNAMICA project TIC2003-07776-C02-02. Moreover, it is funded by the Microsoft Research Cambridge, *"PRISMA: Model Compiler of aspect-oriented component-based software architectures"* Project.

R. Morrison and F. Oquendo (Eds.): EWSA 2005, LNCS 3527, pp. 59–76, 2005.

approaches. However, there is no doubt whatsoever that dynamic evolution of architectures is necessary to overcome changes in the requirements. This evolution must be able to evolve the structure as well as the behaviour of architectures.

PRISMA is an approach to develop complex information systems. This approach provides a model and an architecture description language (ADL). The PRISMA model defines software architectures by integrating aspect-oriented software development (AOSD) [1] and component-based software development (CBSD) [18]. In this paper, we present how the PRISMA model provides a solution for dynamic evolution and supports changes in aspect-oriented architectures requirements by means of a meta-level. The meta-level contains the definitions of architectural elements as data in order to update them by executing evolution services. In this way, the execution of services is reflected in the architecture by its updating the data (the concept of reflection). As a result, the PRISMA meta-level allows for the evolution of components and aspects as well as the dynamic reconfiguration of architectures.

The PRISMA prototype has been developed as a middleware using the .NET technology. This middleware contains the PRISMA meta-level in order to evolve the architectures at run-time. The dynamic reconfiguration of PRISMA approach has been tested using a real case study, the *TeachMover* robot. The *TeachMover* robot belongs to the tele-operation systems domain. One of the main features of systems of this kind is that they must deal with changes in architecture without stopping their execution. In this paper, we briefly introduce the *Teach Mover* robot case study and how the meta-level supports the dynamic reconfiguration of its architecture.

The structure of the paper is as follows: Section 2 presents a brief summary of the PRISMA model and the meta-model. Section 3 details the main characteristics of the PRISMA evolution. Section 4 presents the tele-operation domain and the *TeachMover* case study which is used through out the paper to exemplify the presented evolution techniques. Section 5 explains how the PRISMA evolution has been implemented. Section 6 compares related works on architecture evolution. Finally, conclusions and further work are presented in section 7.

2 Architectural Model

The PRISMA architectural model allows the definition of architectures of complex software systems [12]. Its main contributions are the integration of the AOSD [5] and the CBSD [17] and its reflexive properties. In this way, PRISMA specifies different characteristics (distribution, safety, context-awareness, coordination, etc.) of an architectural element (component, connector) using aspects, and it has a meta-level to evolve its architectural models.

A PRISMA architectural element can be seen from two different views, internal and external. The internal view (see Figure 1) shows an architectural element as a prism. Each side of the prism is an aspect of this architectural element. In this way, we represent that an architectural element of PRISMA is formed by a set of aspects; whereas, the external view (see Figure 1) is an architectural element that encapsulates its functionality as a black box and publishes a set of services that it offers to the rest of the architectural elements.

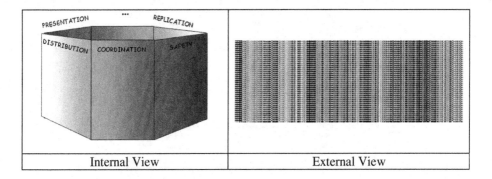

Fig. 1. Views of an Architectural Element

The PRISMA meta-level has been represented by means of a metamodel which contains one metaclass for each PRISMA concept. These metaclasses define the set of properties and evolution services for each considered concept in the model.

In the following, we present the main concepts of the PRISMA metamodel and their metaclasses with their evolution services.

2.1 Aspect

In our work, an aspect represents a specific *concern* (safety, coordination, distribution, etc) that crosscuts the software architecture, this means, those *concerns* that do not crosscut the architecture will not be an aspect. In order to avoid these *crosscutting-concerns*, a PRISMA architectural element is formed by a set of aspects that describe it from the different *concerns* of the architecture. The kind of aspects that form an architectural element depends on the *concerns* of the information system that we are specifying.

PRISMA is based on OASIS [6] to define the semantics of architectural models in a formal way and to preserve its main advantages, that is, the validation and the verification of architectural models and the automatic generation of code from the ADL. Due to the fact that PRISMA is based on OASIS, aspects are defined by attributes, services, preconditions, valuations, triggers and protocols. In addition, an aspect defines a *concern* and may specify the semantics of some interfaces (set of services published by a component). In Figure 2, we present the *aspect* package of the PRISMA metamodel.

The evolution services of the *aspect* metaclass (see Table 1) allow us to create and destroy aspects. Moreover, they permit the modification of their name, the interfaces that they specify, and the kind of characteristics that they define as well as the addition and removal of properties from the aspect.

The *NewAspect* service allows us to create a new aspect; its parameters define its name and the kind of properties that the aspect specifies. However, the *DestroyAspect* service destroys an aspect.

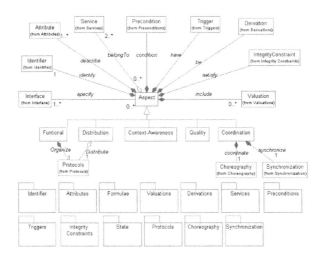

Fig. 2. The aspect package of the PRISMA metamodel

Table 1. Evolution services of the *Aspect* metaclass

```
Metaclass Aspect
 new NewAspect(name: string, type: AspectType¹);
 destroy DestroyAspect;
 usingInterface(name: string);
 removeInterface(name: string);
 changeName (Newname: string);
 changeType(Type: AspectType);
 addAttribute (name: string, Type: type);
 removeAttribute(name: string);
 addServices(name:string, Type:type,
             ParameterList:string);
 removeService(name: string);
 ... ...
End_Metaclass Aspect;
```

---

[1] AspectType is a predefined enumerated type which contains the following list of values: coordination, distribution, quality, presentation, context_awareness, navigational and others. However, the user can also define new kinds of aspects.

In addition, a set of services to modify a specific aspect are provided. For example, the *AddAttribute* service adds a new attribute to the aspect, but the *removeAttribute* service deletes an attribute from the aspect. Finally, services to change the aspect are provided (*changeName, changeType, etc*).

These evolution services have associated constraints which must be satisfied before or after their execution in order to maintain the consistence of the architecture.

- Weaving

Simply defining an aspect (crosscutting concerns) is not enough. The methods indicating how an aspect is weaved (connected) with the rest of the aspects must also be determined. The weaving indicates that the execution of an aspect service can generate the invocation of services in other aspects (see Figure 3). Nevertheless, in order to preserve the independence of the aspect specification from the aspect weaving, the weaving is specified externally to the aspect.

As a PRISMA architectural element is formed by a set of aspects, the weaving is part of the architectural element specification; it is the glue of the aspects forming a prism (Internal View). This glue is achieved using the weaving methods that the model provides. The weaving methods are operations that describe the causality of the weaving services. The weaving methods which are typical of the AOP are the following:

- **after**: aspect1.service is executed **after** aspect2.service
- **before**: aspect1.service is executed **before** aspect2.service
- **instead**: aspect1.service is executed **in place of** aspect2.service

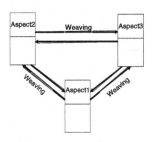

Fig. 3. Aspect weaving

Next, we present the *weaving* package of the PRISMA metamodel (see Figure 4) and the evolution services of the *weaving* metaclass (see Table 2).

Similar to the *aspect* metaclass, the *weaving* metaclass (see table 2) allows us to create and destroy weavings. Moreover, its evolution services permit the modification of its properties. This update is separated into three parts, the first two of them modify one of the services that participate in the weaving and the third one changes the weaving operator.

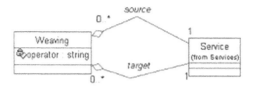

Fig. 4. The weaver package of the PRISMA metamodel

Table 2. Evolution services of the *Weaving* metaclass

```
Metaclass Weaving
   New NewWeaving(SourceAspect: string,
                   SourceService:string,
                   Operator:{after, before, instead},
                   TargetAspect:string,
                   TargetService: string);
   destroy DestroyWeaving();
   ChangeSourceWeaving (NewAspect: string,
                        NewService: string);
   ChangeOperator(NewOperator:{after, before,instead});
   ChangeTargetWeaving (NewAspect: string,
                        NewService: string);
End_Metaclass Weaving;
```

2.2 Architectural Elements

2.2.1 Components

A PRISMA component is an architectural element that captures the functionality of the information system and does not act as a coordinator between other architectural elements. It is formed by an identifier, a set of aspects, its weaving relationships and the ports that offer and request services of a specific interface.

We present the *component* package of the PRISMA metamodel in Figure 5 and the evolution services of the *component* metaclass in Table 3.

The *NewComponent* service allows us to create a new component. However, the *DestroyComponent* service destroys the component. In addition, a set of services to modify a component is provided. For example, the *AddPort* service adds a new port to the component, but the *removePort* service deletes a port from the component.

Table 5. Evolution services of the *System* metaclass

```
Metaclass System
    new NewSystem(Name: string);
    destroy DestroySystem;
    AddComponent(SystemName: Name: string);
    RemoveComponent(name: string);
    AddConnector(Name: string);
    RemoveConnector(name: string);
    AddAttachment(Component: string, Port: string,
                  Connector: string, Role: string);
    RemoveAttachment(name: string);
    AddBinding(Architectural_element: string,
               CPort: string, System: string,
               SPort: string);
    RemoveBinding(name: string);
    AddPort(Name: string, Interface: string);
    RemovePort(name: string);
End_Metaclass System;
```

3 PRISMA Evolution

PRISMA supports software evolution by means of a meta-level and the reflexive properties of its ADL. In this way, PRISMA provides the evolution of aspect-oriented software architectures and their dynamic reconfiguration.

The PRISMA architectures are defined at two different levels of abstraction: the type definition level and the configuration level. The first level defines architectural types (interfaces, aspects, components, connectors and systems) with a high abstraction level. The PRISMA types defined in this level are stored in a PRISMA library so that they can be reused by other types or specific architectures. The second level designs the architecture of software systems by creating and interconnecting instances of the defined architectural types in the previous level. In other words, in this level, we specify the topology of a specific software system.

The fact that PRISMA architectures are defined at two different levels of abstraction implies that the PRISMA evolution can be classified into two kinds: type evolution and configuration evolution (reconfiguration).

The evolution of types is achieved by invoking evolution services that do not affect the structure of the architecture or the communication among architectural elements.

It is important to take into account that there are evolution services that affect the architecture configuration such as the *AddPort* and the *RemovePort* services. The execution of services of this kind leads to the execution of other evolution services in order to adapt the configuration, thereby preserving the consistency of the architecture. For example, if a port is removed, its connections must be deleted.

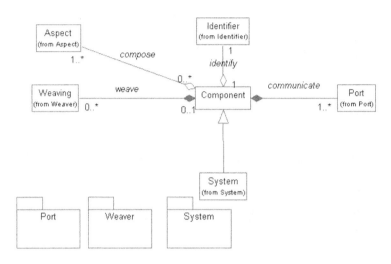

Fig. 5. The component package of the PRISMA metamodel

Table 3. Evolution services of the *Component* metaclass

```
Metaclass Component
   new     NewComponent(Name: string);
   destroy DestroyComponent(Name:string);
           AddAspect (Name: string, type: AspectType);
           RemoveAspect(name: string);
           AddPort(Name: string, Interface: string);
           RemovePort(name: string);
           AddWeaving(InAspect: string,InService:string,
                  OutAspect:string, OutService: string);
           RemoveWeaving(name: string);
End_Metaclass Component;
```

2.2.2 Connectors

A PRISMA connector is an architectural element that acts as a coordinator between other architectural elements. It is formed by an identifier, a set of aspects, its weaving relationships and one or more roles, whose signature is a specific interface. These roles represent points of interaction among components.

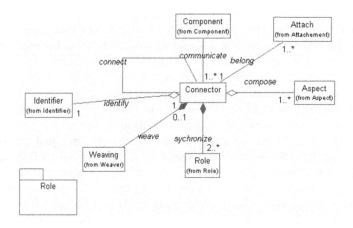

Fig. 6. The connector package of the PRISMA metamodel   .

Table 4. Evolution services of the *Connector* metaclass

```
Metaclass Connector
    new      NewConector(Name: string);
    destroy  DestroyConector();
    AddAspect(Name: string, type: AspectType);
    RemoveAspect(name: string);
    AddRole(Name: string, Interface: string);
    RemoveRole(name: string);
    AddWeaving(InAspect: string,
    InService:string,
    OutAspect:string,
    OutService: string);
    RemoveWeaving(name: string);
End_Metaclass Connector;
```

We present the *connector* package of the PRISMA metamodel in Figure 6 and the evolution services of the *connector* metaclass in Table 4.

Similar to the *component* metaclass, the *connector* metaclass (see table 4) allows us to create and destroy connectors. Moreover, it permits the modification of its properties, and it can affect the architecture configuration.

2.2.3 Systems

PRISMA components can be simple or complex. The complex ones are called systems. A PRISMA system is a component that includes a set of connectors, components and other systems that are correctly attached. Figure 7 presents the *system* package of the PRISMA metamodel and Figure 5 shows the inheritance relationship between the metaclasses component and system.

The evolution services of the *system* metaclass allow us to create and destroy systems. Moreover, the *system* metaclass permits the modification of the system name and the set of components, connectors, attachments, bindings and ports that it includes. A system definition must specify the connection and composition relationships (attachments and bindings, respectively) among the architectural elements that it contains. The attachment relationship establishes the connection among ports of components and roles of connectors. The binding relationship defines the composition between the system and the architectural elements which it contains by means of its ports. The signatures of the metaclass services are presented in Table 5.

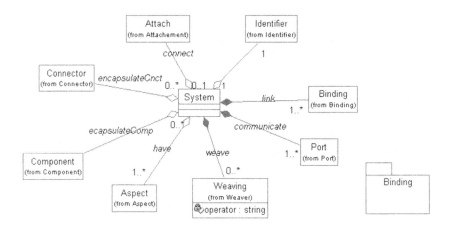

Fig. 7. The system package of the PRISMA metamodel

Similar to the *component* metaclass, the *system* metaclass (see Table 5) allows us to create and destroy systems. Moreover, it permits the modification of its properties, and it can affect the architecture configuration.

These evolution services only update the internal specification of architectural elements (internal view).

An architecture configuration is evolved by invoking evolution services that update the number of architectural elements, the communication among them, and the structure of the architecture. These evolution services affect the external view of the architectural elements and belong to the *interface, port, role, attachment, binding, component, connector* and *system* metaclasses (see Table 3, 4 and 5). The evolution services of the *port and role* metaclasses can modify the architecture configuration because they can create and destroy ports or roles of a specific component or connector, respectively. At the same time, these changes can produce the evolution of the architecture attachments and the architecture bindings by creating, destroying or modifying them. This is due to the fact that attachments and bindings are defined by using ports and roles. In addition, the creation of new instances of components, connectors and systems produces a big change in the architecture because it implies other changes such as new ports, roles, attachments or bindings. In the same way, the destruction of instances of components, connectors and systems produces meaningful changes in the architecture.

Finally, it is important to keep in mind that the evolution of PRISMA architectures can be done at run-time. The evolution at run-time allows the dynamic reconfiguration of PRISMA architectures. This dynamic reconfiguration is achieved by executing evolution services at run-time. In this way, it is possible to enforce the business rules that produce the architectural changes at run-time.

4   A Case Study: The *TeachMover* Robot

We are currently working on the *PRISMA: Model Compiler of Aspect-Oriented Component-Based Software Architectures* Microsoft® Research Cambridge project. This project consists of the specification of industrial systems such as the EFTCoR teleoperation system [13]. EFTCoR is a robotic platform that cleans the hulls of ships and that has strong requirements in terms of adaptability to different devices, safety for operators, response time, etc. These systems need dynamic reconfiguration to overcome their large set of variability sources.

Before developing the software architecture of EFTCoR [3], we specified and implemented the PRISMA architecture of the *TeachMover* robot [19]. The *TeachMover* is simpler than EFTCoR, but it has the same architectural features. We are now implementing EFTCoR reusing the implemented components of the *TeachMover* robot.

The *TeachMover* robot is composed by a set of joints that permit its movement: *Base, Shoulder, Elbow* and *Wrist*. In addition, it has a *Tool* to perform different tasks. In this case study, the tool is a gripper where open and close actions allow it to pick up objects (see Figure 8). The functionality of the *TeachMover* robot is to move objects from an initial position to a final one. The movements of the robot are ordered by an operator from a computer.

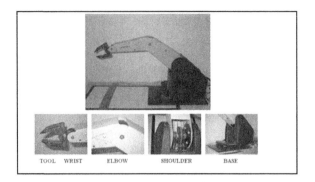

Fig. 8. The *TeachMover* Robot

The *TeachMover* architecture has a lot of components, connectors and attachments at different levels of abstraction. Due to the complexity of the system, in this paper, we only focus on the higher level of abstraction because it is more familiar to the reader and it is easier to understand. Figure 9, shows this level of the *Teach Mover* architecture. It consists of two components, *Operator* and *RUC*(Robot Unit Controller) that are connected through a connector (*CnctMovement*). The components and connector are inside of a system called *Teach Mover*. In addition, this system includes two attachments to link each component with the connector by means of their ports and roles (*Commands*, *Robot*). Figure 9 also shows that the Operator and the Robot are local (they are situated in the same node) as they form part of the same system.

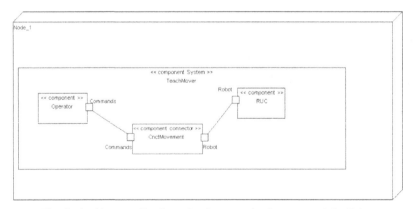

Fig. 9. Architecture Configuration between the Operator and the Robot

5 PRISMA Meta-level Implementation

The main purpose of PRISMA is to become a framework to model software architectures, providing their automatic code generation, evolution and maintaince. Therefore, we have implemented the PRISMA approach using the .Net platform as a middleware to execute PRISMA software architectures. The middleware provides the evolution services of the metalevel to evolve PRISMA software architecture.

This section introduces the PRISMA middleware and explains how the implemented evolution services of the middleware are used in a reconfiguration case of the TeachMover architecture.

5.1 PRISMA Middleware

To implement PRISMA applications, an abstract middleware which sits above the .Net platform has been developed (see Figure 10). This middleware offers the extra functionalities and characteristics of PRISMA which .Net does not directly offer. Thus, each PRISMA type (*Aspects*, *Components*, *Attachments* and *Bindings*) has been mapped to a .Net construct. In this way, the evolution services of the PRISMA metalevel are provided by the middleware.

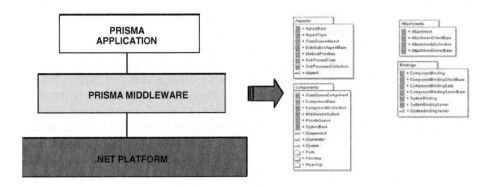

Fig. 10. The PRISMA Middleware

As PRISMA also specifies software architectures of distributed systems, this has also been taken into account in the development of the middleware. A PRISMA middleware has to run on each node where a PRISMA application needs to be executed (see Figure 11). Each middleware manages the architectural element instances that are executing in a specific node, providing the instances with necessary

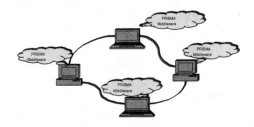

Fig. 11. PRISMA middleware running in distributed nodes

maintenance and evolution services. In order to maintain the consistence of the distributed software architecture and to make the instances work as if they were local instances, each middleware is able to interchange information with the other middlewares of the different nodes of a software architecture. We have used the .Net Remoting technology [10] to implement the distributed communication.

In our case study (see Figure 9), each node of the *Teach Mover* architecture must have a middleware running in order to enable the execution of the software architecture.

5.2 Dynamic Reconfiguration in the *TeachMover* Architecture

In this section we are going to demonstrate how the evolution techniques previously presented are applied to the TeachMover Robot case study and how an evolution service unchains other evolution services to preserve the consistency of the architecture.

As mentioned above, the *TeachMover* robot belongs to the tele-operation domain and one of the main features of systems of this kind is the fact that they need to deal with changes in architecture without stopping their execution. One of the requirements that emerged after the teach mover architecture was implemented is that the operator could move the robot from computers located in different places. Taken into account that the initial configuration of the *TeachMover* architecture is the one shown in Figure 9, our first implementation version of this system does not satisfy this requirement. This is because the operator component is forced to be at the same computer (node) as the robot controller (RUC) component. This restriction exists because these components are inside the same system and the operator component cannot move itself without moving the entire system. For this reason, the initial configuration does not allow the operator component movement from one computer to another and to access to the robot controller (RUC) component in a distributed way. In order to overcome this requirement at execution time, the architecture can reconfigure itself by externalizing the Operator component from the *TeachMover* system. In this way, the Operator component can access the TeachMover system from another node independently of which node it is working at.

Figure 12 shows how the architecture should be configured for the operator be able to move the robot from different places. As Figure 12 shows the Operator component is connected to the TeachMover system in a distributed way and is not part of the system. To perform this change, a set of meta-level services must be executed at run-time. These services are provided through the PRISMA middleware, which contains the meta-level implementation. The set of executed meta-level services is discussed bellow. It is important to keep in mind that the new Node, where the Operator component is going to be moved to, should also have the middleware executing.

When the operator component decides to move to a new node (*Node_2*), it notifies the decision to the middleware of Node_1. This middleware request the *NewComponent(Operator)* service of the meta-class *Component* from the middleware of Node 2 (see Table 3). The same Operator Component exists at both, Node_1 and

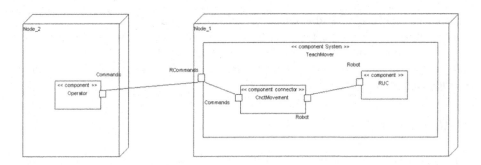

Fig. 12. The reconfiguration of the architecture in Figure 8 caused by the mobility of the Operator

Node_2 (this is performed by serializing the type). When the Operator component is created in Node_2, the middleware of Node_1 is notified and it destroys the Operator component on its site. Node_1 performs this by executing the *DestroyComponent(Operator)* of its meta-class *Component*. The results are shown in Figure 13. The operator component is at Node_2 and the *TeachMover* system, which encapsulates the attached *CnctMovement* and RUC, is at Node_1.

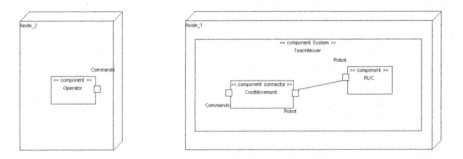

Fig. 13. The result of applying the *NewComponent (Operator)* and *DestroyComponent (Operator)* to the architecture in Figure 9

However, this is not enough to enable the Operator component to communicate with the *RUC* component. Therefore, the middleware of Node_1 requests from the TeachMover system to execute the *AddPort(RCommands, ICommands)* of the meta-class *System* (see Table 5). This service adds a port to the *TeachMover* system called *RCommands* of the *ICommands* interface type. The middleware then requests TeachMover system to execute the *AddBinding(CnctMovement, Commands, TeachMover, RCommands)* of the meta-class *System*. Thus, a binding is created between the *TeachMover* and the *CnctMovement*. Once this is performed, the Node_1 middleware request the execution of the *AddAttachment(Operator, Commands, TeachMover, RCommands)*service to middleware of Node_2 in order to create an attachment between the distributed *TeachMover* and *Operator* [2]. The final configuration of the architecture is achieved without stopping the execution of the system, the final configuration of the architecture (see Figure 12). This proposal allows the operator to become a mobile component which can access the robot in a distributed manner.

6 Related Works

This work is focused on providing a complete framework to support architecture evolution. This evolution framework is for a specific model called PRISMA. PRISMA takes into account various relevant solutions such as Component-Based Design, the Separation of Concerns Aspect-Oriented and a powerful reflexive meta-level.

Many Architecture Definition Languages (ADLs) that support evolution have been proposed. Each one has positive and negative aspects. An interesting comparison between these languages is done in the work by [14]. The proposal by Loques & Leite [7] is very similar to our approach. Their Model R-RIO incorporates dynamic reconfiguration by means of a reflexive architecture, but the use of the meta-level is quite different from ours. Other approaches use meta-programming techniques but at an implementation level such as the work by [9]. In GUARANA [11], a complex meta-level is defined at compilation time in an ad-hoc and independent way.

However, these proposals do not provide technological support for evolution that preserves the features of the model. Moreover, they have not been tested with complex case studies such as tele-operation systems. Furthermore, there is no aspect-oriented ADLs that provide evolution techniques for aspects, components and dynamic reconfiguration of architectures. As a result, PRISMA is presented as a framework to evolve aspect-oriented and component-based software architectures of complex systems at run-time.

7 Conclusions and Future Work

In this paper, the PRISMA model has been briefly presented in order to show how it is possible to define aspect-oriented architectures. The paper classifies evolution into different kinds and explains how the model overcomes each kind of evolution. Thus, a solution for the evolution of aspect-oriented software architectures has been provided. As a result, the cost of people and time invested in the maintenance process of the PRISMA architectural models is reduced.

It is also important to keep in mind that the division of the PRISMA architecture specifications into two levels of abstraction allows us to distinguish between the evolution of reusable types and the evolution of a specific architecture.

---

[2] The connector between the *Operator* component and the *TeachMover* system has been omitted because it is a relay station. The connector is implicitly supported by the existing attachment between the *Operator* and the *TeachMover*.

This paper presents the main concepts of the PRISMA metamodel in detail , it also presents its implementation by means of a middleware and the results that we have achieved executing a real case study such as the TeachMover robot.

Further work will be dedicated to improving the automatic code generation of the middleware. Sometimes, it is not necessary to evolve the whole system. As Díaz states in his work [2], systems can be divided into a static part and a volatile part. The volatile part is the one that can undergo changes due to the modification of business rules; however, the static part cannot undergo changes during the life of the application. Specifically, we want to improve the generation code-time and the run-time of the middleware by means of generating only the part of the metalevel that is needed to evolve the volatile part of a specific architecture.

Over the long term, our work with regard to software evolution will be related to the data evolution problem of software architectures, where we will apply our previous experience about data migration and data evolution of object-oriented conceptual schemas [14, 15, 16].

Bibliography

1. Aspect-Oriented Software Development http://aosd.net
2. Diaz, O., Paton, N. W.: Stimuli and Business Policies as Modelling Constructs: their definition and validation through the event calculus. Proc. CAiSE, Lecture Notes in Computer Science, Vol. 1250. Springer-Verlag,A. Olive and J. Pastor (eds) (1997) 33-46.
3. EFTCoR Project: Friendly and Cost-Effective Technology for Coating Removal. V Programa Marco, Subprograma Growth, G3RD-CT-2002-00794. (2002)
4. Garlan, D., Kompanek, A.: Reconciling the Needs of Architectural Description with Object-Modeling Notations. Proceedings «UML» 2000, Lecture Notes in Computer Science, Vol. 1939. Springer-Verlag, York, UK, October 2-6, (2000) 498-512.
5. Kiczales, G., Hilsdale, E., Huguin, J., Kersten, M., Palm, J., and Griswold, W.G: An Overview of AspectJ. In proceedings of the European Conference on Object-Oriented Programming, Lecture Notes in Computer Science, Vol. 2072. Springer-Verlag (2001)
6. Letelier, P., Sánchez, P., Ramos I., Pastor O.: OASIS 3.0, A formal language for the object oriented conceptual modeling. Polytechnic University of Valencia, SPUPV-98.4011, ISBN 84-7721-663-0 (1998) (In Spanish).
7. Loques, O., Sztajnberg, A., Leite, J., Lobosco, M.: On the Integration of Meta-Level Programming and Configuration Programming. In Reflection and Software Engineering (special edition), Editors: Walter Cazzola, Robert J. Stroud, Francesco Tisato, Lecture Notes in Computer Science Vol. 1826, Springer-Verlag, Heidelberg, Germany, June (2000).191-210.
8. Medvidovic, N., Taylor, R. N.: A classification and Comparison Framework for Software Architecture Description Languages. IEEE Transactions of SW Engineering, Vol. 26, n° 1, January (2000)
9. McGurren, F., Conroy, D.: X-ADAPT: An Architecture for Dynamic Systems. Workshop on Component-Oriented Programming, ECOOP, Málaga, Spain (2002)
10. Microsoft .Net Remoting: A Technical Overview, http://msdn.microsoft.com/library/default.asp?url=/library/en-/dndotnet/html/hawkremoting.asp

11. Oliva, A., Garcia, I. C., Buzato, L. E.: The Reflective Architecture of Guaraná. Technical Report IC-98-14. Computation Institute, Campiñas University, April (1998)

12. Pérez, J., Ramos, I., Jaén, J., Letelier, P., Navarro, E.: PRISMA: Towards Quality, Aspect Oriented and Dynamic Software Architectures. In proceedings of 3rd IEEE International Conference on Quality Software (QSIC 2003), Dallas, Texas, USA, November (2003)

13. Pérez, J., Ali, N.H., Ramos, I, Pastor, J. A., Sánchez, P., Álvarez, B.: Tele-operated Systems Development using the PRISMA approach. VIII conference on Software Engineering and Databases, Alicante, Spain (2003)

14. Pérez, J., Carsí, J A., Ramos, I.: On the implication of application's requirements changes in the persistence layer: an automatic approach. Workshop on the Database Maintenance and Reengineering (DBMR'2002), IEEE International Conference of Software Maintenance, Montreal, ISBN: 84-699-8920-0, Canada, October 1st (2002) 3-16.

15. Pérez J., Carsí J. A. and Ramos I., "ADML: A Language for Automatic Generation of Migration Plans", *The First Eurasian Conference on Advances in Information and Communication Technology*, Tehran, Iran, octubre http://www.eurasia-ict.org/ © Springer LNCS vol n.2510 (2002)

16. Pérez, J., Anaya, V., Cubel, J M., Domínguez, F., Boronat, A., Ramos, I., Carsí, J A.: Data Reverse Engineering of Legacy Databases to Object Oriented Conceptual Schemas. Software Evolution Through Transformations: Towards Uniform Support throughout the Software Life-Cycle Workshop (SET'02), First International Conference on Graph Transformation(ICGT2002), ENTCS vol n. 72.4, Barcelona, Spain, October (2002)

17. D'Souza, D., Wills, A.: Objects, Components and Frameworks with UML. The Catalysis approach. Addison-Wesley (1.999)

18. Szyperski, C.: Component software: beyond object-oriented programming. ACM Press and Addison Wesley, New York, USA (1998).

19. The *TeachMover* Robot, http://www.questechzone.com/microbot/teachmover.htm

Handling Dynamic Behaviour in Software Architectures

Sorana Cîmpan[1], Fabien Leymonerie[1], and Flavio Oquendo[2]

[1] LISTIC, ESIA Ecole Supérieure d'Ingénieurs d'Annecy, Université de Savoie
BP 806, 74016 Annecy, Cedex France
Tel: +33(0)4 50.09.65.86 – Fax: +33(0)4 50.09.65.90
[2] VALORIA , Campus de Tohannic-Bât. Yves Coppens, Université de Bretagne-Sud
BP 573 , 56017 Vannes Cedex , France
Tel : +33(0)2.97.01.72.76 - Fax : +33(0)2.97.01.72.79
{Sorana.Cimpan, Fabien.Leymonerie}@univ-savoie.fr,
Flavio.Oquendo@univ-ubs.fr

Abstract. More and more software applications have to be able to dynamically change during execution in order to adapt to changes in their environment. In the context of architecture-centred software development, this capability has to be expressed at the architectural level, inducing the need of architecture description languages capable of representing dynamic architectures. In this paper we propose an architecture description language for dynamic software architectures, the ArchWare C&C-ADL. This language uses the component-connector view, and is constructed as an architectural style on top of a more generic ADL, the ArchWare π-ADL (formal ADL based on strongly typed π-calculus). The mechanisms the language offers for the management of dynamic behaviour of software systems, as well as all the advantages of the language design are stressed in the paper. We illustrate the language concepts using dynamic client server architectures.

Keywords: software architectures, dynamic systems, architecture description language.

1 Introduction

More and more economic activities rely on software to achieve their business goal, becoming thus software intensive. The change in the economic environment has to be reflected at the level of the software support. The software applications have thus to be able to dynamically change during execution in order to adapt to the environment evolution. We distinguish among static, dynamic and evolvable systems. The *static systems* do not evolve while executing. The *dynamic systems* are generally systems that are able to evolve while executing, according to evolution patterns established at the design phase[1]. The *evolving systems* are systems that are able to evolve while executing, but the evolution has not been necessarily being established at the design phase.

---

[1] A typical example of dynamic system is a client-server with a back-up server. When the main server is down, the system dynamically reconfigure itself such that client requests are redirected towards the back-up server.

R. Morrison and F. Oquendo (Eds.): EWSA 2005, LNCS 3527, pp. 77 – 93, 2005.
© Springer-Verlag Berlin Heidelberg 2005

During the past years, the work on the engineering of software intensive applications considered the software architecture as a central point in the development process: the architecture is specified early in the software lifecycle, and constitutes the model that drives the entire engineering process. Thus, first considered at an abstract level, the architecture is stepwise refined till obtaining a concrete representation which sometimes can be used for automatic code generation. Software properties can be specified and verified early in the development process, where error recovery costs are lower. A formal refinement guaranties property preservation from one step to another.

The adoption of this architecture-centric software development process induced the proposition of several languages to support the definition of software architectures: Architecture Description Languages (ADLs). All the proposed ADLs address the software structure, and give means for describing topological aspects of the architecture. Some of the ADLs allow also the representation of the system behaviour, basing most of the time their behaviour formalization on process algebras [2,3,6,20,19]. For representing dynamic systems, ADLs taking into account behavioural aspects are better suited, as they allow to represent the way the system changes [3,6,20]. ADLs that do not address system behaviour using algebraic foundations may represent dynamic change by combining topology representation with temporal logic [28]. Other generic formalisms were used to reason upon a system architecture dynamic change, like the use of a chemical abstract machine model (based on a general term rewriting system, it describes arbitrary reconfigurations of architectures) [11] and use of graph grammars to describe the allowable topologies of architectures [13].

This paper proposes an innovative ADL called ArchWare C&C-ADL allowing the description of dynamic software architectures. The language proposed is in the alignment of efforts made in language such as Dynamic Wright [3] and π-Space [6] and proposes facilities for handling dynamic behaviour for component connector architectures. The language proposed is original in the way dynamic behaviour is handled, as well as in the way the language is constructed.

The language design, its formal foundations and research context are presented (section 2), followed by the language concepts, insisting on those that differentiate it from other propositions (sections 3). The language is then presented throughout illustrative examples (section 4), and positioned with respect to other existing approaches (section 5).

2 Language Foundations and Design

The work presented here has been partially funded by the European Commission in the framework of the IST ArchWare Project (IST–2001–32360) [1]. The ArchWare project aims to develop and validate an innovative architecture-centric software engineering framework, i.e., architecture description and analysis languages, architectural styles, refinement models, architecture-centric tools, and a customisable software environment. The main concern is to guarantee required quality attributes throughout evolutionary software development (initial development and evolution), taking into account domain-specific architectural styles, reuse of existing components, support for variability on software products and product-lines, and run-time system evolution.

The ADLs proposed in the literature use a component-connector view of architecture design. This component-connector view is the starting point from which specialisation is possible in the form of more specific component types, or trough the use of style mechanisms. The approach adopted in ArchWare was to start not from a component-connector view of software architecture, but from a more generic one, a *core formal language* based on architectural elements, coupled with a *style mechanism* allowing the construction of more specific languages. The component connector language we propose (ArchWare C&C-ADL) is constructed in such a way, as presented here after.

The core formal language – Archware π-ADL [20,7,19] - is based on the high-order π-calculus algebra [18], persistent programming and dynamic system composition and decomposition [10]. Archware π-ADL is a well-formed extension of π-calculus for defining a calculus of communicating and mobile architectural elements. These architectural elements are defined in terms of *behaviours*. A behaviour expresses in scheduled way both the interaction of an architectural element and its internal computation. Behaviours can be connected through connections, along which values can be transmitted. These actions (concerning communication as well as internal computing) are scheduled using similar π-calculus operators for expressing sequence, choice, composition, replication and matching. Architectural constituents are defined by composing behaviours, communicating through connections. An architecture is itself an architectural element. Moreover, π-ADL provides a mechanism for reusing parameterised behaviour definitions which can be embedded in abstractions. Such abstractions are instantiated as behaviours by application.

Architectural styles provide a design vocabulary. In the ArchWare approach, when a style is defined, it is possible to associate a new syntax; thus the style provides a more specialized architecture description language. The basic style mechanism (core style mechanism), consists in associating properties to Archware π-ADL behaviour abstractions. The properties are expressed using another language of the ArchWare family: the Archware Analysis Language[2], or Archware AAL [3].

A more elaborated language is built on top of this basic style mechanism, allowing style formalisation – ArchWare Architectural Style Language, or ArchWare ASL 158. Using ArchWare ASL, one formalises styles around three main concepts: *style constraints* (rules that architectures must follows to satisfy a style), *style analyses* (used to evaluate particular architecture characteristics) and *style constructors* (reusable parameterised ArchWare π-ADL definitions).

Style constraints are the essence of a style and delimit a design space in which every architecture satisfies a common set of properties, i.e., they characterise an architecture family corresponding to the style. The language offers the possibility to constrain structural, behavioural and non-functional characteristics of architectures, using a formalism based on predicate logic. This formalism is a sub-part of ArchWare AAL [4].

Style constructors provide support for the design of architectures following the style, by allowing their rapid creation through an instantiation mechanism. They constitute a library of reusable elements.

---

[2] The AAL is a formal language defined as an extended calculus subsuming the modal μ-calculus [10] and the predicate calculus for expressing structural and behavioural properties on software architectures.

The architectures following a styles respect all the style constraints, i.e. they share common properties. *Style analysis* permit to go further in the analysis of properties, by evaluating additional properties on architectures following the style. The system is open, in the sense that analysis can be described in model specific languages performed by external tools.

This paper presents the ArchWare C&C-ADL [8,15], a component – connector language for the definition of dynamic software systems architectures. The language is the associated notation of a Component-Connector Style defined using ArchWare ASL. The concepts of components and connectors are architectural element styles. They can be easily specified, or changed in order to better suit users expectations. For instance, a component is an architectural element style. It has an associated style constructor, allowing to actually define a component (by instantiating the constructor). As the instantiation of a component result is a ArchWare π-ADL description, the language is a formal one.

The component and connector style proposed imposes a minimum set of constraints, allowing for instance the connection of two connectors. In order to obtain a more restrictive component-connector language, one can do it by simply defining a sub-style of the component-connector style we propose. If one agrees with the proposed concepts (and associated constraints) but doesn't like the syntax, it can again easily adapt it to best suit her/his needs.

The ArchWare C&C-ADL design provides the benefits of giving a formal foundation as well as adaptable concepts and notations. The paper presents the language, and not the associated style defined using ArchWare ASL, style for which details can be found in [15,8]. The following section presents the main concepts of the language.

3 ArchWare C&C-ADL Concepts

Most of the existing ADLs propose to model software architectures using a compositional approach, components and connectors. Components entail system functionalities, while connectors allow the communication between components. The components and connectors interfaces are generally structured using ports (or other equivalent concepts), allowing to more easily see whether different components and connectors can be attached (the compatibility check is made at the port level rather than at the component level).

Parts of the Archware C&C-ADL concepts we propose are similar to some proposed by other ADLs for representing the structure (ports, components, connectors) or the behaviour (based on process algebras), and will be rapidly introduced (cf. section 3.1). We will focus then on concepts that make the originality of our proposition, which is most related to the way dynamic aspects of architectures are represented and handled (cf. section 3.2).

3.1 Architecture Description Basic Concepts

The language takes a compositional approach for building architectures. Components and connectors are first class citizens. They can be either atomic, either composed by other components and connectors.

Atomic architectural elements[3] have a behaviour, represented in ArchWare π-ADL, basically expressed in terms of communication actions along connections, enhanced with dynamic specific actions (cf. section 3.2). The component interface, represented by a set of connections, is structured in ports. Each port has a protocol (which is a projection of the element behaviour).

Composite architectural elements are composed by several components and connectors. A composite behaviour results from the parallel composition of the behaviours of elements that compose it, which at a lower level, comes to parallel composition of ArchWare π-ADL behaviours. In order to interact, the compatible ports of components and connectors are attached. The composite has its own ports, to which ports of the composing elements are bound.

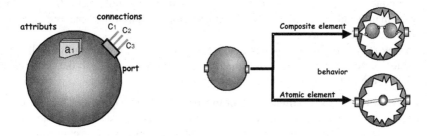

Fig. 1. Architectural elements structure

Atomic as well as composite elements may also have attributes, which store different properties. Attributes can be used in the architectural element parameterisation, as behaviour actions can be guarded by conditions related to attribute values. We will see further how this can be achieved, when presenting the language illustration (section 4).

3.2 Dynamism Related Architecture Description Concepts

The dynamism of architectures can be considered at different levels, and three such levels are proposed9. The lowest one named *first-level* or *interactive dynamism*, just requires the dynamic communication of data in a fixed structure. Languages that do represent architectural behaviour are at this level of dynamism. We found in this class all the languages which are based on process algebras, like [6,5,3,2,1,9]. The second level allows the modification of this structure, usually expressed as the creation and removal of component instances and links; this could be named *structural dynamism* and it's the one found in most of current proposals. The third level allows the modification of the infrastructure in which structures are defined; that is, the dynamic (re)definition of new component types, named *architectural dynamism* [9].

Our proposition allows to represent the three levels of dynamism. This is possible due to its construction on top of ArchWare π-ADL, completed with *dynamics specific behavioural actions*, *meta-entities* and *choreographers*, as presented hereafter.

---

[3] We will use the term architectural element to talk about components or connectors, in cases where there are no differences between the two.

Dynamics Specific Behavioural Actions. As mentioned, our architectural elements behaviour representation is based on ArchWare π-ADL. In order to ease the representation of the topology modifications, we enriched the ArchWare π-ADL behaviour actions with actions dedicated to the dynamic creation (of connections, ports and architectural elements) and reconfiguration (dynamic attachment and detachment, inclusion and exclusion of architectural elements. In the case of atomic architectural elements these actions concern connections and ports.

Meta-entities – Everything Is Dynamic. In our approach everything is potentially dynamic, which means that whatever entity, from connection to composite architectural elements, can be duplicated several times. An architectural entity definition can serve at the dynamic creation of several occurrences. In order to handle this, we introduce the concept of *meta-entity*, as a matrix containing an entity definition together with information allowing the creation, suppression (dynamic or not) and management of several occurrences.

A meta-entity is defined by: a name which references it, a production unit allowing the creation of new occurrences, a list containing references towards all the occurrences created from the meta-entity, a reference (position on the list) for the latest occurrence[4].

Choreographer – Management of Composite Elements Dynamics. Components and connectors are seen as black-boxes when they are composed (the verification of their compatibility can be made by analysing their ports). The interconnections are made by explicit ports attachments. How can this architecture evolve? Who should handle it? When defined, components and connectors have no knowledge of the environment in which they will be used (composed), and thus we consider they cannot be the one that handle the topology of the system for which they are a part. We propose (as in other languages [3,13,25,27]) a special entity explicitly modelled for handling the composite dynamics: the *choreographer*. The latter is in charge of changing the topology when needed, namely by:

- changing the attachments between architectural elements,
- create dynamically new instances of architectural elements,
- exclude elements from the architecture (make the decoupling),
- include existing element that arrive into the architecture (couple them with the rest of the architecture).

This section focused on the language concepts, without whatsoever syntactic resentation. The following section presents the language (its syntax) through examples.

4   ArchWare C&C-ADL Illustration by Examples

In this section the ArchWare C&C-ADL is presented using dynamic client-server architectures, where clients and servers are defined by meta-components which are then instantiated in an architecture. A version in which the server is dynamic, and the architectures takes into account the server breakdown in order to reconfigure is presented in section 4.1. This architecture is then enhanced, and clients can join the architecture dynamically (cf. section 4.2).

---

[4] This is of course completely transparent to the language users.

4.1   Client – Server Architecture

Let us consider an architecture which has one client, one connector and one server. Whenever the server goes down, a new instance is dynamically created and linked to the connector, in a transparent manner to the clients that request the server services. The server can only go down between two request proceedings.

The architecture is presented in an incremental way. First a simple port definition is explained, then the definition of a client that entails the port definition. Tthe server and the link connector are then examined, to finally get to the global view where all the elements are put together and the dynamic change of the server is handled.

Ports definitions have three parts. The first is dedicated to the declaration of connections. These declarations correspond to meta-connections. The second part is dedicated to the initial configuration, i.e., what connections are created when the port is instantiated. The third part is dedicated to the port protocol, described using Arch-Ware π-ADL.

Let us have a look at the following port definition:

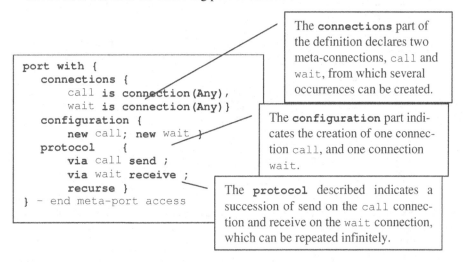

```
port with {
    connections {
        call is connection(Any),
        wait is connection(Any) }
    configuration {
        new call; new wait }
    protocol    {
        via call send ;
        via wait receive ;
        recurse }
} - end meta-port access
```

The **connections** part of the definition declares two meta-connections, `call` and `wait`, from which several occurrences can be created.

The **configuration** part indicates the creation of one connection `call`, and one connection `wait`.

The **protocol** described indicates a succession of send on the `call` connection and receive on the `wait` connection, which can be repeated infinitely.

The previous definition can be used inside a component or connector definition, where a meta-port with this definition can be declared:

```
access is  port with { … }
```

The Client Component. Atomic components have three main parts. The first is dedicated to the meta-ports declaration. A configuration part indicates which are the port occurrences initially created, while a computation part indicates the component behaviour. The following declaration of a Client meta-component declares in a ports part of its definition a port `access` with the previous definition.

```
Client is component with{
   ports {
      access is port with { /… }
   }
   configuration { new access }
   computation {
      via access~call send any();
      unobservable;
      via access~wait
        receive reply:Any;
      recurse }
} – end meta-component Client
```

Declaration of meta-port `access`

One instance of the `access` meta-port in the initial configuration

The client behaviour consists on sending a request on the `call` connection of the `access` port, do something and then receive a reply on the `access` port `wait` connection.

The Server Component. The following definition concerns the server meta-component, which is also defined as an atomic component.

```
Server is component with{
   ports {
     sAccess is port with {
      connections {
       request is connection(Any),
       reply is connection(Any)   }
      configuration { new request;  new reply }
      protocol  {
       via request receive request:Any ;
       via reply send any();
       recurse }
      }
   }
   attributes {down: boolean default value is false }
   configuration { new sAccess }
   computation {
    via attribute~down
       receive v:Boolean;
    if not(v) then {
     choose
       { via sAccess~request
          receive request:Any;
        unobservable;
        via sAccess~reply
          send any() }
     or
       { via attribute~down
          send true}
        then recurse
    }  }
}– end meta-component Server
```

Definition of meta-port `sAccess` with two connections `request` and `reply`

attribute `down` stores the state of the server.

The value of the `down` attribute is constantly checked. If the server is not down it can either handle a request (receive, treat, send reply) or stop (set the down attribute value to true). Thus the server cannot stop while processing a request. After making the choice, the servers recourses (attribute is checked, and then the choice is made, etc.

The server has a port via which requests can be addressed and answered. The server posses a Boolean attribute (down) which stores its state, with the default value false. If the server is not down then there are two choices: it can stop or receive a request, treat it, and send a response. At this level of abstraction, the internal procedure of the request is not important, and is represented by an unobservable action. In this way it is modelled at the architectural level that the server cannot stop while handling a request.

Attributes values are accessed via communication actions along a port with the name attribute. Thus in order to read the value of the down attribute, the server makes a receive on the down connection of the port attribute, in the beginning of its computation. In order to modify the attribute value, the server makes a send on the same connection.

The Link Connector. The connector between the Client and the Server is and atomic connector named Link. It has two ports, one for communicating with the server (serverAccess, with two connections request and reply) and one for communicating with the client (clientAccess with two connections call and wait)[5]. One instance of each is created in the configuration part. The connector behaviour (represented in the routing part of its definition), consists in receiving a request from the client, send it to the server, then receive a response from the server and send it to the client.

```
Link is connector with{
   ports { clientAccess is port with { … },
           serverAccess is port with { … }
   }
   configuration { new clientAccess ; new serverAccess }
   routing {
        via clientAccess~call receive request:Any;
        via serverAccess~request send request;
        via serverAccess~reply receive reply:Any;
        via clientAccess~wait send reply;
        recurse
   }
}- end meta-connector Link
```

DynamicClientServer Composite. The global architecture is defined as a composite component, named DynamicClientServer. A composite component has a part dedicated to the meta-ports declarations as well as one to the different constituents (meta components and meta-connectors). The configuration part specifies the initial occurrences of ports and constituents, as well as the attachments between the constituents' ports or the bindings to the composite ports. The choreographer describes the dynamic behaviour.

For the DynamicClientServer, three meta-elements are declared in the constituents part, corresponding to the previous definitions of Client, Server and

---

[5] We do not detail the port definitions.

Link. The configuration gives the initial topology, composed by a client, a server and a link connector.

The dynamic change of the server (and associated attachments) is handled by the choreographer. The later constantly looks at the down attribute for the current server. The current instance is referenced by Server#last. If the server is down, it is detached from the connector. A new instance is created and attached to the connector. The choreographer has access to all the ports of all the composite elements (the attachment is implicit, and thus not specified at the level of the configuration part). The attributes of a component which is part of the composite can be accessed by the choreographer by giving the component name, and then by following the procedure already explained in the server presentation.

Note that the DynamicClientServer composite has no ports, thus the architecture is closed. The following section presents an enhanced version of this architecture, with mobile clients joining the architecture.

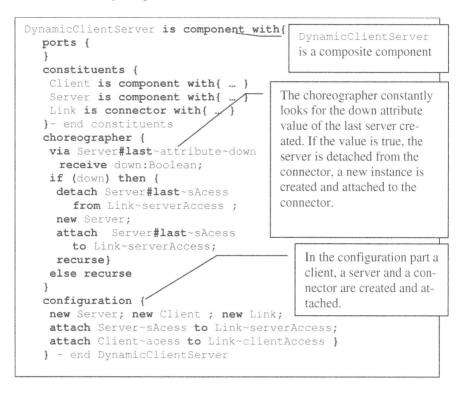

4.2 Client-Server Architecture with Mobile Clients

Here after is a new version, where mobile clients can enter the architecture dynamically. The architecture, which we call EnhancedDynamicClientServer, contains the same meta-components (Client and Server). The connector Link is replaced by the DynamicLink and the choreographer definition changes also.

DynamicLink Connector. The connector becomes dynamic in the sense that whenever a new client joins the architecture, it has to adapt, so that the client can be attached to it (a new port is created), and that the requests coming from the client are transmitted to the server.

```
DynamicLink is connector with{
  ports {
    clientAccess is port with { ... },
    serverAccess is port with { ... },
    newClient is port with {
     connections {
      createI is connection(Any),
      createO is connection(Any) }
     configuration { new createI; new createO }
     protocol {
       via createIn receive;
       via createOut send ;
       recurse
      }
     }
  configuration {
      new clientAccess ;
      new serverAccess }
    routing {
     choose {
      via clientAccess#any=i~call
        receive requete:Any;
      via serverAccess~request
        send requete;
      via serverAccess~reply
        receive reponse:Any;
      via clientAccess#i~wait
        send reponse      }
      or {
       via newClient~createIn receive;
       new clientAccess;
       via newClient~createOut send }
      then recurse
      }
}- end meta-connector DynamicLink
```

The connector receives on one of its clientAcess ports referenced by clientAccess**#any** a request. The actual occurrence number is stored in the variable i. The connector transmits the request to the server, and then receives the reply and gives it to the client that requested it (clientAccess#i).

The connector makes a interaction via its newClient port, which means that a new client joined the architecture. It creates a new clientAccess port and notifies by a send on the newClient port that it's definition changed.

The ports definition include the ones of the Link connector (clientAcess and serverAccess), one occurrence of each being created in the configuration part. A port newClient is added, via which the connector can be notified about the fact that a new client joined the architecture. The routing part indicates that the connector can either handle a request (get the request from a client, send it to the server, receive the replay, and send it back to the client), either handle the arrival of a new client.

We recall that each meta-entity entails a sequence of all its occurrences, thus the clientAcess meta-port handles the sequences of occurrences. By clientAccess**#any**, we make reference to whatever element of the sequence. When the connector creates a new `clientAccess` occurrence, the port is added to the sequence, and thus become eligible for receiving requests.

The connector topology and behaviour changes thus dynamically.

EnhancedDynamicClientServer Composite. The new composite has a port, along which mobile clients can join the architecture. This port, named `newClient`, has two connections along which clients can transit.

```
EnhancedDynamicClientServer is component with{
  ports {
   newClient is port with {
    connections {
     createIn is connection(Client),
     createOut is connection(Client) }
    configuration { new createIn; new createOut}
    protocol {
     via createIn receive c:Client ;
     via createOut send c;
     recurse }
  }
  constituents {
   Client is component with{ … }
   Server is component with{ … }
   DynamicLink is connector with{ … }
  }- end constituents
  configuration {
   new Server; new Client ; new DynamicLink;
   attach Server~sAcess to DynamicLink~serverAccess;
   attach Client~acess to DynamicLink~clientAccess }
  choreographer {
   choose {
    via Server#last~attribute~down receive down:Boolean;
    if (down) {
      detach Server#last~sAcess
        from DynamicLink~serverAccess ;
      new Server;
      attach Server#last~sAcess
         to DynamicLink~serverAccess }
      }
    or {
       via newClient~createOut receive c : Client;
       insert component c in Client ;
       via DynamicLink~newClient~createIn send ;
       via DynamicLink~newClient~createOut receive ;
       attach DynamicLink~clientAccess#last to c~access
       }
     then recurse }
   }
} - end DynamicClientServer
```

The `Server` and `Client` constituents are the same as the ones in our previous archi-tecture, the `Link` connector is replaced by the `DynamicLink` connector we just pre-sented. The configuration part creates one occurrence of each, and makes the proper at-tachments. Note that the `newClient` port is not bound to none of the constituents com-ponents. The choreographer uses this port, and it has implicit access to it.

The choreographer has always the choice to either respond to a server breakdown (made in the same way as `DynamicClientServer`), or handle the arrival of a new client.

When a new client arrives it joins the architecture via the `createOut` connection of the `newClient` port. The choreographer receives it and inserts it into the architec-ture, in the meta-element `Client`. This actually adds the client to the list of occur-rences handled by the meta-element `Client`[6]. The choreographer makes a communi-cation with the `DynamicLink` connector, which is announced about the client arrival. When it receives a message from the connector, this means that the connector has a new `clientAccess` port created for the client connection, port which can be refer-enced by `DynamicLink~clientAccess#last` in order to attach the new client to it.

5 Related Work

In architecture research, there are two widely accepted approaches to software archi-tecture description: one concentrates on the problem of "coordination", the other on the "refinement of abstract specifications"[7]. Our work clearly inserts in the second ap-proach, where several ADLs have been proposed. Good presentations of the state of the art can be found in the literature [17,14]. Rather than giving an extensive over-view, we will focus here on the languages which are more relevant to our proposition, namely π-Space [6] and Dynamic Wright [3], which equally use a component-connector view of the architecture, represent behaviour and allow representing dy-namic architectures. Other generic formalisms were used to reason upon a system ar-chitecture, like the use of a chemical abstract machine model (based on a general term rewriting system, it describes arbitrary reconfigurations of architectures) [11] and use of graph grammars to describe the allowable topologies of architectures [13].

π-Space [6] is a language for dynamic architecture and architecture behaviour de-scriptions. Wright [2] is a language for modelling and analysis behaviour of concur-rent systems, which Dynamic Wright [3] with additional mechanisms for handling dynamic architectures.

Dynamic Wright uses CSP for representing behaviour, an algebra which (unlike the π-calculus used by π-Space) does not allow to represent dynamic behaviour. In order to represent dynamic behaviour, Dynamic Wright introduces special control ac-tions and the *configuror*, which establishes several configurations among which one can alternate during execution.

In ArchWare C&C-ADL composite elements dynamic change is equally handled by a special entity, the choreographer. For composite architectural elements, the ini-tial configuration is established in the configuration part, which indicates which meta-

---

[6] It is also possible for elements different than the ones already existing in the architecture to join the architecture, as the elements transit connections with their meta-definition attached.

[7] 9 presents some of the common aspects between the two approaches.

entities are first instantiated. Once the first occurrences are created, the system can execute (in the sense that the components run), or it can dynamically change. The choreographer has the global view and controls the dynamic change. The Dynamic-ClientServer example illustrated the structural dynamism, with the creation of instances and links. The EnhancedDynamicClientServer show how new elements can join the architecture.

The DynamicLink connector is an example of atomic connector, which dynamically adapts to the insertion of a new client. This can be seen as architectural dynamism [9], as the connector internal behaviour changes, so that it takes into account the new client.

π-Space [6] is the ADL that is closer to our proposition, as it is also based on π-calculus[8], and allows to represent dynamic architectures. π-Space targets the elements that are potentially dynamic in an architecture, limiting the dynamic change of the architecture. The initial configuration includes an instance of all declared elements, and attachments are described in the *where* part of the composite (corresponding to our configuration part). The dynamic change is managed in composite elements by rules (described in a dedicated part *whenever*) which explain topological changes due to the creation of new elements. An example of such a rule is that the creation of a new client induces the creation of a new port on the connector and attaches the client to the connector. The dynamic change of a composite can be triggered by one of its composite components.

The main differences on how dynamic change is handled in ArchWare C&C-ADL and π-Space are the following. Firstly, by making each entity potentially dynamic we have simplified to the user the entity definition (targeting no longer needed), and we have increased the reusability of components definitions (elements which were not "dynamic" in some usages, become so in others). The way we handle dynamic change is different. In π-Space a dynamic change (an attachment for instance) is initiated by an atomic component. In order to increase components and connectors reuse, we consider them at a composite level as black boxes; they are defined independently of their environment and have no knowledge of their attachments to other elements, the choreographer being the one that entirely orchestrates the creation of new instances, the attachments and detachments between components. ArchWare C&C-ADL goes further equally towards mobile architecture description[9], by allowing the transition of architectures along connections, while π-Space limits to connection mobility.

Most ADLs (including the two cited above), essentially provide a built-in model of architecture description and formalise topological constraints. The reason of this is that most ADLs enforce a hard coded component-and-connector model and that structure is certainly the most understandable and visible part of an architecture. But one can notice, that behavioural and attribute aspects are often taken into account, and they are certainly an essential point of the work on architecture description.

---

[8] Unlike ArchWare π-ADL, π-Space is not strongly typed, which reduces the number of verifications that can be performed at architectural level. Actually it is based on an un-typed version of π-calculus.

[9] Lots of aspects related to mobility are of course still to be studied. We do not claim the description of mobile architectures, but we provide some basic mechanisms to do it.

ArchWare π-ADL is a general-purpose ADL providing features for building user-defined component-and-connector viewpoints (ArchWare C&C-ADL is such a viewpoint) and architectural styles, including structural, behavioural and semantic properties. It was designed following a compliant architectural model (in a layered style) in order to support compliant software applications that are dynamic and evolvable.

Being based on ArchWare π-ADL, ArchWare C&C-ADL takes advantage of all the interesting features ArchWare π-ADL possesses (formal foundation with property checking, behaviour description, on-the-fly dynamicity and mobility). It gives a component-and-connector view which is not too restrictive, allowing constructing further user-specific component-connectors views of architectural description.

6 Further Considerations

This paper presented the ArchWare C&C-ADL, a language for describing dynamic software architectures, addressing the structural as well as the architectural dynamism 9. As illustrated by the examples provided, on the fly changes may concern the connectivity between architectural elements, creation of new element occurrences, change in the definition of existing elements, as well as the introduction of new elements in architectures. The language gives the possibility to indicate at the architectural level when the change may take place. Thus for the server example, it is possible to indicate that the server should stop only between two requests. Further in the refinement process up to implementation, this can be backed by mechanisms allowing recovering if the failure occurs while processing a request. The server change was completely transparent to the clients that send requests to it. Other examples in the literature considered a simpler architecture, with a main server and a backup one [3].

In our enhanced client server architecture, we show how mobile architectural elements can join the architecture at whatever point in time. The connector changed in order to take into account the new client arrival, in a transparent manner for the server that processes the requests as well as for the clients already present in the architecture. The language permits equally to detach elements from a composite and send them to migrate in other composite elements.

The ArchWare C&C-ADL is constructed as associated syntax of an architectural style defined in a formal language. This gives a lot of flexibility and increases the language usability. The style constraints are not too restrictive, such that the user can adapt it to its proper needs. The change can also be made only at the syntactic level. In this paper we show how one can use the language in order to create architectures. More specific styles can be created from the Component-Connector style, and then instantiated. We created several such sub-styles (including client-server, the pipe-and-filter, data indirection and layered) in the ArchWare project, which form the ArchWare Foundation Styles Library [8]. The Component-Connector style (which entails the semantics of the ArchWare C&C-ADL) consists the root of the library. The ArchWare C&C-ADL has been extensively used by our industrial as well as academic project partners, but also by other research actors, outside the project [23]. The use of the language is often made in conjunction with the use of the associated style, in order to create more specific styles. Nevertheless, ArchWare C&C-ADL is not imposed in order to use the ArchWare environment, and we have cases in which styles have been built for specific domains not from component-connector style, but in the same way as the component-connector style [24].

Architecture descriptions written in ArchWare C&C-ADL correspond to architectural style instantiations, which lead to ArchWare π-ADL descriptions. As the associated component-connector style is written using ArchWare ASL, the associated toolkit is used in order to generate the architectures (the toolkit includes an architecture instantiator) [16]. Once the ArchWare π-ADL descriptions obtained (the definition is complained with the style), the user has the possibility use several other tools in the ArchWare environment, including the ArchWare Animator [26], which allows to animate the architectural descriptions, or verification tools for verifying additional architectural properties. The architecture can be executed with the virtual machine, or it can be refined towards a target language.

Currently the language handles anticipated changes, like in our example a new client joining the architecture. Future work will consider unanticipated change, and investigate mechanisms allowing the choreographer to handle such changes. Another aspect that has also to be further investigated is the case of distributed systems, and how that impacts the choreographer current design.

References

1. ArchWare project team, Architecting evolvable software, ARCHWARE, European RTD Project IST-2001-32360, 2001-2004.
2. R.Allen, A Formal Approach to Software Architectures. PhD thesis, TR# CMU-CS-97-144, Carnegie Mellon University, School of Computer Science, May 1997.
3. R. Allen, R. Douence & D. Garlan, Specifying and Analyzing Dynamic Software Architectures. Proceedings on Fundamental Approaches to Software Engineering, Lisbon, Portugal, March 1998.
4. I. Alloui, H. Garavel, R. Mateescu, F. Oquendo, The Archware Architecture Analysis Language. ARCHWARE European RTD Project IST-2001-32360, Deliverable D3.1b, 2002.
5. M.Bernardo, P.Ciancarini, L.Donatiello, Architecting Systems with Process Algebras. Technical Report UBLCS-2001-7, July 2001.
6. C.Chaudet, F.Oquendo, π-SPACE: A Formal Architecture Description Language Based on Process Algebra for Evolving Software Systems, Proceedings of 15th IEEE International Conference on Automated Software Engineering (ASE'00), September 11 - 15, 2000, Grenoble, France.
7. S. Cîmpan, F. Oquendo, D. Balasubramaniam, G. Kirby, R. Morrison, The ArchWare ADL: Definition of The Textual Concrete Syntax, ARCHWARE European RTD Project IST-2001-32360, Deliverable D1.2b, 2002.
8. S. Cîmpan, F. Leymonerie, F. Oquendo, The ADL Foundation Styles Library. ARCHWARE European RTD Project IST-2001-32360, ArchWare Report R1.3b, June 2003.
9. C.Cuesta, P. de la Fuente, M. Barrio-Solorzano, Dynamic Coordination Architecture through the use of Reflection. Proceedings of the 2001 ACM symposium on Applied computing, Las Vegas, Nevada, United States, pp: 134 - 140, 2001
10. M. Greenwood, D. Balasubramaniam, S. Cîmpan, N.C. Kirby, K. Mickan, R. Morrison, F. Oquendo, I. Robertson, W. Seet, R. Snowdon, B. Warboys, E. Zirintsis. Process Support for Evolving Active Architectures. Proceedings of the 9th Europeean Workshop on Software Process Technology, EWSPT 2003, Helsinki, Finlande, 2003, pp. 112-127.

11. P.Inverardi, A.Wolf, Formal Specification an Analysis of Software Architectures Using the Chemical Abstract Machine Model. IEEE transactions on Software Engineering, vol. 21, no.4. April 1995.
12. D. Kozen, Results on the Propositional Mu-Calculus. Theoretical Computer Science, 1983, n. 27, pp. 333-354.
13. D. LeMétayer, Describing software architecture styles using graph grammars. IEEE Transactions on Software Engineering, 24(7):521–553, July 1998.
14. F. Leymonerie, S. Cîmpan, F. Oquendo, Classification and Comparison for ADL formalising style, Revue Génie Logiciel no. 62, pp 8-14, 2002.
15. F. Leymonerie. ASL language and tools for architectural styles. Contribution to dynamic architectures description. PhD thesis, University of Savoie, December 2004.
16. F. Leymonerie, S. Cimpan, F. Oquendo, Lionel Blanc Dit Jolicoeur, David Le Berre, Fredéric Pourraz, Régis Dindeleux, André Montaud, The Style-Based Customizer – Release 1, ARCHWARE European RTD Project IST-2001-32360, Deliverable D2.4b, July 2004.
17. N. Medvidovic, R. N. Taylor, A Framework for classifying and comparing architecture description languages. In Proceedings of ESEC/FSE'97, pages 60–76.ACM Press, Sept. 1997.
18. R. Milner, J. Parrow, D. Walker, A Calculus Of Mobile Processes. Information and Computation, pp 1-40, 1992.
19. F. Oquendo, π-ADL: an Architecture Description Language based on the higher-order typed π-calculus for specifying dynamic and mobile software architectures. ACM SIGSOFT Software Engineering Notes Volume 29, Issue 3, May 2004, pp. 1-14
20. F. Oquendo, I. Alloui, S. Cîmpan, H. Verjus, The ArchWare ADL: Definition of The Abstract Syntax and Formal Semantics. ARCHWARE European RTD Project IST-2001-32360, Deliverable D1.1b, 2002.
21. F. Oquendo and Al, Positioning Archware ADL w.r.t. the State of the Art. ARCHWARE European RTD Project IST-2001-32360, 2002.
22. D.E. Perry, A.L. Wolf, Foundations for the Study of Software Architecture. ACM SIGSOFT Software Engineering Notes vol. 17 no. 4 pp 40, 1992.
23. Ratcliffe O., Cimpan S., Oquendo F., Scibile L., Formalization of an HCI Style for Accelerator Restart Monitoring. First European Workshop on Software Architecture (EWSA 2004), St. Andrews, Royaume Uni, May 2004, pp. 167-181
24. Revillard J., Benoit E., Cimpan S., Oquendo F., Software Architecture for Intelligent Instrument Design. 16th Int. Conf. on Software & Systems Engineering and their Apllications (ICSSEA 2003), Vol. 3-17, Paris, France, December 2003, pp. 1-10.
25. S. Stuurman and J. Van Katwijk. On-line change mechanisms: The software architectural level. In 6th International Symposium on the Foundations of Software Engineering, 1998.
26. H. Verjus, F. Pourraz, S. Azzaiez, Final ArchWare Architecture Animator – Release 1 – Prototype. ARCHWARE European RTD Project IST-2001-32360, Deliverable D2.2b, 2003.
27. M. A. Wermelinger, Specification of Software Architecture Reconfiguration. PhD thesis, Universidade Nova de Lisboa, Sept. 1999.
28. D.Wile, AML: An Architecture Meta Language. Proceedings of the 14th International Conference on Automated Software Engineering, pp. 183-190. Cocoa Beach. October 1999.

Pattern-Based Architectural Design Driven by Quality Properties: A Platform to Model Scientific Calculation

Francisca Losavio[1], Nicole Levy[2], Parinaz Davari[2], and François Colonna[3]

[1] LaTecS Laboratory, Centro ISYS, Universidad Central de Venezuela
flosav@cantv.net
[2] Laboratoire PRISM, Université de Versailles St Quentin
{nlevy, dap}@prism.uvsq.fr
[3] Laboratoire de Chimie Thórique, Université Paris VI
colonna@lct.jussieu.fr

Abstract. There is a general agreement on the fact that architectural design is crucial to build software that meets initial needs. Nonfunctional properties play an important role, however methods are not still mature. We have defined a pattern-based architectural design method driven by quality properties. Our goal is to apply it to design a platform to model scientific calculation. We do not intend to re-write a new Simulation Code (Quantum Chemistry, Molecular Dynamics etc ...) nor to integrate various existing Codes inside an external envelope, with some scripting language, which is the usual practice in most of these calculation environments. Our intention is rather to spend the necessary time to design rationally the architecture and the objects of a modeling framework. In this platform the architecture is crucial to handle a unique calculation structure, shared by all the components of the platform.

1 Introduction

Architectural design is a stepwise process which identifies the key strategies for the large-scale organization of systems under development [17]. Most of the existing methods consider that nonfunctional requirements are crucial, especially when the application must respond to critical issues and to a changing environment. However, the usage of requirements that drive the architectural decisions is poorly addressed by methodologists and practitioners, even if nonfunctional requirements engineering is now considered in recent research trends as a key issue for the design of adaptable architectures [6, 11, 19, 20, 25, 26, 28]. On the other hand, the reuse of catalogued pattern is made difficult for the lack of unambiguous and standard textual descriptions and graphic notations. The proposed method is an architectural design process, focused on the use of architectural patterns [30] defined as <problem-solution> couples, specified in UML 2.0 [31]. Both problem and solution include functional and nonfunctional requirements. The architectural decisions taken to obtain acceptable solutions are driven by quality goals that are associated to the nonfunctional requirements [25].

The main goal of this paper is to discuss the application of the above architectural design method to define an open and homogeneous platform for scientific calculation,

R. Morrison and F. Oquendo (Eds.): EWSA 2005, LNCS 3527, pp. 94–112, 2005.

integrating the main activities performed by scientists in the domains of theoretical chemistry, biology and physics (project FRAMES, **FR**amework for **A**tomic, **M**olecular and **E**xtended **S**ystems). We do not intend to re-write a new Simulation Code (Quantum Chemistry, Molecular Dynamics etc ...) or to integrate various existing codes inside an external envelope, with some scripting language which is the usual practice in most of these calculation environments. Our intention is rather to spend the necessary time to design rationally the architecture and the objects of a modeling framework. The FRAMES platform should allow a friendly development of new calculations, reusing also existing old FORTRAN code and should facilitate to scientists the specification and execution of a calculation. The platform will manipulate a main object, a "calculation", that may use other calculations and integrate different elements in order to achieve the main functionalities. The "openness" of the platform is required to offer the scientific community free access to programs and/or results.

In the scientific domains using extensively computer models, the user is most of the time also a programmer. This make the code evolve rapidly and in an anarchical way. To avoid this defect common to all software developed in these domains, a preliminary architectural design of these particular requirements has necessarily to be done.

This paper is structured as follows, besides this introduction: Section 2 describes the definition structure of the patterns. The pattern-based architectural design process is described in Section 3. Section 4 presents the FRAMES platform and the application of the method Section 5 discusses some related works on architectural design. The conclusion presents final remarks and perspectives.

2   Architectural Patterns

Several patterns libraries are available [5, 9, 30]. These libraries describe patterns focusing on the solutions proposed. But the problem is only informally described [15]. As a consequence, it is really difficult to choose the adequate pattern to solve a current problem [24]. We aim at providing help to guide the choice and application of architectural patterns. To do so, we add to the actual pattern description the precise definition of the problem part in terms of functional and nonfunctional requirements. The pattern structure usually contains several clauses concerning both the *problem part* and the *solution part*. The problem is described within several clauses:

- Specific design problems are informally stated in the Intent clause. We explicitly include the problem functionality. Scenarios may be given in the *Motivation* clause.
- *Participants* are classes or objects already existing that can be used as parameters of the pattern. They are partially described or defined in the Structure.
- The *Applicability* clause contains a list of situations in which the pattern can be applied.

In addition, we add the following information:

- In the *Context* clause, the nonfunctional requirements.
- The new *Quality* clause contains a quality model [14, 23] related to the problem context, expressing the expected quality properties as measurable items. It is used

to associate quality characteristics to functional and nonfunctional requirements. Goals may be assigned to each characteristic. Here, and at this step of the development, we have chosen as a ranking: *high, medium, low*. This ranking can be refined during later development steps into finer ranking. The goals guide the choice of a solution according to nonfunctional requirement priorities. Goal rankings and priorities can be assigned by the stakeholders involved using existing techniques such as voting or consensus.

Patterns are defined by experimented software engineers to describe their solution proved in practice. However, it is important when dealing with critical systems, to ensure their correctness that the problem stated will effectively be solved by the pattern. Pattern validation consists in proving :

- That the solution preserves the behavior described in the problem part of the pattern [1]
- That the solution respects the quality goals specified in the pattern.

Example of a pattern description: Repository (based on Shared Memory [22, 29]). **Problem definition**.

- *Intent*: Several components of a software system need to communicate directly or indirectly, that is exchange (share) potentially large and evolving data in order to meet system requirements.
- *Functional requirements*: data sharing (provide and require data) (Figure 1).

Structure of the problem: The UML architectural description is decorated with tags denoting the characteristics from the Quality Model.

- Components are executed on different processors, notification mechanisms are generally implemented to notify the concurrent components of any change of the shared data

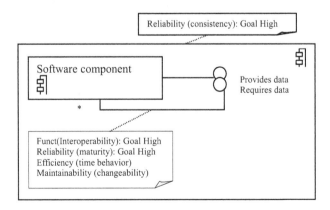

Fig. 1. Data Sharing

- Additional mechanisms need to be provided to implement the control part. They depend on the application characteristics and the execution platform.
- *Nonfunctional requirements and quality model*:
  - Data are shared:
    - ➤ Functionality (Interoperability) Attribute: presence of a mechanism; Metrics: Boolean; Goal: High
  - Data must be completely and correctly transmitted.
    - ➤ Reliability: Maturity (robustness) provide mechanisms to avoid failures; Attribute: presence of a mechanism; Metrics: Boolean; Goal: High
  - Limited transmission time.
    - ➤ Efficiency: Performance with respect to time behavior; Attribute: latency; Metrics: time behavior percentage; Goal: Low
  - Communication must be flexible to meet changing requirements, since relationships between components can evolve statically and dynamically.
    - ➤ Maintainability: Changeability (flexibility) of the components relationships; Attribute: size; Metrics: measure of complexity; Goal: Low
  - Components can be changed or replaced over time:
    - ➤ Reliability: Consistency: provide a mechanism (e.g. to replace a component interface); Attribute: presence of a mechanism; Metrics: Boolean; Goal: High

Structure of the Solution:

- A set of software components, containing the knowledge of the domain, communicate to each other to meet system requirements. They do not know each other (indirect communication); they are only defined by their needs to perform the computations (their inputs) and the results they can provide (their outputs). When a component produces some information that is of interest for other components, it stores it in the shared repository. The other components will retrieve it if needed.
- A repository that is accessible by every component (read and write accesses). This repository can store all the data that need to be exchanged by components during system execution.

Notice that the repository is a centralized solution (it may become unavailable in case of communication failure) that implies indirect communication among the components; hence a new maintainability (decoupling) requirement has been added to the problems domain quality model.

3   Pattern-Based Architectural Design Process

The basic idea behind the proposed process is to focus on the problem and not to go straight to the design of its solution [3, 15]. In our case, the problem statement is characterized by both its functional and nonfunctional requirements. The functional requirements are generally derived from the users needs and the nonfunctional requirements are more related with the problems environment, domain or context, which can have different views according to the stage of the development, such as the problems real

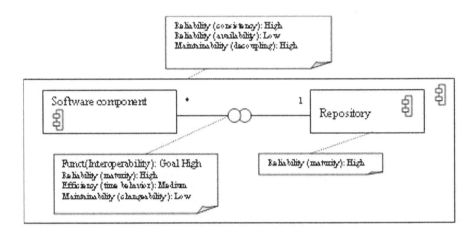

Fig. 2. Data sharing with Repository

world and the systems operational environment [25]. However, in problem domains where time and resources are critical or changing, each functionality can be also associated with a quality goal that must be satisfied to ensure the accomplishment of the functionality in the final software system, running in a specific operational environment. Moreover, when a nonfunctional requirement such as the fact that an ad hoc network has no supporting infrastructure, is formulated, it implies that a new functionality or implicit functionality, such as the handling of transient connections, has to be considered in the applications designed for such an environment. The quality properties related to functional and nonfunctional requirements are specified in the quality model associated to the problem domain. Notice that the solutions can introduce new quality features that must be added to the quality model.

Our pattern-based architectural development process is a top-down stepwise approach. At each step, an architectural pattern has to be chosen in order to solve some functional or nonfunctional requirement. A pattern is defined as a <problem-solution> couple. The problem part permits to choose the right pattern that will solve some problem of the current underdevelopment system. The general pattern-based architectural design process is the following:

Initial Input: Problem definition ("cahier des charges")

I. Requirement Engineering

a) Identification of the business requirements: users, environment & operation and data requirements

Artifacts:
- Use Case Model to express user (functional) requirements,
- UML Sequence Diagrams and State charts, to express the systems behavior
- Formal specification to guarantee the consistency and completeness of the requirements

b) **Identification of the nonfunctional requirements**
   Artifacts:
   - Quality Model to express the quality properties related to the nonfunctional requirements.
c) **For each functionality: identification of the quality characteristics**
   Artifacts:
   - Quality properties for each functionality
d) **First definition of the architecture**
   Artifacts:
   - UML 2.0 model of the architecture: a configuration including components and connectors and decorated by tags denoting the quality properties and constraints. Tags can decorate components, connectors and/or the configuration.

II. Iterative development of the Architecture

1. **Choice and application of an architectural pattern**
   An applicable architectural pattern is selected from an available patterns library. A pattern is applicable if:
   i. its problem functional part matches with the functional description of the problem to be solved
   ii. it gives a solution to a nonfunctional requirement. Pattern application consists in replacing the identified problem that matches with the chosen pattern problem part, by the pattern solution part.
   Artifacts:
   - UML 2.0 model of the architecture under development
2. **Step a is applied iteratively** until all the quality characteristics have been considered for each functionality. Existing techniques to outline and solve conflicts and tradeoffs can be applied at this stage [7, 8, 10, 11]. At the end of this process, the architecture has been developed satisfying the nonfunctional requirements.

The requirement engineering process is detailed in what follows.

Initial Input: the problem definition ("cahier des charges") is provided by the organization giving the problem.

I. Requirement Engineering

a) **Identification of the business requirements: users, environment & operation and data requirements**
   These requirements can be elicited using a four step process [21] which is an extension of the method proposed by Heisel and Souquires [13]. A classification of requirements has been added to facilitate the identification of nonfunctional requirements and derive the corresponding quality properties [25]. This method to perform the early phases of the software life cycle in a systematic way, supports two phases, namely requirements elicitation and specification development. It starts with a brainstorming process where the problem domain and the requirements are described in natural language [12]. This informal description is then transformed into a formal representation. On the formal representation, interaction analyses are performed. Their purpose is to obtain a consistent set of requirements. It is described in four steps, as follows:

1. Interaction Analysis. The objective of this first step is to understand the business requirements given by the client and expressed informally by the cahier des charges in order to identify the users or actors (humans and non humans) and the actions (functionalities derived from the user requirements) that are important for the software system. UML Use Cases are defined providing the artifact for this step.

2. Invariant Properties Analysis. Then it is important to understand the software system itself and its interactions with its environment or context. Three kinds of properties are described to help the requirements identification: facts, hypothesis and needs. The facts are static properties concerning the problem domain, the trivial knowledge about the application domain that the analyst can hardly invent. Here will be described the objects that will have to be modeled by the system, their states and attributes. The preconditions on transitions or modifications of their state will also be identified, as should be the physical limitations. The hypotheses are properties concerning the software system environment that is supposed to be always satisfied. These properties can change during the development process. They are in general simplifications that are considered at the beginning of a process. The expected behavior of the environment will be also described here. The needs concern the desired behavior of the software system and they must meet specific quality goals. They are in general temporal or structural properties. Facts, hypothesis and needs are basically constraints which are included in the business rules [25]. They comprise policy, data processing and technology constraints and they are used to precise the quality properties corresponding to the nonfunctional requirements. They must be specified, for example, by means of a quality model related to the problem domain. These properties are written in natural language but must be traced during the whole development.

3. Description of the Desired Behavior. The comprehension of the dynamic behavior of the future system is obtained by the description of the manner the actors will interact with it. Two steps are necessary: first, UML Sequence Diagrams are defined in order to describe some typical behavior. Second, the complete expected behavior of the system is described. UML State Charts are defined to describe the global interaction of a software system with each actor of its environment. OCL expressions can also be used to specify both the invariant properties and the behavior.

4. Complete Description of the System. In order to guarantee the correctness of the requirements, that is their consistency and their completeness, it is important to be able to put together all the information distributed among the different documents already written. To do so, all the existing documents are translated into a formal specification [27]. Formal specifications can be expressed using the B development method [1] that covers the software process from the specification to the implementation. B notation is based on set theory, the language of generalized substitutions and first order logic. Specifications are composed of abstract machines similar to modules or classes; they consist of a set of variables, properties on these variables called the invariant and operations. The

state of the system is only modifiable by operations. Several relations can link the machines of a specification.

b) Identification of the nonfunctional requirements

According to ISO 9126-1 [14], *quality* is defined as a set of features and characteristics of a product or service that bear on its ability to satisfy stated or implied needs. Different perspectives of quality can be considered: internal quality (measured during the development process), external quality (measured when the system is accomplished but not yet delivered) and quality in use (measured when the system is running on the end-user environment) views. The overall quality of a product can be the expressed by a combination of the different views. The internal and external quality models propose a set of six independent high-level quality characteristics (*functionality, reliability, efficiency, maintainability, portability, usability*), (see Table 1) which are defined as a set of attributes of a software product by which its quality is described and evaluated. In practice, some influence could appear among the characteristics, however, in this work they will be considered independently to simplify our presentation. The quality characteristics are used as the targets for validation at the various stages of development.

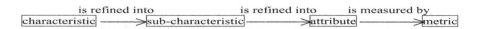

Fig. 3. Relations among the quality model elements

They are refined (see Figure 3) into sub-characteristics, until the *attributes* or *measurable properties* are obtained. In this context, *metric* or *measure* is defined as a *measurement* method and measurement means to use a metric or measure to assign a value.

In order to monitor and control software quality during the development process and on the final product, the internal and/or external quality characteristics must be related to the requirements of the intermediate products or artifacts such as the architecture, obtained from development activities, [23, 24, 25]. This mapping and selection of the attributes is a non-trivial activity [11], depending much on the stakeholder personal experience, unless the organization provides an infrastructure to collect and to analyze previous experience on completed projects. The model should be adapted or customized to the specific problem domain. In this sense, for a particular software product we could have a subset of the six characteristics. In the ISO 9126-1 standard, no guidelines are given about this customization [23, 24].

c) For each functionality: identification of the quality characteristics

The quality model defined for the problem domain is used to characterize the quality properties that hold when some functionality is accomplished. The goals can be used to guide the choice of the patterns to be applied in Step II.

Note that similar properties and metrics can be found in [22]. However the qualities are presented neither as a domains standard quality model, nor they are related with the problem requirements.

d) First definition of the architecture A first UML 2.0 model of the architecture is described as a configuration including components and connectors and decorated by tags denoting the quality properties and constraints.

Table 1. ISO 9126-1 Generic Quality Model

Characteristic	Description
Functionality	The capability of the software product to provide functions which meet stated and implied needs when the software is used under specified conditions (what the software does to fulfill needs)
Reliability	The capability of the software product to maintain its level of performance under stated conditions for a stated period of time
Usability	The capability of the software product to be understood, learned, used and attractive to the user, when used under specified conditions (the effort needed for use)
Efficiency	The capability of the software product to provide appropriate performance, relative to the amount of resources used, under stated conditions
Maintainability	The capability of the software product to be modified. Modifications may include corrections, improvements or adaptations of the software to changes in the environment and in the requirements and functional specifications (the effort needed to be modified)
Portability	The capability of the software product to be transferred from one environment to another. The environment may include organizational, hardware or software environment

4   The FRAMES Platform

The FRAMES platform should allow carrying out complex calculations. It should help the not-expert user to define a new calculation, and will be able to check both the a priori coherence of a calculation request and the a posteriori validity and precision of the obtained result.

In what follows we will describe the design process of the architecture of the FRAMES platform taking into account some nonfunctional requirements. We apply the pattern-based architectural development process. The platform should propose two main functionalities: (i) write a calculation, that is defining an algorithm to solve some problem describing the context in which it should be calculated and its parameters, and (ii) make a calculation. To do so, a non programmer user has to choose a calculation and to give its parameters.

4.1   Requirements Engineering

a. Identification of the Business Requirements

To abridge this presentation, this step will not be detailed. Only the use case model is presented in Figure 4. Two main functionalities are identified: *write a new calculation* by a "programmer" user and *make a calculation.* "Make" means that the "non programmer user" must provide easily all the information required to execute a calculation or a simulation.

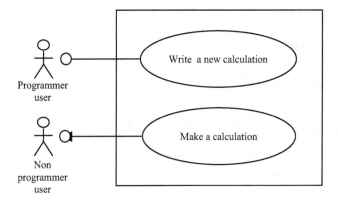

Fig. 4. Use case model for FRAMES

b. Identification of Nonfunctional Requirements

Main nonfunctional requirements for FRAMES are:

- calculations must be validated and should support flexibility to dynamic changes and extensions;
- the Input language used to define a calculation must be attractive and easy to use for an experimenced scientific user;
- the users tasks must be helped whenever possible; resources (time and space) utilization must be checked before and during the calculation to ensure acceptable performance levels;
- the results of the calculations should be available, accurate, exportable and reusable;
- the existing old code is meant to be reused but not changed; it should also be accurate and interoperable within the platform.

The quality model. The nonfunctional requirements for the FRAMES platform are related with the ISO 9126-1 quality model. A goal, ranked low, medium and high according to its importance, is used to prioritize a quality property, whenever possible. Goal values are assigned on a vote basis by the stakeholders. At this stage of the development,most of thequality properties will be associated to an attribute whose Boolean value will become true when some mechanism will be provided to take into account the quality. Instead, the attribute for efficiency and maintainability is size, whose metrics involve complexity measures.

Quality Model for FRAMES

Nonfunctional requirement: Calculations must be validated and support flexibility to changes and extensions

- **Functionality:**
  - **Suitability Goal:** High

- **Reliability**
  - ○ **Maturity** to avoid failures, **Recoverability, fault tolerance Goal** : Medium
- **Maintainability**
  - ○ **Changeability:** to handle multiple versions of a calculation Goal: High
  - ○ **Testability: Goal:** High

Nonfunctional requirement: Input language used to define a calculation must be attractive and easy to use for an experimented scientific user

- **Functionality:**
  - ○ **Suitability Goal:** High
- **Usability**
  - ○ **Understandability, Learnability Goal:** High

Nonfunctional requirement: Users must be helped whenever possible

- **Functionality:**
  - ○ **Suitability Goal:** High
- **Usability**
  - ○ **Understandability,Operability Goal:** High

Nonfunctional requirement: Resources (time and space) utilization must be checked before and during the calculation to ensure acceptable performance levels

- **Efficiency:**
  - ○ **Time behavior, Ressource behavior Goal:** High

Nonfunctional requirement: The calculations results should be available, accurate, exportable and reusable

- **Functionality:**
  - ○ **Accuracy Goal:** High
- **Portability:**
  - ○ **Adaptability Goal:** High
- **Reliability:**
  - ○ **Availability Goal:** High

Nonfunctional requirement: Existing old code is to be reused;

- **Functionality:**
  - ○ **Interoperability Goal:** High
- **Reliability:**
  - ○ **Availability Goal:** High
- **Maintainability: of existing old code**
  - ○ **Changeability Goal:** None

c. For each functionality: identification of the quality characteristics

The main functionalities concerning directly the calculation have been refined and related with their corresponding quality characteristics, taken from the FRAMES quality model, specifying also the expected quality goals for each functionality.

Functional requirement: Make a Calculation.

Request (execute) and validate a calculation in a friendly and easy to use context.

The non programmer needs reliable edition mechanisms for the input language and efficient execution of the calculation

- **Functionality:**
  - **Suitability** to provide an appropriate set of functions to guarantee that the required calculations are obtained **Goal:** High
- **Efficiency:**
  - **Time Behavior** while introducing the algorithm to execute the calculation. (property of the input language) **Goal:** High
- **Reliability:**
  - **Maturity** to avoid failure **Goal:** Medium
  - **Recoverability** (properties of the input language) **Goal:** Medium
  - **Consistency** to deal with multiple versions of a calculation. **Goal:** Medium
- **Usability:**
  - **Attractiveness Goal:** High
  - **Operability Goal:** High
  - **Learnability Goal:** High

Functional requirement: Make a Calculation.

Read results: non programmer users need powerful visualization and analysis mechanisms to understand and interprete the results

- **Functionality:**
  - **Accuracy Goal:** High
- **Efficiency:**
  - **Resource utilization** to store and update results **Goal:** High
- **Portability:**
  - **Adaptability** to export the results to other platforms **Goal:** High
- **Reliability:**
  - **Consistency** in storage and update of results. **Goal:** High
- **Usability:**
  - **Understandability Goal:** High

Functional requirement: Write a new Calculation.

Addition of new algorithm (code), reusing also legacy (old) code. The programmer user needs efficient mechanisms, for example an editor to write and a compiler to execute the program

- **Functionality:**
  - **Interoperability** with legacy code **Goal:** High
- **Efficiency:**
  - **Time behavior** during execution **Goal:** High
- **Reliability:**
  - **Availability** of legacy code **Goal:** High
- **Maintainability:**
  - **Changeability, testability** to validate the new code. **Goal:** High

d. Architecture of the FRAMES Platform

Figure 5 shows the problem, stated according to the "cahier des charges". The Library component is introduced here as existing old code that has to be reused and cannot be modified. Note that the properties in the tags are just to denote the properties of the quality model.

The first solution presented in Figure 6 introduces two components to take into account the main functionalities of the FRAMES platform as expressed by the use case model (Figure 3). Each architectural element is decorated by tags with the required quality properties. Interoperability for the connector means that the data exchanged must be understood by the components.

The quality properties are associated to each component and connector. Now we have to take them into account choosing an adequate solution that is for example a pattern that will solve the problem. For example, we notice that all connectors require interoperability. That means that these components share the calculations. The solution shown in Figure 7 shows the introduction of a new component, a **"Calculation Manager"** acting as a repository, as a mechanism to handle the *interoperability requirement*. With Repository we achieve in addition high changeability and reliability (Figure 2).

Following the same approach, all the components of Figure 7 should be analyzed with respect to nonfunctional requirements and new component introduced as solutions should be justified by their quality properties. For example, if the problem is to ensure usability and reliability issues in Make a calculation, an "Interpreter" new component to handle the input language for entering the calculation could be introduced using the interpreter pattern [9]. In the same way, for Calculation Manager, looking at the nonfunctional requirements *"Calculations must be validated and support flexibility to*

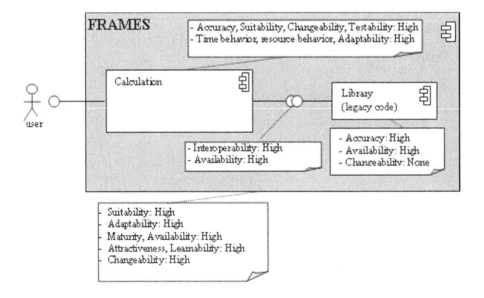

Fig. 5. Problem: FRAMES platform for scientific calculation

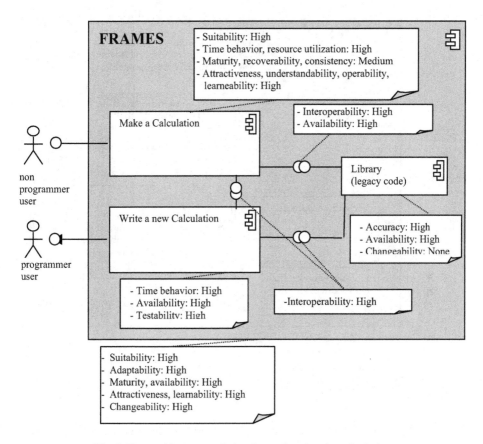

FRAMES
- Suitability: High
- Time behavior, resource utilization: High
- Maturity, recoverability, consistency: Medium
- Attractiveness, understandability, operability,
   learneability: High

Make a Calculation

- Interoperability: High
- Availability: High

non
programmer
user

Library
(legacy code)

Write a new Calculation

programmer
user

- Accuracy: High
- Availability: High
- Changeability: None

- Time behavior: High
- Availability: High
- Testability: High

-Interoperability: High

- Suitability: High
- Adaptability: High
- Maturity, availability: High
- Attractiveness, learnability: High
- Changeability: High

Fig. 6. First architecture: solution for performing the calculation

changes and extensions" and *"Resources (time and space) utilization must be checked to ensure acceptable performance levels"* and their quality properties, we could think to introduce two new components, one responsible for the execution of the calculation, **"Programming Environment"** (a *compiler* or *interpreter* to achieve fault-tolerance, performance and testability) and the other for the storage and update of results, **"Calculation Results Manager"** (a *repository* pattern to achieve consistency, space administration and changeability). Moreover, to analyze (understandability issue) and export (adaptability issue) the results of the calculation, a new **"Visualization and Analysis Tools"** component can be introduced offering powerful visualization mechanisms. Finally, in order to fulfill the properties for the FRAMES configuration, a **"GUI"** component is introduced, to provide access to the overall functionality (suitability). The user interface should comply with user interface design standards, to assure attractiveness, changeability and maturity. Adaptability to export the results will be accomplished by the visualization & analysis component, through the GUI component. Figure 8 shows the resulting architecture (http://galileo.lct.jussieu.fr/~FRAMES/en/).

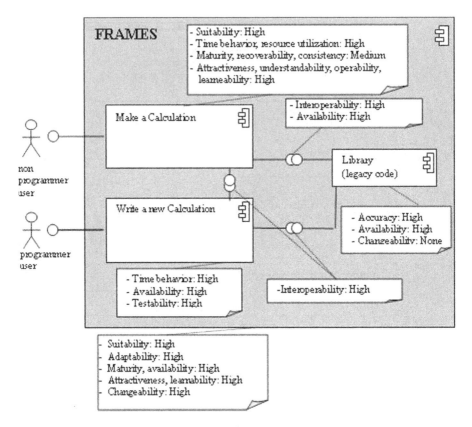

Fig. 7. Second architecture: solution to handle interoperability between the maincomponents

5   Related Works

Architectural Design Process

Architectural design [5, 7, 26], on one hand identifies the key strategies for the large-scale organization of the system under development [17]. These strategies include for example, the mapping of packages to processors, bus and protocol selection, at a quite low level of abstraction. On the other hand, at a higher level, a rough structure or architectural style or pattern, like for example layers, is identified. This style is considered as a starting point for further refinement or transformation. The first selection or evaluation can be made on the basis of prioritizing on a scenario the quality characteristics related to the style and to the architectural patterns constituting the style. This is the approach taken by Clements et al [7] using the ATAM (Attribute Tradeoff Analysis Method). Conflicts and tradeoffs are analyzed and outlined but not solved. Architectural refinement or choice of architectural patterns is not considered. Other methods and/or techniques complement ATAM for this purpose. Some of our works extend this approach [23, 24] by introducing a standard quality model and general architectural metrics. The

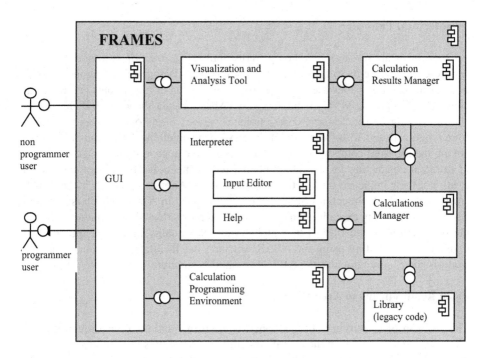

FRAMES

Visualization and Analysis Tool

Calculation Results Manager

Interpreter

Input Editor

Help

Calculations Manager

Calculation Programming Environment

Library (legacy code)

GUI

non programmer user

programmer user

Fig. 8. FRAMES Architecture

evaluation and selection of the architecture is then performed on the basis of the goal values of the quality attributes computed for some of the quality characteristic. In this sense, architectures are responses to specific quality requirements [8, 28]. In [32], the authors propose to extend the ATAM approach for enterprise information systems (EIS) automating the performance and reliability analysis, on the basis of a specific architectural style. The approach followed by J. Bosch [4] is based on the transformation of the initial architecture. Each transformation (quality attribute-optimizing solution), generally improves one or more quality attributes, affecting others negatively. The process stops when an evaluation of the architecture indicates that the quality goals initially established for the systems are reached to an acceptable extent. Formal or semiformal specification of the architecture, using for example an ADL (Architecture Description Language), is recommended to apply a simulation technique. The Rational Unified Process (RUP) [17] is a general architecture centered framework for software development. Architectural design is considered a crucial early stage for minimizing the risks involved in the overall software project development. Main functionalities relevant to the architecture should be selected and prioritized in order to propose an initial candidate architecture. Detailed guidelines on the process are left to users framework customization [26]. However, neither P. Krutchen [17], nor J. Bosch [4], even acknowledging its importance, provide precise guidelines to specify quality characteristics and measures for the architectural quality attributes [26]. Notice that architectural choices are made at high abstraction level, at early stages of software development, where an execution environment is not always present.

Architectural Patterns

Another important research based on patterns libraries [2, 5, 9, 30], is to provide a pattern description schema to give support to architectural design, improving the descriptions of the existing catalogues. The approach of Lucena et al [2] considers different views, according to an MVC model, the ADV (Abstract Data View) model. This model allows creating design patterns descriptions at various levels of granularity, ranging from program design to software architecture, while maintaining separation of concerns among the different components. However, even if the approach allows the modeling of different abstraction levels, nonfunctional requirements issues are not considered at all, nor their influence on functional requirements. Another approach is the ABAS (Attribute-Based Architectural Style) [16], now included in ATAM, which is a pattern description including explicitly the quality characteristics related to the pattern. In [23] the introduction of the ISO 9126-1 global view of a quality model for the problem domain, defined before using the ABAS structure, has facilitated and accelerated the analysis stage, enriching also the ABAS information structure.

From Requirements to Architectures

The problem of identifying nonfunctional requirements and the related quality properties needed to accomplish the overall systems functionality is in general superficially treated or even not addressed at all. The main functionality of the problem related with the architecture has to be identified in order to be implemented and tested early, according to [17]. However, it is not clear how to identify or prioritize them. In [24], an architectural evaluation method that can be used as an ATAM step is proposed, which takes into account the quality properties related to the problem domain. These are associated with the problems main functionalities in order to rank them according to the importance of the initial quality requirements. In [11] a classification of requirements is used to relate them with the architectural elements (components, connectors and configurations). In our approach we also use a classification, considering early the requirements of the problem context, constraining a first architectural solution. UML tags are used to relate the requirements and their quality values to the architectural elements expressed in UML 2.0. In [11] requirements relevant to the architecture are chosen, refined and prioritized using consensus or voting techniques. We use a standard quality model to specify the quality properties for each requirement. Priorities and conflicts are solved on consensus or vote basis, but these issues are not explicitly treated in this presentation. The properties of the problems context are considered in [11] as a consequence of the refinement and related to the C2 architectural style as a last step of the process. Choice of styles or patterns is not considered. In the present work, the quality model associated to the problem domain is driven from the problems nonfunctional requirements, which mainly affect the problems context. The functional requirements are then related with the corresponding quality properties, which are also expressed as a standard quality model. A. van Lamsweerde [20] proposes a pattern-based architecture refinement process. This process starts from a first architectural description based on the functional requirements. Then, at each step of the refinement process, a pattern is applied to take into account one nonfunctional goal. L. Chung et al. [6] consider also patterns solving one nonfunctional requirement. Let us note that none of them defines formally the refinement. We have done it using the refinement notion from the B Method applied to the patterns (the solution part of a pattern refines its problem part). These processes imply tradeoff analysis that must be carried out using a qualitative reasoning [10] based on degree of consensus and vote [11].

6   Conclusion

In this paper, we have investigated the development process to construct the FRAMES platform. This project is of wide importance and its architecture is crucial: it will condition the allocation of the tasks to be done among the different FRAME project participants. The idea is to find the architectural patterns that will propose a solution to take into account all the nonfunctional properties listed above. The contribution of this process is to take into account very early in the development the quality requirements. The process has led us to introduce some components whose functionality is to take in charge some non functional requirement so the architecture defined will satisfy them. These architectural elements are introduced in the configuration as a response to precise quality goals. Naturally, the functional requirement must be satisfied by the architecture and this can be verified by proving that the defined architecture is a refinement of the initial one. Concerning the Calculation Manager, it appears that this component is quite complex. The data stored are huge and persistency must be handled. Our process can be applied to refine precisely this component. Note that the configuration properties have to be maintained and their goals fulfilled by the FRAMES platform.

References

1. J.R. Abrial. The B Book Assigning Programs to Meanings. Cambridge University Press, 1996. ISBN 0521496195.
2. P. S. C. Alencar, D. D. Cowan, C.J.P. Lucena A Formal Approach to Architectural Design Patterns. FME '96: Industrial Benefit and Advances in Formal Methods, Vol. 1051, Springer Verlag, Oxford, editors J. Woodcock M.-C. Gaudel, 1996, pp. 576-594.
3. C. Alexander The timeless way of building. Oxford University Press, 1979.
4. J. Bosch. Design and Use of Software Architecture. Addison Wesley, Harlow, England, 2000.
5. F. Buschmann., R. Meunier, H. Rhonert, P. Sommerlad, M. Stal. Pattern-Oriented Software Architecture. A System of Patterns, John Wiley & Sons, New York, 1996.
6. L. Chung, K. Cooper, A. Yi. Developing adaptable software architectures using design patterns: an NFR approach. Computer Standards & Interfaces 25 (2003) 253-260
7. P. Clements, R. Kazman, and M. Klein. Evaluating Software Architecture. Methods and Case Studies. SEI Series in Software Engineering. Addison-Wesley, 2002.
8. P. Clements, F. Bachmann, L. Bass, D. Garlan, J. Ivers, R. Little, R. Nord, and J. Stafford, Documenting Software Architectures: Views and Beyond. Addison Wesley, September 2002.
9. E Gamma., R. Helm, R. Johnson. J. Vlissides. Design Patterns. Elements of Reusable Object-Oriented Software. Addison Wesley, Reading, Massachusetts, 1995.

10. D. Gross, E. Yu, From Non-Functional Requirements to Design Through Patterns, Requirements Engineering Journal, Vol 6, 2001, 18-36
11. P. Grnbacher, A. Egyed, N. Medvidovic, Reconciling Software Requirements and Architectures: the CBSP Approach. Journal of Software and Systems Modeling (SOSYM), to appear.
12. M. Heisel and J. Souquires. A Method for Requirements Elicitation and Formal Specification. In J. Akoka, M. Bouzeghoub, I. ComynWattiau, and E. Mtais, editors, Proc. 18t Int. conf. on Conceptual Modelling, ER'99, LNCS 1728, pages 309–324. SpringerVerlag, 1999.
13. M. Heisel and J. Souquires. A heuristic algorithm to detect feature interactions in requirements. In S. Gilmore and M. Ryan, editors, Language Constructs for Describing Features, pages 143–162. Springer Verlag, 2000.
14. ISO/IEC 9126-1. Software Engineering - Product Quality. Part 1: Quality Model, 2001.
15. M. Jackson. Problem Frames, Addison Wesley, Harlow, England, 2001.
16. M. Klein and R. Kazman. Attribute-Based Architectural Styles. CMU/SEI-99-TR-022, ESC-TR-99-022, October 1999.
17. P. Krutchen. The Rational Unified Process. Addison Wesley, Reading, Massachusetts, 1999.
18. P. Lalanda. Shared repository pattern. PLOP 1998
19. A. van Lamsweerde. Elaborating security requirements by construction of intentional anti-models. 26th ICSE 04, 148-157, Edinburgh, 2004
20. A. van Lamsweerde. From system goals to software architecture. Formal Methods for Software Architectures, M. Bernardo & P. Inverardi (eds.), LNCS, Springer-Verlag, 2003
21. N. Levy, R, Marcano, J. Souquires. From requirements to formal specification using UML and B, International Conference on Computer Systems and Technologies CompSysTech2002
22. . J Liu, V. Issarny. QoS-aware Service Location in Mobile Ad-Hoc Networks, MDM 2001, Berkeley, C.A, USA, January 2001.
23. F. Losavio, L. Chirinos, M. Prez. Quality Models to Design Software Architecture. In IEEE TOOLS, March 2001, Zurich, pp 123-135.
24. F Losavio., L. Chirinos, N. Lvy, A. Ramdane-Cherif. Quality Characteristics for Software Architecture. Journal of Object Technology, Vol 2, No. 2, March/April 2003. pp. 133-150, http://www.jot.fm/issues/issue_2003_03/article2
25. F. Losavio, L. Chirinos, A. Matteo. Identifying Quality-Based Requirements. Information Systems Management (ISYM), Auerbach Publications, Vol. 21, No. 1 (15-21), Winter 2004.
26. F. Losavio, L. Chirinos, A. Matteo,, N. Lvy, A. Ramdane-Cherif. Designing Quality Architecture: Incorporating ISO Standards into the Unified Process, Information Systems Management (ISYM), Auerbach Publications, Vol. 21, No. 1 (27-44), 2004.
27. R. Marcano and N. Levy. Using B formal specifications for analysis and verfication of UML/OCL models. Workshop on consistency problems in UML-based software development. 5th International Conference on the Unified Modeling Language. Dresden, Germany, October 2002.
28. V. Poladian, J. P. Sousa., D. Garlan, M. Shaw. Dynamic Reconfiguration of Resource-Aware Services, 26th ICSE 04, 604-613, Edinburgh, 2004
29. M. Shaw, D. Garlan. Software Architecture. Perspectives on an Emerging Discipline. Prentice Hall, New Jersey, 1996.
30. D. Schmidt, M. Stal, H. Rhonert, F. Buschmann. Pattern-Oriented Software Architecture, Patterns for Concurrent and Networked Objects. Vol 2, Wiley, Chichester, 2000.
31. UML Resource Page, http://www.omg.org/UML
32. A. Zarras, V. Issarny. Quality Analysis of Enterprise Information Systems. In Concurrency in Dependable Systems, pages 127-146. Paul Ezhilchelvan and Alexander Romanovsky editors. Kluwer Academic Publishers, Boston Hardbound, ISBN 1-4020-7043-8, June 2002.

Concern-Based Development of Pattern Systems

Imed Hammouda, Markku Hakala, Mika Pussinen,
Mika Katara, and Tommi Mikkonen

Institute of Software Systems,
Tampere University of Technology,
P.O.BOX 553, FI-33101 Tampere, Finland
{firstname.lastname}@tut.fi

Abstract. The problem of constructing pattern systems is two-fold. First, the individual patterns should be identified and documented. Second, proper methodologies for abstracting the relationships between the patterns should be used. This paper proposes using *concern architecture views* for building and documenting pattern systems. It further shows how an individual concern can be treated with pattern composition leading to a better alignment between requirements, design, and code. A novel algorithm for *pattern composition* is therefore presented. As an example, we build and document a pattern system for annotating a specialization interface of the J2EE framework using a prototype tool environment supporting the approach.

Keywords: Software architecture, pattern systems, concern architecture views, pattern composition.

1 Introduction

Pattern systems are collections of patterns each of which solves a specific design issue. While individual patterns are essential tools in software development, the power behind many of the well-known patterns is unleashed only when applying them together [1]. However, although individual patterns are easy to understand and apply given adequate documentation and tools, pattern systems are generally much more complex.

While patterns solve design problems, the alignment between requirements, design and code remains a challenge. The main causes of misalignment can be traced to modularity issues. At the requirements level, there are no notions for a class or a pattern, which are only introduced at later development stages when applying object-oriented analysis and design. This causes problems with scattering and tangling, as a requirement can be addressed by more than one class each of which also treats other requirements.

The aspect-oriented solution [2] is to base units of modularity on concerns, cutting across several conventional units such as classes. Ideally, each concern, i.e. a conceptual matter of interest such as a user requirement, should be modularized into an entity that treats only this particular concern and nothing else,

R. Morrison and F. Oquendo (Eds.): EWSA 2005, LNCS 3527, pp. 113–129, 2005.

thus providing better alignment. Early identification of concerns is profitable to identifying elements in the solution domain [3], which helps e.g. in establishing critical trade-offs before the system architecture is derived [4].

In this paper, we introduce a modularization concept for pattern systems, based on concern architecture views [5]. Instead of using concerns to capture entities cutting across classes, our concerns cut across the patterns which form a pattern system. To tackle the complexity resulting from scattering and tangling by providing a one-to-one match between concerns and the corresponding patterns, we should be able to compose the patterns treating any concern into a single more complex pattern. Thus, a composition operation for patterns is needed. Ideally, this operation produces a composite pattern matching whatever concern implemented by the pattern system. Instead of operating on design patterns [6], we use a more general role-based pattern concept which allows concern-based architecting with different domains and notations, such as J2EE and UML. In order to validate our concepts, we have built a prototype tool environment known as MADE [7].

The rest of the paper is organized as follows. In the next section, we discuss our methodology for documenting pattern structures and introduce concern architecture views for abstracting the relationships in pattern systems. Furthermore, we discuss how concerns can be treated as a composition of patterns and we briefly introduce our toolset. An approach for pattern composition is presented in Section 3. In Section 4, we apply our methodology to build and document an annotation for the specialization interface of J2EE framework. Section 5 compares the work to other existing solutions and concepts. Finally, Section 6 draws conclusions.

2   Pattern Systems and Concern Architecture Views

In this section, we first describe our approach for building and documenting pattern systems. Then, our notation for describing the internal structure of patterns is presented. We further discuss how the patterns are applied and composed treating individual concerns. An overview of our toolset ends the section.

2.1   Concern Architecture Views of Pattern Systems

Building pattern systems is a challenging task; a pattern system is more than a plain list of disjoint patterns [1]. A pattern system should describe three main issues: the rationale of the system, the way the individual patterns are collaborating, and their effective use and instantiation order. The building process can be regarded as a two phase activity. Firstly, the individual patterns are identified (identification phase). Secondly, the patterns are put together in a unified context reflecting their main characteristics and inter-relationships as well as defining the way they should be applied (documentation phase).

Figure 1 describes our approach for building and documenting pattern systems. Firstly, the requirements of the system under development are identified.

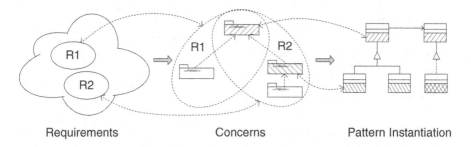

Fig. 1. Process for building and documenting pattern systems

This is illustrated in the left part of the figure in the example case of R1 and R2. Secondly, each of the identified requirements is encapsulated by a separate concern, shown in the middle part of the figure. At this phase, possible overlapping between the concerns are identified. The overall concern structure is referred to as concern architecture view. In order to address each concern in the concern architecture view, proper patterns treating that particular concern are identified. The relationships between the patterns are made explicit in the sense that related patterns are grouped under the same concern and their inter-dependencies are highlighted, indicating the possible instantiation orders.

The right-hand side of the figure shows a possible instantiation of the pattern system. The same pattern can be instantiated several times. When instantiated, a pattern has roles bound to a number of concrete elements. Thus, each pattern ties together the code points implementing part of the concern treated by that pattern. This leads to better traceability and alignment in the sense that there is a one-to-one match between concerns and the corresponding patterns. To achieve this, however, we need to compose the patterns treating any concern in the concern architecture view into a single more complex pattern. Therefore, our methodology defines a composition operation for patterns and presents a pattern composition algorithm.

2.2   Pattern Structure

A pattern is an arrangement of software elements for solving a particular problem. Depending on the nature of the problem, we may speak of architectural patterns [1], design patterns [6], etc. In this work, we will give a simple structural characterization of a generic pattern concept.

A pattern is a structural entity composed of a number of roles. The role concept has been already widely discussed [8, 9]. In our methodology, each role has a type that corresponds to the kind of concrete element (class, method, field) bound to the role. Roles may have properties like dependencies on other roles, cardinality, and constraints. To illustrate these properties, let us consider two pattern roles classRoleA and classRoleB that stand for class roles. Role classRoleA is said to be dependent upon classRoleB if the class bound to classRoleA depends on the class bound to classRoleB, for example if the first class inherits the second. The cardinality of classRoleA specifies the number of classes that may play the role. An example constraint on classRoleA could be an "inheritance constraint" meaning that the class bound to classRoleA should extend the class bound to classRoleB. A more detailed discussion on the role-based pattern concept, we use in this paper, is presented in [10].

2.3 Applying Patterns

In order to illustrate the relationship between patterns and concern architecture views, an example of a simple J2EE system consisting of two concerns 'Synchronous Communication' (SC) and 'Asynchronous Communication' (AC) is depicted in Figure 2(a). SC and AC represent two possible techniques for achieving more optimized communication with entity beans over the network. In case of synchronous communication, a 'Session Facade' solution using a session bean should be used whereas in case of asynchronous communication, a 'Message Facade' solution relying on a message-driven bean should be considered [11]. However, since the application might need both types of communication, both concerns might interact with the same bean, say an entity bean. This is represented in the overlapping region in the concerns.

Generally, once the system concerns are identified, proper patterns for solving these concerns are defined. Figure 2(a), for example, shows three patterns EntityEJB, SessionEJB, and MessageEJB. Patterns SessionEJB and EntityEJB solve concern SC and patterns MessageEJB and EntityEJB solve concern AC. In addition to identifying the patterns, Figure 2(a) documents the concerns of the pattern system. The figure depicts the relationships and dependencies between patterns and the concern structure. The purpose of every pattern is explicitly specified, this is implied by the concern it implements. Moreover, the dependencies between the patterns shows the partial order of applying the patterns. Therefore, the way the individual patterns should be instantiated becomes straightforward, as discussed next.

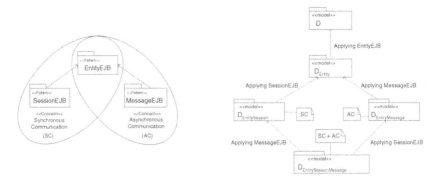

(a) Concern architecture view of patterns   (b) Resulting models

Fig. 2. Applying patterns

Figure 2(b) depicts the instantiations of the patterns shown in Figure 2(a) and documents the effects of applying the patterns in the order implied by the dependencies depicted in the concern architecture view. The design is started from scratch, denoted by an empty model D in Figure 2(b). First, pattern EntityEJB is instantiated by defining the concrete classes, objects, and methods etc. needed and binding those to the pattern roles. Obviously, because we started from scratch, there are no predefined elements to bind to the pattern roles. The model obtained by instantiating the pattern EntityEJB specializes D and is denoted by D_{Entity}.

Let us then consider the branch on the left-hand side of Figure 2(b). Pattern SessionEJB is instantiated by binding some of the units defined by D_{Entity} to SessionEJB's roles. Additionally, new elements might need to be defined to be bound to the remaining unbound roles. This way a new model $D_{EntitySession}$, a specialization of D_{Entity}, is created. Similarly, pattern MessageEJB is instantiated after SessionEJB, creating $D_{EntitySessionMessage}$ treating both concerns. However, the instances of SessionEJB and MessageEJB are independent. The independence implies that the application order of the patterns could have been the other way around. This option is illustrated by the branch on the right-hand side of Figure 2(b).

The concern architecture view described above helps us to separate important concerns related to the problem which the pattern system solves. On the one hand, if the solution corresponding to concern AC needs to be examined in isolation, the corresponding model $D_{EntityMessage}$ can be easily obtained and pattern SessionEJB is discarded. On the other hand, if SC needs to be changed and the changes occur only in SessionEJB, we can replace SessionEJB with some other pattern, for instance. This enables us to solve the problem without touching MessageEJB. However, if the changes occur in EntityEJB, the concern architecture view tells us to be careful also with MessageEJB.

2.4 Composing Patterns Treating Concerns

Based on the discussion above, our methodology defines a one-to-one mapping between concerns and patterns. In general, however, a concern is defined by multiple patterns. Thus, the requirement encapsulated in the concern becomes scattered over the different patterns. The solution to this problem is to treat each concern in the concern architecture view as one large pattern instead of a collection of small patterns. A pattern composition operation is needed that forms a composite pattern out of other individual patterns.

Assuming a role-based pattern specification, we need to define proper abstractions and techniques for pattern composition. Our approach, however, is not to statically create a new composite pattern and add it to the pattern system. Instead, every concern in the concern architecture view defines a composition and treats the concern as a single pattern leaving it possible to identify the individual constituent patterns. The advantage of this is that pattern composition becomes more dynamic and flexible in the sense that new combinations of the patterns can be easily created (and later removed) without the need of changing the pattern catalogue. In addition, this can be useful in tool development, as-suming that we recover the constituent patterns. For instance, we might wish to expose in the solution domain the effects of different patterns in the generated instance models. Naturally, pattern composition can be performed recursively, i.e. composite pattern can be further composed.

2.5   MADE Toolset

In order to validate our methodology, we have developed a concern-based pattern-driven tool environment known as MADE [7]. MADE patterns are role-based structures supporting different formalisms such as Java, UML and XML no-tations. The MADE platform itself is the result of integrating three differ-ent tools: JavaFrames [10], xUMLi [12] and Rational Rose. JavaFrames is a pattern-oriented development environment built on top of Eclipse, whose soft-ware development facilities are also used extensively. Rational Rose is used as UML editor. The third component, xUMLi, is a tool-independent platform for processing UML models and is used for integrating JavaFrames and Rational Rose.

Figure 3 shows an overview of the MADE environment. Rational Rose repre-sents the upper part of the environment. As an example of an integrated editor, implementation code is displayed in a Java editor (middle view). The left view represents the part of the environment where concerns and the patterns they treat are specified and applied. In this case, the view displays the concerns and

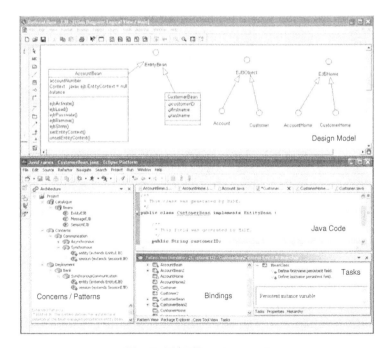

Fig. 3. MADE environment

the patterns identified in 2(a). When a pattern is selected, MADE transforms the pattern into a task list. This is done by generating a task for each unbound role that can be bound in the current situation, taking into account the dependencies and cardinalities of roles.

Tasks are displayed in the Task view. Typically, by performing a task, the user generates the default element to be bound to the role, as specified by the pattern. The user, however, might bind the role to an existing element. This is the case, for instance, when the role is overlapping with another role which has already been bound in a different pattern treating the same concern. It is essential that both roles are bound to the same element. Otherwise, the two patterns would combine in a wrong way leading to an undesirable implementation of the concern.

The bindings between roles and concrete elements are recorded by the tool and are shown in the bindings view of Figure 3. In this way, the environment preserves the information how concerns are addressed in the model. In Section 4, we discuss various features of the MADE tool leading to a better alignment in a J2EE pattern system.

3 Pattern Composition

In this section, we show how pattern composition can be defined and applied using the role-based pattern concept. We also present a novel algorithm for role-based pattern composition. We finally show how composition is achieved in the MADE toolset.

3.1 Definition

First of all, the composition of two patterns corresponding to a concern results in a pattern. The composition operator we define is a binary operator that takes two arbitrary patterns and returns a possibly larger one. Given two arbitrary patterns X and Y, if roleX and roleY are overlapping roles in patterns X and Y respectively, then the composition of X and Y can be expressed as $Z = +(X, Y, \{(roleX, roleY)\})$. Z is said to be the composite pattern of X and Y. The composition formula specifies the two patterns to be composed followed by a set of tuples defining the overlapping roles. In the composite pattern Z, the role representing the overlapping of roleX and roleY, say roleZ, is said to be the unified role of roleX and roleY.

Given the above definition, we can define the following composition properties:

- Two roles roleX and roleY can overlap only if they are of the same role type.
- Two roles roleX and roleY can overlap only if the parent roles of roleX and roleY (the roles where roleX and roleY are contained), if any, are overlapping too.
- If roleX and roleY are two overlapping roles, then the cardinality of the unified role roleZ is reduced to the more restricted cardinality of the two roles.

- If roleZ is the unified role of roleX and roleY, then roleZ has at most the total number of dependencies (both outgoing and incoming) of roleX and roleY. If roleX has n dependencies and roleY has m dependencies, then roleZ has at most n+m dependencies and at least max(n, m) dependencies. This is because some of the dependencies (dependencies having the same target role) of roleX and roleY can be the same.
- Similarly, roleZ is associated with the constraints of roleX and roleY. If roleX has n constraints and roleY has m constraints, then roleZ has at most n+m constraints and at least max(n, m) constraints. The constraints having the same type and value are treated to be the same.
- Patterns X and Y are said to be disjoint if they have no overlapping roles. X and Y are said to be fully composed if there is a one-to-one mapping between all roles of X and Y.

In order to present our composition methodology, we treat a role-based pattern as a directed graph: nodes denote roles whereas edges denote dependencies. When composing two arbitrary patterns, the two directed graphs (each representing one pattern) are not statically composed. Instead, we compose them on the y in order not to loose the identity of the constituent patterns.

3.2   Towards Tool Support for Pattern Composition

In the following, we present a concrete algorithm realizing the composition properties discussed earlier. The algorithm has been implemented in the MADE toolset. Figure 4(a) shows three graphs representing patterns P, Q, and S. The patterns, each defining its own role structure, treat the same concern X. For this, the concern has references denoted by Rp for pattern p, Rq for pattern Q, and Rs for pattern S. In addition, concern X enforces a set of composition rules. In this case, the composition rules say that roleA in pattern P overlaps with roleD in pattern Q. This is denoted by the expression Rp.RoleA = Rq.RoleD. We refer to such a diagram as pattern composition graph. The reason behind this particular representation is that our target, as we have mentioned in the previous section, is not to statically create a new composite pattern.

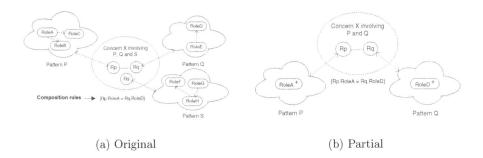

(a) Original   (b) Partial

Fig. 4. Pattern composition graph

Figure 4(b) shows a partial version of Figure 4(a). The graph shows the patterns and the roles that are involved in the composition operation. In order to make the case more interesting, we assume that there can be multiple instances of roles roleA and roleD. This is marked by the '+' sign attached to the role. In this case, when creating an instance for the two overlapping roles, say a first instance, the algorithm creates a separate binding for each role. Then, it associates the two bindings forcing them to point to the same instance. However, since the algorithm is executed stepwise, the binding in one pattern should not be allowed if the other pattern does not provide the corresponding binding. This situation is described in more details in the next discussion. In the case where the cardinality of either roles is '1', there is exactly one instantiation. The composition, therefore, becomes trivial.

Figure 5 shows four steps for applying concern X in Figure 4(b). X1, P1, and Q1 are respectively the instances of concern X and patterns P and Q. In step 1, the algorithm attempts to create an instance of roleA (denoted by a striped role A1 in P1). However, this operation cannot be completed since the corresponding node in Q1 has not been created. The state of the node A1 is said to be 'not doable'. This is marked in Figure 5 by the label on top of the striped node. In step 2, the algorithm creates the node D1. Initially, the state of D1 is 'not doable' but because a 'not doable' instance of roleA exists, the state of A1 and D1 is changed to 'doable' and the association between A1 and D1 is performed. This

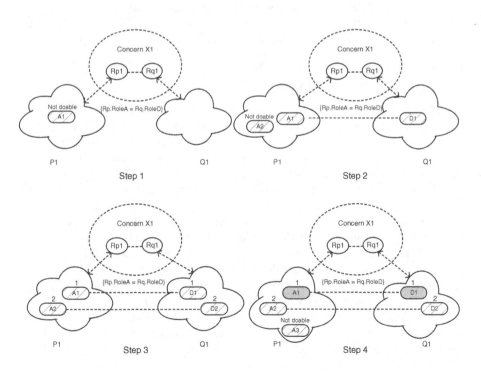

Fig. 5. Instantiation steps

means that the task of creating an instance for roles roleA and roleD (which is the same instance for both roles) can be done. The association is marked by a dashed line linking the two striped nodes. Striped nodes without labels indicate that the instantiation of the role is 'doable'. Because the cardinality of roleA and roleD is '+', other instances of roleA and roleD can be created. In step 2, for example, a new node A2 is prepared for being instantiated. In step 3, the corresponding node D2 is created and linked to A2. As a result, A2 changes state from 'not doable' to 'doable'. The instantiation order is marked on top of the node. A2, for example, has instantiation order 2 meaning that it is the second instantiation of roleA. In step 4, a concrete element for the tuple (A1, D1) has been created. This is marked by the linked dark nodes A1 and D1. In addition, a third node A3 has been created and is prepared for a possible instantiation.

3.3   Proof of Correctness

In brief, when composing patterns P and Q, each instance of roleA must be identical to its corresponding instance of roleD. The composition algorithm should not yield to situations where instances of roleA and roleD have wrong correspondences. In other words, the instances of roleA and roleD should not be linked in an erroneous mode. In order to prove the correctness of the above pattern composition algorithm, we have to prove two important conditions. The first is that, given a fixed number of instantiations, the algorithm should eventually terminate. The second condition ensures partial correctness. The partial correctness is expressed in terms of a set of invariants that should hold before and after the execution of every iteration in the algorithm. A complete proof of correctness along with a discussion are presented in [13].

3.4   Composition in MADE

Figure 6 shows how patterns are organized and applied in the MADE tool environment. Patterns are organized using architecture nodes. There are three types of architecture nodes: catalogue, concern, and deployment. Individual patterns are created under the Catalogue root node. At this stage, each pattern is regarded as a separate entity treating a specific concern in a software system and completely unrelated to other patterns. For example, there are two patterns named P and Q as discussed in Figure 4(b). The concerns of a software system are represented using concern nodes and are hierarchically represented under the Concerns root node, as shown in Figure 6. The figure, for example, depicts a concern named X. This concern is treated by the composition of two patterns: P and Q. The concern defines rules how the two patterns are composed. The composition rules are textually specified using pairs of pattern roles. In this case, the role RoleA in pattern P overlaps with the role RoleD in pattern Q.

Application development is carried out by considering those concerns relevant to the application needs. Using MADE, the developer selects which concern she wants to realize. The environment then takes care of which patterns to instantiate. The Deployment root node in Figure 6 shows the situation where concern X is considered. During the instantiation process, when a developer binds

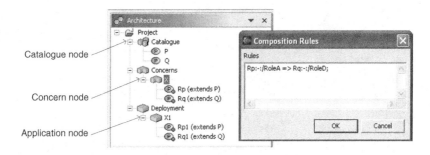

Catalogue node

Concern node

Application node

Fig. 6. Composing patterns in MADE

a role that has an overlapping counterpart, the overlapping role is automatically bound to the same concrete element.

4 Example: J2EE

In this section, we apply our approach to build and document a pattern system for annotating a part of the J2EE framework. We first identify the requirements, the concerns encapsulating these requirements, and the patterns treating these particular concerns. We further show an example of a J2EE pattern composition and finally discuss the benefits of using our methodology.

4.1 Building a J2EE Pattern System

In order to illustrate our concepts, we have applied our approach to build a pattern system for developing J2EE applications. For simplicity, however, we do not discuss all the patterns. An example requirement for J2EE development environments is the ability to generate bean-managed persistence entity beans. In addition, such environments should be able to optimize the communication between the container and the bean, decouple client code from the business logic implementing the bean, and enable support for multiple datasources. We treat each of these requirements as a separate concern. Figure 7 shows the concern architecture view corresponding to the above requirements. The view consists of the following concerns:

- BMP Entity Bean Concern: This concerns abstracts the creation of bean-managed persistence entity beans. It consists of two overlapping sub-concerns:
  - Optimization Concern: Optimizes the communication between the bean and the container.
  - Database Transparency Concern: Separates the data layer from business logic layer.
- Decoupling Client from Business Concern: Abstracts the non-functional requirement of separating client code from business-logic code.

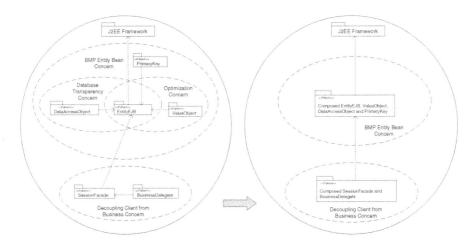

Fig. 7. J2EE concern architecture view

For implementing the above concerns, the following patterns are identified. Figure 7 shows the relationships between the patterns:

– EntityEJB Pattern: Defines the architectural skeleton of the bean-managed-persistence entity bean.
– PrimaryKey Pattern: Encapsulates the use of a primary key class for every generated entity bean.
– DataAccessObject Pattern: Makes the enterprise components transparent to the actual persistent store.
– ValueObject Pattern: Optimizes the number of remote calls over the network.
– SessionFacade Pattern: Interface that reduces the number of business objects exposed to the client over the network and encapsulates the complexity of their interaction.
– BusinessDelegate Pattern: Loose coupling between clients at the presentation tier and the services implemented in the enterprise beans.

4.2   Composing J2EE Patterns

The left part of Figure 7 shows all the patterns forming the pattern system and the concerns abstracting their purpose and relationships. The right part of the figure shows the concern architecture view after composing these patterns. Patterns EntityEJB, ValueObject, DataAccessObject, and PrimaryKey are composed into a larger pattern. In addition, patterns SessionFacade and BusinessDelegate are similarly combined into a single pattern. Conceptually, the first composite pattern, for example, represents a better solution for implementing entity beans. Therefore, the goal of the composition, in this case, is to provide the user with a single pattern managing the construction of entity beans.

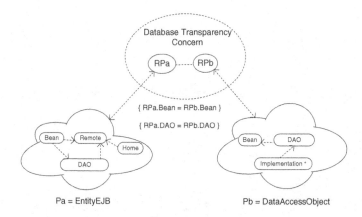

Pa = EntityEJB   Pb = DataAccessObject

Fig. 8. Composition graph of EntityEJB and DataAccessObject

In order to show how the above composition is achieved, we consider the case of the 'Database Transparency' concern shown in Figure 7. The concern is composed of two patterns EntityEJB and DataAccessObject, which have overlapping roles: Bean and DAO. Role Bean defines the methods in the bean implementation class whereas role DAO specifies concrete database implementation for these methods. Bean role is logically part of the EntityEJB pattern whereas DAO role is logically part of the DataAccessObject pattern. When generating a new entity bean, the pattern system user should instantiate both patterns and the results of the first are used for the second. Thus, the user of the pattern system wants to treat the two pattern instantiations as one instantiation. The solution is to compose the two patterns and to treat the 'Database Connectivity' concern as a composite pattern of EntityEJB and DataAccessObject. The composition rules of the two patterns discussed above are shown in Figure 8. Roles Bean and DAO are a part of both patterns and are treated as overlapping roles.

An example MADE annotation of the above J2EE pattern system is shown in the Architecture view of Figure 9. The pattern system has been used to develop a simple J2EE application generating both UML class diagrams and Java code. The application is a web-based to-do list where a list of users and their associated tasks are accessed in a relational database. The BMP Entity Bean concern, for example, has been considered to implement an entity bean for representing users. Using MADE, it is possible to align concerns with the patterns they treat and the model elements they implement. Furthermore, it is possible to trace the model elements back to the patterns and concerns they address.

The above situation is illustrated in Figure 9. Database Transparency concern, addressed by patterns EntityEJB and DataAccessObject, is highlighted in the generated models. In the Rose model, where all the UML model elements addressing the user entity bean are shown, the highlighted model elements are displayed in darker color. Furthermore, the Concern view at the top left of the

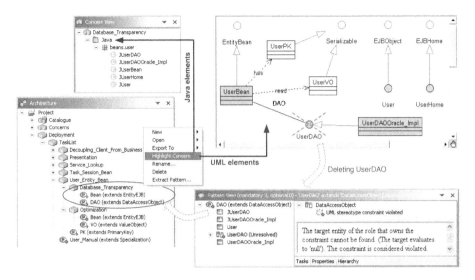

Fig. 9. Alignment in MADE

figure shows Java elements that correspond to the highlighted concern. The Java elements can further be displayed in the Java editor.

4.3   Evaluation

Buschmann et al. specified a number of requirements that pattern systems in general should meet [1]. In what follows, we show how our methodology helps in realizing these requirements.

- Providing a sufficient base of patterns: The concerns in the concern architecture view, such as the one shown in Figure 7, are used to build the proper patterns, each addressing a specific problem. As a result, a basic pattern catalogue is built. The patterns are then composed and specified in the MADE tool.
- Describing all the patterns uniformly: The purpose of each pattern in the pattern system is highlighted in the concern architecture view. Moreover, concern architecture views help comparing the patterns to each other. In the MADE tool, all patterns are specified using the same properties.
- Exposing the various relationships between the patterns: The concern architecture view depicts various relationships among the patterns such as the inter-pattern dependencies and their relationship to the different concerns. In MADE, these are used to impose a certain pattern instantiation order.
- Organizing the constituent patterns: The patterns annotating the J2EE framework specialization interface, for example, are organized into a number of concerns. The collaborations of the patterns are also highlighted. Using the MADE tool, concern nodes are used to compose related patterns.
- Supporting the construction of software systems: The various relationships depicted in the concern architecture view entail the partial order of applying

the patterns. In addition, the MADE environment reveals which patterns to instantiate in order to realize a certain concern.

– Support for system evolution: Our methodology realizes this requirement in different ways. Firstly, new patterns can be added to the pattern system by augmenting the existing concerns with new patterns or by considering completely new concerns. Secondly, our technique for pattern composition can be used to build new patterns from existing ones. Thirdly, concern architecture views tell which concerns are affected when a pattern is removed from or added to the pattern system. In the MADE tool, new patterns can be added while others can be deleted.

5   Related Work

In our methodology, a pattern corresponds to a specific aspect in the pattern system. The relationship between patterns and aspects have been identified in earlier works. An AspectJ implementation of design patterns described in [14] shows modularity improvements in 17 of the 23 GOF patterns.

The idea of structuring software artifacts based on concerns they treat has also been used in the Hyperspace approach [15, 16]. Hyperspace is a conceptual model for advanced separation of concerns that must be instantiated for some language or notation before applicable. A system is described using hyperslices which can be seen to correspond to our patterns. Hyperslices can be composed recursively to hypermodules which contain composition rules for the component slices. In principle, the Hyperspace model could be instantiated for pattern systems. However, in contrast to the concern architecture view utilized in our approach, Hyperspace does not provide a direct support for an architectural view where the relationships between different patterns would be given explicitly.

The most related UML-based approach is Theme [17, 18], which can be seen as an instantiation of the Hyperspace approach. Theme is based on ideas of Subject-Oriented Design [19] combined recently with a support for requirements capturing and management. Subject-Oriented Design facilitates finding and managing the design subjects (concerns) of the system. Moreover, so-called Composition Patterns define rules for composing (possibly overlapping) design subjects. Compared to Theme, we enforce architectural relationship between concerns and the role-based patterns constituting them, and have implemented our composition algorithm for patterns in the MADE toolset.

In [20], an approach for using role diagrams to document object collaboration based patterns is presented. The approach defines the notion of composite pattern to be a pattern described as a composition of other patterns and suggests a technique to cope with the complexity of the composition. However, the methodology does not define a proper scope in which the pattern composition rules should be defined. In our approach, concerns define the scope of the pattern composition. Every time a concern is instantiated, the composition rules defined in the concern are used in the role binding process. Moreover, our work defines an algorithm for pattern composition. The algorithm ensures that the binding process does not yield to instantiation problems and can be easily implemented by role-based pattern tools.

Composition has been regarded as an essential operation in various fields of software engineering. Batory et al. treat models as a series of layered refinements [21]. Individual features (reflecting different concerns) are composed together in a step-wise refinement fashion to form complex models. Models can be programs or other non-code representations. In order to support their concepts, the authors have developed a toolset for feature composition, called AHEAD. The toolset provides similar functions to those of the MADE tool. The MADE environment, however, solves two problems not otherwise addressed in [21]: Tracing concerns in the generated models and checking the validity of models against the architectural rules.

6   Conclusions

A pattern system is made of a number of patterns that interact with each other. Unfortunately, these patterns are tangled in the final design and their documentation becomes complicated. In this paper, we have proposed using concern architecture views for building and documenting pattern systems. Each concern in the concern architecture view captures a specific area of interest in the problem being solved by the pattern system. Concerns are used to identify the constituent patterns. Concern architecture views can then be used to abstract the relationships between the individual patterns and the way they should be instantiated. As a single concern can be scattered over multiple patterns, we treat concerns as a composition of patterns. For this, we have proposed an algorithm for pattern composition.

We have applied our approach to build and document a pattern system for annotating a part of the J2EE framework. Our approach allows individual patterns to be easily identified and the relationships between the patterns to be clearly highlighted. Furthermore, the presented methodology enables the key requirements of pattern systems to be conveniently realized. In [7], we have presented a tool environment supporting our approach and built a concern-based development environment for Symbian applications. In order to be able to combine patterns treating the same concern, we have extended the tool to support pattern composition.

References

1. Buschmann, F., Meunier, R., Rohnert, H., Sommerland, P., Stal, M.: Pattern-Oriented Software Architecture: A System of Patterns. Wiley (1996)
2. Filman, R.E., Elrad, T., Clarke, S., Akşit, M., eds.: Aspect-Oriented Software Development. Addison-Wesley (2004)
3. Nuseibeh, B.: Crosscutting requirements. In: Proc. AOSD 2004, Lancaster, UK (2004) 3–4

4. Rashid, A., Moreira, A., Araujo, J.: Modularisation and composition of aspectual requirements. In: Proc. AOSD 2003, Boston, Massachusetts (2003) 11–20
5. Katara, M., Katz, S.: Architectural views of aspects. In: Proc. AOSD 2003, Boston, Massachusetts (2003) 1–10
6. Gamma, E., Helm, R., Johnson, R., Vlissides, J.: Design Patterns: Elements of Reusable Object-Oriented Software. Addison-Wesley (1994)
7. Hammouda, I., Koskinen, J., Pussinen, M., Katara, M., Mikkonen, T.: Adaptable concern-based framework specialization in UML. In: Proc. ASE 2004, Linz, Austria (2004) 78–87
8. Gottlob, G., Schrefl, M., Röck, B.: Extending object-oriented systems with roles. ACM Transactions on Information Systems **14** (1996) 268–296
9. Pernici, B.: Objects with roles. In: Proc. OIS 1990. (1990) 205–215
10. Hakala, M., Hautamäki, J., Koskimies, K., Paakki, J., Viljamaa, A., Viljamaa, J.: Generating application development environments for Java frameworks. In: Proc. CGSE 2001, Erfurt, Germany, Springer-Verlag (2001) 163–176
11. Marinescu, F.: EJB Design Patterns: Advanced Patterns, Processes, and Idioms. Wiley Computer Publishing (2002)
12. Peltonen, I., Selonen, P.: An approach and a platform for building UML processing tools. In: Proc. WoDiSEE 2004, Edinburgh, Scotland (2004) 51–57
13. Hammouda, I.: Towards tool-support for pattern composition. Technical report, Tampere University of Technology, http://www.cs.tut.fi/~imed/reports/PatternComposition.pdf (2004)
14. Hannemann, J., Kiczales, G.: Design pattern implementation in Java and AspectJ. In: Proceedings of OOPSLA '02. (2002) 161–173
15. Tarr, P., Ossher, H., Harrison, W., Sutton, Jr., S.M.: *N* degrees of separation: Multi-dimensional separation of concerns. In: Proc. ICSE'99, Los Angeles, CA, USA, ACM Press (1999) 107–119
16. Ossher, H., Tarr, P.: Multi-dimensional separation of concerns and the hyperspace approach. In: Proc. Software Architectures and Component Technology. The State of the Art in Software Development, Kluwer (2000)
17. Baniassad, E., Clarke, S.: Theme: An approach for aspect-oriented analysis and design. In: Proc. ICSE 2004, Edinburgh, Scotland (2004) 158–167
18. Clarke, S.: Extending standard UML with model composition semantics. Science of Computer Programming **44** (2002) 71–100
19. Clarke, S., Harrison, W., Ossher, H., Tarr, P.: Subject-oriented design: towards improved alignment of requirements, design, and code. ACM SIGPLAN Notices **34** (1999) 325–339
20. Riehle, D.: Composite design patterns. In: Proc. OOPSLA 1997. (1997) 218–228
21. Batory, D., Sarvela, J.N., Rauschmayer, A.: Scaling stepwise refinement. In: Proc. ICSE 2003, Portland, USA (2003) 187–197

Engineering MDA into Compositional Reasoning for Analyzing Middleware-Based Applications

Mauro Caporuscio, Davide Di Ruscio, Paola Inverardi,
Patrizio Pelliccione, and Alfonso Pierantonio

Dipartimento di Informatica,
Università degli Studi di L'Aquila,
67100 L'Aquila, Italy
{caporusc, diruscio, inverard,
pellicci, alfonso}@di.univaq.it

Abstract. Behavioral analysis of middleware-based applications typically requires the analysis of the middleware and the application, in a
monolithic way. In terms of model-checking, this is a complex task and
may result in the well known "state-explosion" problem. These considerations led us to investigate a *compositional verification* approach which
decomposes the system in accordance with its Software Architecture.
The *architectural decomposability* theorem we defined in previous work
decomposes the system into three logical layer: (i) *application components*, (ii) *proxies* and, (iii) *middleware*. This logical separation allows
for reducing the global system validation to the verification of local behaviors.

In this paper, we engineer the architectural decomposability theorem
to the analysis of middleware-based applications by automatically generating the proxies needed by the components in order to properly interact
with each other via the middleware. In particular, following the *Model
Driven Architecture* approach and by making use of the *Abstract State
Machine* formalism, we describe a set of transformation rules that allow
for deriving correct proxies for using CORBA. By means of the proposed
transformations, the correctness of the proxy behavioral models is guaranteed without the need to validate them with respect to the assumptions
posed by the theorem.

1   Introduction

Due to the widespread diffusion of network-based applications, middleware technologies [1] increased in significance. They cover a wide range of software systems,
including distributed objects and components, message-oriented communication,
and mobile application support. Thus, methodologies and tools are in need to
analyze and verify middleware-based applications since the early stages of the
software life-cycle.

Recently model checking has been proposed to verify an entire system [2, 3, 4],
i.e. both the middleware and the application, in a monolithic way. The approach

R. Morrison and F. Oquendo (Eds.): EWSA 2005, LNCS 3527, pp. 130–145, 2005.

turned out to have two major drawbacks: (i) it may result in the well known "state-explosion" problem and, (ii) the middleware needs to be verified every time. These considerations naturally have led us to investigate the *compositional verification* approach [5, 6, 7] in order to validate the middleware once and for all and reusing the results of the validation as base for verifying the applications built on top of such middleware. The key idea of compositional verification is to decompose the system specification into properties that describe the behavior of its subsystems. In general, checking local properties over subsystems does not imply the correctness of the entire system. The problem is due to the existence of mutual dependencies among components.

In [8] we presented the *architectural decomposability* theorem that allows the decomposition of software applications built on top of a middleware by exploiting the structure imposed on the system by the Software Architecture (SA) [9]. This allows the verification of middleware-based applications since the early phases of the software life-cycle. In fact, once the application specification (behavioral and structural) has been defined, the designer might want to validate it with respect to some desired behaviors. Next, the communication facilities are provided to the application by means of a middleware infrastructure. In essence, the high level SA is refined in order to realize the desired communication policy by means of additional components. These are the *proxy* components[1] towards the middleware that allow the application to transparently access the services offered by the middleware. The decision of using services offered by a middleware may invalidate all behaviors stated at the previous phases. In fact, middlewares usually have a well defined business-logic that could not be suitable for the application purposes. Consequently, the system has to be re-verified by considering also a full-featured model of the middleware. In such a context, the *architectural decomposability* theorem helps the designer to choose the right middleware by (i) freeing him from the middleware model implementation and, (ii) hiding low-level details. Actually, the designer must have a deep knowledge about the middleware and its internal mechanisms needed to identify and properly model the *Proxy* entities.

In this paper, we present techniques and tools to engineer the architecture decomposability theorem. In particular, we propose an approach that, following the Model Driven Architecture [10] (MDA) methodology, automatically generates the proxy models that correctly use the middleware. MDA separates the application logic from the underlying platform technology and represents this logic with precise semantic platform independent models (PIMs), i.e. abstract descriptions that do not refer to the underling technologies. The proposed approach starts from the system SA and the components behaviors, given as PIMs. Then by applying several transformation rules, formally described by means of Abstract State Machines (ASMs) [11], the models of proxies are obtained. By means of the proposed transformations, the correctness of such models, w.r.t.

---

[1] While in [8] we referred to these components as *interfaces*, here we make use of the term *proxies* in order to distinguish them from the well defined CORBA Interfaces.

the use of the middleware, is guaranteed without the need of validation of the hypothesis required by the theorem. In order to illustrate the approach, we use an ATM distributed system implemented on top of the CORBA middleware [12], as running example throughout the entire paper. Due to space limits, we only give a fragment of the system.

The paper is organized as follows. Section 2 presents some preliminary concepts, Section 3 briefly introduces the architectural decomposability theorem and applies the overall approach to the running example. Finally, Section 4 draws some conclusions and discusses future work.

2   Background

2.1   Model Driven Architecture

The Model-Driven Architecture [10] (MDA) approach pursues the conceptual separation between the abstract specification of a system and the specification of its implementation w.r.t. a specific technology. Models play a central role in MDA and they can be distinguished in those describing the system in a platform-independent manner (PIMs – Platform Independent Models) and in others describing the same system but bound to a specific target platform (PSMs – Platform Specific Models). Mapping a description at a higher level of abstraction to a lower one is performed by transforming models. The transformation process encodes the refinement knowledge which used to make the target models concrete and aware of the technological assets being used. At the moment, there is no standard language for defining transformation among models, although OMG issued a Meta-Object Facilities (MOF) Query/View/Transformation (QVT) request for proposal [13] which is expected to provide a standard mechanism for transforming models.

2.2   Abstract State Machines

The ability to simulate arbitrary algorithms on their natural levels of abstraction, without implementing them, makes Abstract State Machines [14] (ASMs) appropriate for high-level system design and analysis (see [15]) and a candidate for specifying model transformation. Generating models in a formal setting not only facilitates traceability, reuse and evolution of software systems, but also represents a basis to reason about the properties of the generation process as encoded into unambiguous transformation descriptions.

Due to space limitation, we briefly introduce ASMs here and we refer to [14, 11] for a detailed description. ASMs are intended to bridge the gap between specification and computation by providing more versatile Turing-complete machines. They form a variant of first-order logic with equality, where the fundamental concept is that functions are defined over a set $\mathcal{U}$ and can be changed point-wise. The set $\mathcal{U}$ referred to as the *superuniverse* in ASM parlance, always contains the distinct elements *true*, *false*, and *undef*. Apart from these, $\mathcal{U}$ can contain numbers, strings, and possibly anything, depending on the application domain. Being slightly more formal, we define the *state* λ of a system as a mapping from a signature Σ (which is a collection of function symbols) to actual functions. We write f_λ for denoting the function which interprets the symbol f in the state λ. Subsets of $\mathcal{U}$, called universes, are modeled by unary functions from $\mathcal{U}$ to *true, false*. Such a function returns *true* for all elements belonging to the universe, and *false* otherwise. A function f from a universe U to a universe V is a unary operation on the superuniverse such that for all $a \in U$, $f(a) \in V$ and $f(a) = undef$ otherwise. The universe *Boolean* consists of *true* and *false*.

A basic ASM *transition rule* is of the form

$$f(t_1, \ldots, t_n) := t_0$$

where $f(t_1, \ldots, t_n)$ and t_0 are closed terms (i.e. terms containing no free variables) in the signature Σ. The semantics of such a rule is to evaluate all the terms in the given state, and update the function corresponding to f at the value of the tuple resulting out of evaluating $(t_1, \ldots, t_n)$ to the value obtained by evaluating t_0. Rules are composed in a parallel fashion, so the corresponding updates are all executed at once. Of course not all functions can be updated, for instance the basic arithmetic operations (such as addition) are typically not redefinable.

3   Compositional Verification of Middleware-Based SA

In this section, we illustrate compositional verification by means of an example which is going to be used throughtly the paper. Given an architectural description of the system and a set of properties which presents the desired behaviors, specified by means of message sequence charts [16] (MSC), the architectural decomposability theorem states that the verification of the entire system is guaranteed provided that the components satisfy the hypothesis[2].

Let us consider the high-level SA description (depicted in Fig. 1.a) of an ATM system that allows users to: (i) buy a refill card for its mobile phone and, (ii) check its bank account. The system has been designed as the composition of a set of distributed components whose behavior is described as state machines (an example is shown in Fig. 2): a *User*, the *Phone Company*, the *Bank Account* and a *Transaction Manager* that manages all the interactions between the user and the other entities. In Fig. 1.b a property of the ATM system behavior, represented as an MSC (in the remainder referred to as Z), is satisfied by the high level SA. The property states that every time a refill card is bought, the corresponding credit is withdrawn from the user's bank account.

As already mentioned, the development of distributed applications often relies on a middleware infrastructure which provides the required communication services. In architectural terms this means that the high-level SA will be refined

---

[2] The interested reader can find more details about the theorem on [8], although it is not required to follow the approach we present.

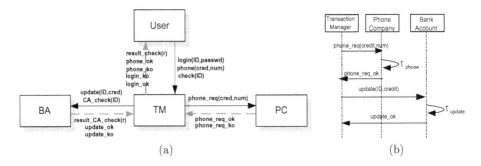

Fig. 1. a) ATM application; b) Z property

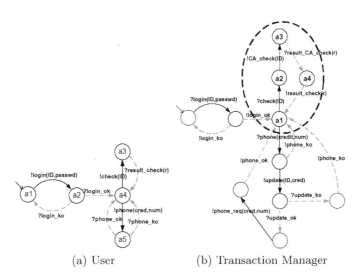

(a) User   (b) Transaction Manager

Fig. 2. Component Behavior Descriptions

in a more detailed SA that presents additional components, i.e. the middleware and the proxies. In Fig. 3.a, the CORBA middleware communicates through the proxies with the application components *User*, *Transaction Manager*, *Phone company* and *Bank Account*. In this context, the designer's challenge is to understand if Z is still valid on the refined architecture. In fact, due to the introduction of CORBA that offers services to the application, the property Z may be falsified by the new SA.

In Fig. 3.b and Fig. 4 the architectural decomposability theorem has been instantiated on the ATM system and Z is split in a set of local properties that the subparts of the system must satisfy. In this new contest a relabelling function is applied to the components in order to let them to communicate through the middleware (for example the components in Fig. 2 have been relabelled as shown in Fig. 5). The properties that have to be proved are graphically denoted

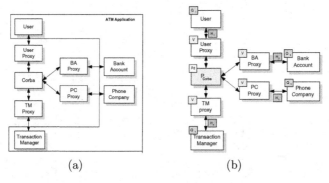

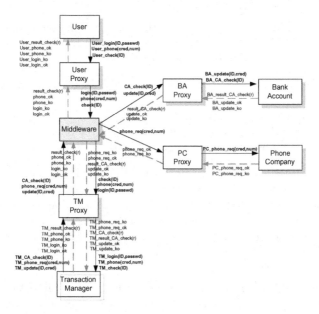

(a)   (b)

Fig. 3. Architectural Refinement

Fig. 4. Detailing SA

in the upper left corner of each component. For verification purposes, CORBA is substituted with a set of properties P that characterizes its behavior. The properties we consider for CORBA are reported in the Appendix (they are written in Linear Temporal Logic (LTL) [17]). In the following we define the set of properties V, defined in LTL, that assess the correct usage of CORBA.

V Properties

1. $\Box(\neg get\_IOR(ID) \cup reg\_IOR(ID))$
   In order to retrieve the object reference, the object has to be already registered.

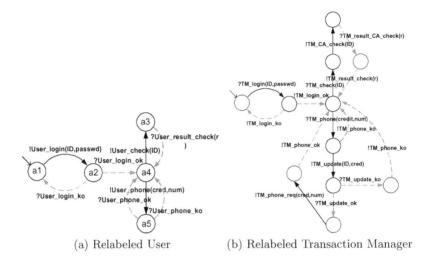

(a) Relabeled User   (b) Relabeled Transaction Manager

Fig. 5. Components Relabelling

2. $\Box(\neg < METHOD > \cup get\_IOR(ID))$

In order to use the object methods [3] the object reference must be obtained. It is obtained by asking for it $(get\_IOR(ID))$.

The approach described in [8] assumes that the proxies models are explicitly given and then verified with respect to the set V.

In the following we show how these two steps can be collapsed by only assuming the component models and the constraints V through a set of transformation rules which allow, by construction, the generation of correct proxies.

3.1   Proxy Generation

The model transformations presented in this section are specified through ASMs, a mathematical setting which already showed a certain effectiveness in system analysis and verification (see [11]). The transformation process (depicted in Fig. 6) starts with an encoding step which takes the model of a component and returns an algebra encoding it. The ASM rules are applied on the source algebra to generate another algebra which contains an algebraic representation of the state machine of the proxy. For instance, if we consider the TM component in the ATM application described in Sect. 3, in order to let it communicate with the other components via CORBA it requires a proxy component which is obtained by transforming the component model itself. The state machine of the transaction manager and of the associated proxy are illustrated in Fig. 9, respectively.

---

[3] In the formula, <METHOD> is just a placeholder that must be replaced by an actual method signature

Fig. 6. The transformation process

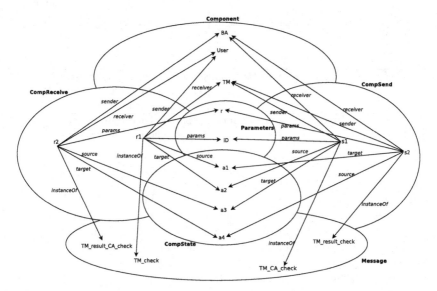

Fig. 7. The algebra $A(M)$ of the TM model

From State Machines to Algebras. A state machine M defines an algebra $A(M)$ whose sets $A(M)_{State}$ contains the representatives of all states in the model M, while $A(M)_{MessageInstance}$ contains individuals corresponding to the transitions in M. The parameters used to invoke methods are represented in $A(M)_{Parameter}$ as tuples of parameter identifiers of the form $< p_1, p_2, \ldots, p_n >$. By applying iteratively the rules we obtain algebras which encode the target models. During the transitions the elements representing the source model are not deleted, thus the target algebra contains both the source and target model. This causes certain domains to be subsorted in order to distinguish among source and target elements of the same kind.

A number of functions are given to represent properly the information given by the models and some of them are reported in Table 1. As an example, Fig. 7 depicts the algebra obtained from the fragment of the state machine model depicted in Fig. 5.b.

Transformation Rules. The transformations are given in XASM, an ASM implementation whose compiler is freely available [18]. Due to space limitation

Table 1. Some functions

Function symbol	Description
$source : MessageInstance \rightarrow State$	given an element in *MessageInstance* returns the source state of the message
$target : MessageInstance \rightarrow State$	given an element in *MessageInstance* returns the target state of the message
$sender : MessageInstance \rightarrow Component$	given an element in *MessageInstance* returns the component that sends the message
$receiver : MessageInstance \rightarrow Component$	given an element in *MessageInstance* returns the component that receives the message
$instanceOf : MessageInstance \rightarrow Message$	given an element in *MessageInstance* returns the message of which the message is an instance
$params : MessageInstance \rightarrow Parameters^*$	given an element in *Message* returns the parameters used in the message

only the most important rules are reported here. The transformation process consists of two macro steps: the first one initializes the target algebra, while the second iteratively extends it by transforming the method instances of the source algebra. The transformation rules are designed in order to preserve the message sequences given in the source model, assuming that the communication via CORBA is synchronous. This is accomplished by means of an auxiliary function *border* which keeps track of the states whose outgoing messages still have to be transformed. At each iteration a state in the *border* is taken into account and all its outgoing messages are transformed. Additionally, a state is added in the *border* if it is a non-visited target state of the message under transformation. The rules which implement such transformation strategy are the following:

– *Main:* it is the main rule and triggers the other ones, in particular it defines all universes and functions, and has some control over the states which has to be *visited* according to the information held by the *border* function as follows

  asm MAIN **is**
  universes – Universe declarations section

  $\vdots$

  function – Function declarations section

  $\vdots$

  function initial
  init
     – Initializations describing the source model

  $\vdots$

```
      endinit
      if initial=undef
      then
        executed:=REGS
        executed:=RESOLVE
        border(sourceInitState):=true
        initial:=true
      endif
      choose x in CompState : border(x)=true
        executed:=VISIT(x)
      endchoose
    endasm
```

– *Regs:* it generates the registration CORBA dependent of the component whose proxy is being generated, by extending the target algebra with a *reg* message having as parameter the name of the component which have to be registered as follows

```
    asm REGS -> Bool
      used as function in MAIN
      is
      if (exists y in CompReceive: type(y)=INVOCATION)
      then
        extend ProxyState with a,b and ProxySend with m
          source(m):=a
          target(m):=b
          instanceOf(m):=getMessage("reg_IOR")
          params(m):=[getPar(name(component)),getPar(ior(component))]
          sender(m):=proxy
          receiver(m):=middleware
            ⋮
        endextend
          ⋮
      endif
      return true
    endasm
```

– *Resolve:* it generates the resolutions CORBA dependent in order to retrieve the identifier of all components with whom to communicate as follows

```
asm RESOLVE -> Bool
  used as function in MAIN
  is
  choose x in CompSend:(type(x)=INVOCATION) and (considered(receiver(x))=undef)
    extend ProxySend with m and ProxyReceive with m2 and ProxyState with b,c,d
      if ( anchorInitialState!=undef)
      then
```

```
        source(m):=anchorInitialState
    else extend ProxyState with a
        source(m):=a
      endextend
    endif
    target(m):=b
    instanceOf(m):=getMessage("get_IOR")
    params(m):=[getPar(name(receiver(x)))]
    type(m):=INVOCATION
    sender(m):=proxy
    receiver(m):=middleware
    source(m2):=b
    target(m2):=c
    instanceOf(m2):=getMessage("result")
    params(m2):=[getPar(ior(receiver(x)))]
    type(m2):=RETURN
    sender(m2):=middleware
    receiver(m2):=proxy
    extend ProxyMessageInstance with m3
      instanceOf(m3):=getMessage("condition")
        ⋮
    endextend
  endextend
    ⋮
  endchoose
  return true
endasm
```

– *Visit:* given a state of the source model it transforms all outgoing messages and manages the function *border* explained above. An extract of the rule is the following:

```
asm VISIT(sourceCurrState:CompState) -> Bool
  used as function in MAIN
  is
  function – Function declarations section
    ⋮
  do forall x in CompMessageInstance
    if (type(x)=INVOCATION) and (source(x)=sourceCurrState)
    then
      if CompSend(x)=true
      then
        executed:=SENDTRANSF(x)
      else
        executed:=RECEIVETRANSF(x)
      endif
      if (transformed(target(x))=undef)
      then border(target(x)):=true
```

```
      endif
    endif
  enddo
  do forall x in CompMessageInstance
    if (type(x)=RETURN) and (source(x)=sourceCurrState)
    then
      if CompSend(x)=true
      then
        executed:=SENDTRANSF(x)
      else
        executed:=RECEIVETRANSF(x)
      endif
      if transformed(target(x))=undef
      then
        border(target(x)):=true
      endif
    endif
  enddo
  if VISITED(sourceCurrState)
  then
    border(sourceCurrState):=undef
  endif
  return true
endasm
```

- *Visited:* given a state in the source model return if it has been visited or if there are messages which are not yet transformed.
- *SendTransf:* given a sending message in the source model it generates the transformed one extending the target algebra as reported in the following extract:

```
asm SENDTRANSF(m:CompMessageInstance) -> Bool
  used as function in VISIT
  is
  extend ProxyState with b and ProxyReceive with m1 and ProxySend with m2
    if (transformed(source(m)) = undef)
    then
      source(m1):=anchorInitialState
    else
      source(m1):=transformed(source(m))
    endif
    target(m1):=b
    instanceOf(m1):=instanceOf(m)
    params(m1):=params(m)
    sender(m1):=component
    receiver(m1):=proxy
    source(m2):=b
    if transformed(target(m))=undef
    then
```

```
        extend ProxyState with c
          transformed(target(m)):=c
          target(m2):=c
        endextend
      else
        target(m2):=transformed(target(m))
      endif
        ⋮

      params(m2):=params(m)
      sender(m2):=proxy
      receiver(m2):=middleware
        ⋮

    endextend
    return true
  endasm
```

- *ReceiveTransf:* given a receiving message in the source model it generates the transformed in the target algebra following a similar logic of the *Sender-Transf* rule.

Figure 8 depicts a fragment of the target algebra representing the subpart of the state machine model in Fig. 9.b obtained by means of the transformation on the source algebra given in Fig. 7.

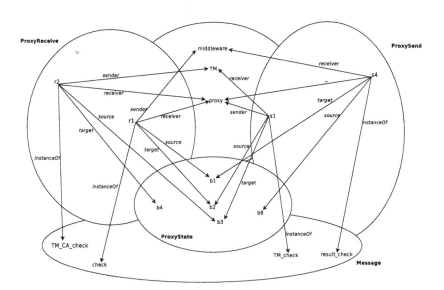

Fig. 8. The algebra $A(M)$ of the TM proxy model

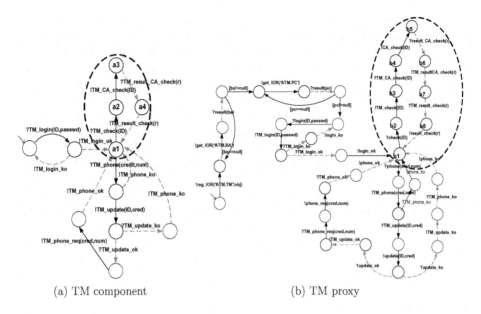

(a) TM component   (b) TM proxy

Fig. 9. TM State Machine models

Properties Preserving Transformations. As already discussed, by automating the application of the architectural decomposability theorem, the correctness of the target models is granted without the need to validate each of them w.r.t. the theorem hypothesis. In particular, we need to prove that the generated state machines are satisfying the V properties listed in Sec. 3 by construction. The following sketches such proof.

A generated state machine is obtained by means of precise transformation steps which consist of an initialization step and subsequent message transformations. The first step generates a fragment of the target model which includes the registration of the component whose proxy is being generated and the identification of all the components with whom it communicates via CORBA. The initialization step suffices to guarantee that the properties $V1$ and $V2$ are preserved. In fact, the model fragments are generated by means of the *Regs* and *Resolve* rules described in the previous section. The rule *Regs* assures the preservation of the registration property $V1$ by generating a component registration message (and the corresponding source and target states) as shown in Fig. 9.b. Analogously, the property $V2$ is guaranteed by the rule *Resolve* since such a rule generates the resolve messages to the middleware to retrieve the component identifiers as stated by the $V2$.

4   Conclusion and Future Work

The paper illustrates how to engineer the architectural decomposability theorem to the analysis of middleware-based applications by automatically generating the proxies needed by the components in order to properly interact with each other via the CORBA middleware. In particular, model transformations, proper of the MDA approach, are used to generate the proxy models required by the middleware-based SA. Such transformations are expressed formally and unambiguously in terms of ASMs, which allows the verification of the correctness of the transformation w.r.t. the properties of interest.

The transformations have been *implemented* by means of the XASM compiler and both the sources and the binaries are available for download (please refer to [19]). A stronger tool support is to be pursued in future work in order to assist the designer in all the stages described in this work: (i) design the high-level application SA and validate it with respect to desired behaviors, (ii) choose an appropriate middleware, (iii) automatically refine the high-level SA by proxies generation and validate it with respect to the behaviors defined in (i), (iv) automatically generate the source code of the proxies. Once again, code generation should exploit as much as possible the potential of MDA by means of refinement mappings.

References

1. Emmerich, W.: Software engineering and middleware: a roadmap. In: Proceedings of the conference on The future of Software engineering (ICSE 2000) - Future of SE Track, Limerick, Ireland, ACM Press (2000) 117–129
2. Garlan, D., Khersonsky, S., Kim, J.S.: Model Checking Publish/Subscribe Systems. In: Proceedings of The 10th International SPIN Workshop on Model Checking of Software (SPIN 03), Portland, Oregon (2003)
3. J.Bradbury, Dingel, J.: Evaluating and Improving the Automatic Analysis of Implicit Invocation Systems. In: European Software Engineering Conference and ACM SIGSOFT Symposium on the Foundations of Software Engineering. (ESEC/FSE 2003), Helsinki, Finland, ACM Press (2003)
4. Kaveh, N., Emmerich, W.: Validating distributed object and component designs. In Bernardo, M., Inverardi, P., eds.: Formal Methods for Software Architecture. Volume 2804 of Lecture Notes in Computer Science. (2003)
5. Grumberg, O., Long, D.E.: Model Checking and Modular Verification. ACM Transaction on Programming Languages and Systems **16** (1994) 846–872
6. Long, D.: Model Checking, Abstraction and Compositional Reasoning. PhD thesis, Carnegie Mellon University (1993)
7. Clarke, E.M., Grumberg, O., Peled, D.A.: Model Checking. The MIT Press (2001)
8. Caporuscio, M., Inverardi, P., Pelliccione, P.: Compositional verification of middleware-based software architecture descriptions. In: Proceedings of the International Conference on Software Engineering (ICSE 2004), Edinburgh (2004.)
9. Perry, D.E., Wolf, A.L.: Foundations for the study of software architecture. In: SIGSOFT Software Engineering Notes. Volume 17. (1992) 40–52
10. Object Management Group (OMG): OMG/Model Driven Architecture - A Technical Perspective (2001) OMG Document: ormsc/01-07-01.
11. E.Börger, R.Stärk: Abstract State Machines - A Method for High-Level System Design and Analysis. Springer Verlag (2003)
12. Object Management Group: (Common Object Request Broker Architecture (CORBA/IIOP), v3.0.3) OMG document formal/04-03-01.

13. Object Management Group: MOF 2.0 Query/View/Transformation RFP (2002) OMG document ad/02-04-10.
14. E.Börger: The origins and the development of the asm method for high level system design and analysis". Journal of Universal Computer Science **8** (2002) 2–74
15. Börger, E.: High level system design and analysis using abstract state machines. In: Procs. FM–Trends 98, Current Trends in Applied Formal Methods. Volume 1641 of LNCS., Springer (1999) 1–43
16. ITU-T Recommendation Z.120.: Message Sequence Charts. (ITU Telecommunication Standardisation Sector)
17. Manna, Z., Pnueli, A.: The temporal logic of reactive and concurrent systems. Springer-Verlag New York, Inc. (1992)
18. Anlauff, M.: XASM – An Extensible, Component-Based Abstract State Machines Language. In Y. Gurevich and P. Kutter and M. Odersky and L. Thiele, ed.: Abstract State Machines: Theory and Applications. Volume 1912 of LNCS., Springer-Verlag (2000) 69–90
19. M.Caporuscio, D.Di Ruscio, P.Inverardi, P.Pelliccione, A.Pierantonio: Tranformation rules (2004) Available at http://www.di.univaq.it/diruscio.

Appendix

P Properties

1. after an object registration request, the object reference has been stored into the IOR repository:

$$\Box((reg\_IOR(o)) \rightarrow \Diamond serverRegistered[o])$$

2. after an object retrieve request, the object reference, if it exist, will be returned:

$$\Box((get\_IOR(o)) \rightarrow (\Diamond(result\_IOR(ref_o))W(\neg serverRegistered[o])))$$

3. A synchronous method invocation is eventually followed by a return message:

$$\Box(sync\_meth\_inv \rightarrow \Diamond return)$$

4. (a) An asynchronous method invocation is eventually received by the suitable server:

$$\Box(async\_meth\_inv \rightarrow \Diamond ServerRecv)$$

   (b) An asynchronous result retrieval is eventually followed by the return:

$$\Box(result\_inv \rightarrow \Diamond return)$$

Context-Awareness in Software Architectures

Antónia Lopes[1] and José Luiz Fiadeiro[2]

[1] Department of Informatics, Faculty of Sciences, University of Lisbon,
Campo Grande, 1749-016 Lisboa, Portugal
mal@di.fc.ul.pt
[2] Department of Computer Science, University of Leicester,
University Road, Leicester LE1 7RH, UK
jose@fiadeiro.org

Abstract. The growing importance of context-awareness in the construction of adaptable systems requires the development of formal models and notations that can bring this new dimension from middleware concerns into the higher levels of modelling. In this paper, we propose a formal approach to the design of context-aware systems that is well integrated with the concepts and techniques that have been proposed for software architectures. This approach is based on a set of primitives through which the notion of context can be modelled as a first-class entity and context-awareness addressed explicitly as an additional dimension of architectural elements. We illustrate the approach around an image search system.

1 Introduction

In recent years, we have been witnessing a growing interest for software systems that are able to adapt autonomously at run-time. This is justified in part by the need for developing applications that can cope with highly dynamic execution environments. Typical examples are distributed applications with components executed in distinct devices under a wide range of operational conditions that can change over time. This new breed of applications are usually known as *context-aware* systems because they must be responsive to the context in which they execute in order to adapt to changes as they occur.

Much of the work in what has become known as *context-aware computing* is being devoted to the development of middleware infrastructures that facilitate the implementation of this new generation of systems (e.g., [3,7,8,19,20]). In these approaches, the context-aware aspects are divided between the application logic and an infrastructure responsible for the gathering, management and dissemination of contextual information [6,13]. As a result, software developers can concentrate on the application logic without having to be concerned with the way context information needs to be sensed. This separation is important because it promotes the development of general context widgets that can be used, and reused, as components in different configurations of the infrastructure [8].

The added level of complexity that this new dimension brings to software development suggests that context-awareness should be also addressed at higher levels of

R. Morrison and F. Oquendo (Eds.): EWSA 2005, LNCS 3527, pp. 146 – 161, 2005.

abstraction and in earlier phases of the development lifecycle. As remarked in [22], formal models and high-level notations are needed that provide suitable support for modelling and designing context-aware systems before infrastructural concerns come into play. Software designers should have the means for exploring different design solutions that take advantage of contextual information and defining the specific notions of context that are best suited for the systems that are envisaged.

Consider, as an example, the problem of searching a database of images stored in a remote site. Assume that a cheap algorithm is available that quickly identifies images that are potentially interesting. We may think of several different solutions depending on how much awareness the system can have of the context in which it is operating. For instance, a simple and context-unaware solution consists in deciding that all the images must be downloaded from the server and then processed locally. A more flexible solution proposed in [2] consists in executing the cheap algorithm remotely and, depending on the size of the selected images and the current bandwidth, deciding if the remaining more intensive computation should be performed remotely or if the selected images should be dispatched to be locally processed. Other context information, such as the processing power that is available, could be used for taking the decision on where to process the selected images, giving rise to different design solutions for the problem.

In most approaches to software development, context-awareness is not addressed explicitly and, hence, it is not possible to represent explicitly this kind of design decisions: they are simply programmed. This implies that if, for some reason, one needs to change the system to operate according to a different strategy, the system needs to be reprogrammed, possibly interfering with the way orthogonal concerns have been captured in the code. In this paper, we address the design of context-aware systems at the higher architectural levels where such decisions can be modelled in terms of first-class entities and evolved in a compositional way.

Given that context-awareness is especially relevant in the presence of distribution and mobility, we focus our attention in software architectures that address location-dependence explicitly. More concretely, we show how the description of context-awareness aspects of systems can be integrated with the techniques that we have been developing within the IST-2001-32747 project *AGILE – Architectures for Mobility* for supporting distribution and mobility in software architectures [14,15]. The resulting architectural approach promotes the separation of concerns by awarding first-class status to the notion of context. On the one hand, it supports the description of context dependencies of a system's architecture in an explicit way through *context models* that can be understood independently of the specification of the system behaviour. On the other hand, it allows these aspects to be refined and evolved independently of the other concerns.

As such, this paper extends preliminary work presented in [16] where we have focused on the algebraic semantics of much simpler and less expressive design abstractions for context-awareness. We decided to use the same example so that the reader who is familiar with that first proposal can appreciate the added expressive power that we are now proposing. On the other hand, we are now omitting much of the algebraic semantics of the whole approach, and concentrate on the new and revised features.

Most of the added expressive power comes from context models, which are also explored in this paper as requirement specifications for the gathering and dissemination of contextual information. Indeed, context models provide an important abstraction mechanism for modelling, in a formal way, context information in middleware infrastructures that support context sensing.

In Section 2, we briefly review the basic principles of our approach to architectural modelling of distributed and mobile systems and the way it is supported in CommUnity, a prototype language for architectural description. In Section 3, we discuss the context-sensitive behaviour of distributed systems and present the primitives through which architectural models can be made context-aware. We show how higher level notions of context can be modelled and how they can support separation of concerns. In Section 4, we address context modelling in the development of systems that are responsible for the gathering and dissemination of contextual information. We conclude in Section 5 by discussing related and future work.

2 Distributed and Mobile Architectures in CommUnity

As already mentioned, context-awareness is particularly relevant in the presence of mobility. When components are allowed to move across networks, the availability and responsiveness of resources and services are often difficult to predict and out of control [1]. For instance, when visiting a site, a piece of mobile code may fail to link with the libraries that it requires for execution according to its specification. Computational resources such as CPU and memory can no longer be assumed to be fixed as in conventional computing.

Given that, in these situations, the context that a component perceives is to a great extent related with its location, it is important that context-awareness be addressed in approaches that, like CommUnity [10], do not adopt location-transparency as an abstraction principle and address distribution as a first-class concern in par with computation and coordination. In this section, we provide a brief review of the primitives that are used in CommUnity to capture distribution and mobility and illustrate how they support the description of mobile systems at an architectural level of design. A more detailed account of this approach can be found in [14,15].

CommUnity is a parallel program design language in the style of Unity [5] and Interaction Processes [11] that we have been developing for formalising architecture description primitives. A CommUnity design is defined in terms of *channels*, *actions* and *location variables*.

Channels provide the means for the exchange of data between different components. The declaration of a channel as *input* or *output* defines its role in the exchange of data with the environment. Declaring a channel to be *private* means that it models internal exchanges of data, i.e. between different parts of the component, and that these exchanges are not perceived by the environment. Output and private channels are said to be *local* because they are controlled by the component, i.e. the environment cannot modify the values that are made available on these channels. Input channels are used by the component to read data from the environment.

Actions provide points for rendez-vous synchronisation. Each action is associated with a set of guarded commands that is executed atomically. These commands are of the form

```
exp → x1:=exp1 || x2:=exp2 || …
```

and define computations over the data that is available in the channels. The expression *exp* defines the enabling condition of the command. When the command is executed, all the assignments are preformed atomically.

Location variables act as "containers" for data and code that can be moved across a communication network. Every local channel x is statically associated with a location variable l (we write $x@l$). The same happens for the guarded commands associated with actions. The idea is that the position of the space where the values of a channel are available or a command is executed is determined by the position of the container in which the channel or the command was placed.

We start with a very simple design of one of the components of the image search system – the filter. The role of this component in the system is to interact with the database in order to obtain the images that are potentially interesting and calculate the size of these images.

```
design Filter is
inloc  lf:Loc
in     db:set(image)
out    img@lf:set(image), size@lf:nat
prv    s@lf:[0..4]
do     beg@lf: s=0 → s:=1
[]     req@lf: s=1 → s:=2
[]     filt@lf: s=2 → s:=3 || img:=filterop(db)
[]     rel@lf: s=3 → s:=4 || size:=imgsize(img)
[]     end@lf: s=4 → skip
```

Fig. 1. The design *Filter*

According to this design, the database is made available by the environment through the input channel *db*. Once the filter is requested to begin its activity through the execution of the action *beg,* it first requests access to the database (action *req)*, then it proceeds with the filtering activity, after which it computes the size of the images. The selected images and their size are made available to the environment through the output channels *img* and *size*. After releasing the database (action *rel)*, action *end* becomes enabled meaning that the activities of the filter have ceased.

Designs are defined over a collection of data types that are used for structuring the data that the channels transmit and define the operations that perform the computations that are required. In order to remain independent of any specific language for the definition of these data types, we take them in the form of an algebraic specification. In the example, the images are modelled through a data type that involves the-domain *image*. *Filter* also makes use of the operations *filterop* and *imgsize* that abstract the selection process of the images considered to be of interest and the computation of the size of these images, respectively.

In what concerns distribution, the design *Filter* models a centralised component because all its constituents are located at the same variable *lf*. The fact that *lf* is declared as input means that it is under the control of the environment, i.e. the position where the filter performs its activities is determined by the rest of the system in which it is integrated as a component. The underlying space of distribution and mobility is constituted by the set of possible values of a special data sort *Loc* and whatever operations are necessary to characterise locations such as hierarchies or taxonomies.

By taking advantage of mobility, we may opt for the migration of the filter to the host of the database. This decision can be integrated in the design of the filter as follows.

```
design MobileFilter is
inloc  lr, lc:Loc
outloc lf:Loc
in     db:set(image)
out    img@lf:set(image), size@lf:nat
prv    s@lf:[0..4], q@lf:[0..2]
do     beg@lf: s=0 ∧ q=0 → s:=1|| q:=1
[]     move@lf: q=1 → q:=2
             @lc: true → lf:=lr
[]     req@lf: s=1 ∧ q=2 → s:=2
[]     filt@lf: s=2 → s:=3|| img:=filterop(db)
[]     rel@lf: s=3 → s:=4|| size:=imgsize(img)
[]     end@lf: s=4 → skip
```

Fig. 2. The design *MobileFilter*

This design has two input location variables *lr* and *lc* accounting for the location of the database server and the client application, respectively. The location of the filter (*lf*) is now captured by an output variable because it became under the control of the extended component. *MobileFilter* models a filter that can only migrate after it has begun its activities. Furthermore, it can only request access to the database after it has been moved to the database host. The command that gives rise to the migration, modelled by the assignment *lf:=lr*, is issued at the location of the client.

It is important to notice that the design decisions concerning filter migration can be modelled in an independent way through the following "mobility controller":

```
design MobCont is
inloc  lr, lc: Loc
outloc l: Loc
prv    q@l:[0..2]
do     pre@l: q=0 → q:=1
[]     move@l: q=1 → q:=2
             @lc: true → l:=lr
[]     pos@l: q=2 → skip
```

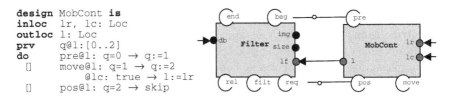

Fig. 3. Externalisation of the design decisions concerning the mobility of the filter

This controller externalises design decisions into an explicit connector that can be superposed over different components. In particular, it can be applied to the filter at hand, as depicted above.

In CommUnity, interaction between a component and its environment relies on the synchronisation of actions and exchange of data through input and output channels. The design of interactions between different components is supported through configurations; these are diagrams that exhibit interconnections between components. In configuration diagrams, components only depict their public elements. The lines connecting actions establish synchronisation points – these actions have to be executed synchronously. The lines connecting channels or location variables establish I/O communication. In contrast with most architecture description languages, these "boxes and lines" have a mathematical semantics: configuration diagrams are in fact diagrams in a category of CommUnity designs whose morphisms capture notions of superposition [10]. The semantics of such a diagram is given by its colimit [9]. In the case of the configuration above, this colimit returns exactly the design *MobileFilter*.

For completeness, we conclude this section by providing the architecture of an image search system. In this system, the filter algorithm is executed remotely. Upon its termination, the filtered images are downloaded by the *Checker* and checked locally, wherever the client is located.

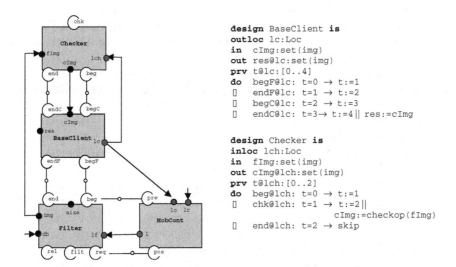

Fig. 4. An architecture of an *Image Search System*

3   Context-Aware Architectures in CommUnity

Section 2 introduced the primitives made available in CommUnity for the design of mobile systems and illustrated how they support the explicit representation of distribution/mobility in software architectures. In this section, we show how context-awareness can be integrated in this architectural approach in a way that supports the definition of application specific notions of context and the design of components and connectors that have to deal with changes of context as part of their intrinsic behaviour.

In our approach, "local contexts" exist in the positions of the underlying space of mobility. They are all instances of a given type. This type captures static properties of contexts, i.e. features that are common to all instances as available in given locations. However, not all instances need to be the same, of course. Hence, for instance, when an action migrates from a location to another, the type of the resources that it needs for its computations will have been statically determined, i.e. at design time, but the actual resources available (say arithmetic precision) will only be known at run time.

3.1 Context-Sensitiveness

So far, we have neglected how behaviour is affected by factors like network connectivity or the set of services that are available at each location. Consider, for instance, *MobileFilter* as presented in Section 2. The filter may not be able to migrate to the database host for reasons such as restrictive security policies enforced at the destination or simply because of lack of connectivity. Once at the database host, the behaviour of the filter still depends on the context of execution. For instance, the filtering of the images cannot be performed if the computational services that this activity requires cannot be found at the given location.

This shows that there exists a dimension of context-sensitiveness that is orthogonal to context-awareness: even a component that, like *MobileFilter*, does not take advantage of context information, has a context-sensitive behaviour. This dimension is related with what was identified in [6] as the *active aspect* of context – the aspect that concerns the characteristics of the surrounding environment that are *determinant* in the behaviour of mobile computing systems. In contrast, the *passive aspect* of context consists of the characteristics that are *relevant* but not critical.

In CommUnity, each of the architectural dimensions – computation, communication and distribution – depends on different characteristics of the environment: *Computations*, as performed by individual components, are constrained by the *resources* and *services* available at the positions where the components are located; *Communication* among components can only take place when they are located in positions that are *"in touch"* with each other; *Movement* of components from one position to another is constrained by *"reachability"*.

Therefore, in CommUnity, the active aspect of context consists of *computational resources*, *computational services*, *connectivity* and *reachability*. These characteristics of the environment are considered as part of the context of any system design, regardless of its particular application domain.

More concretely, a *context type* in CommUnity has an application-independent part defined by the four special observables *<rsc,serv,bt,reach>*. The intuition behind these observables and the nature of their observations is given below.

– The observations of *rsc* are natural numbers and should be regarded as measures of the computational resources available locally.

- The observable *serv* provides access to the local interpretations (in the sense of implementations) of the operations of the underlying data type specification. Given an operation $f\!:\!s_1...s_n \to s$, $serv(f)$ can be undefined, meaning that there is not a local interpretation of f. If defined, $serv(f)$ is a pair (F,amm) where F is a computational service that transforms n-tuples of values of type $s_1...s_n$ in a value of type s and amm is a natural number that represents the level of resources required by F. In order to remain independent of any language for the definition of these computational services, we take them simply as mathematical functions. We shall use $[s_1...s_n \to s]$ to denote the type of (F,amm).
- The observations of *bt* and *reach* are sets of positions of the space (i.e., values of type *Loc*). They represent the positions reachable from the *self* position through, respectively, communication and movement.

These observables play a determinant role in the behaviour of a system, which is captured by the context-sensitive semantics of CommUnity designs as formally defined in [16]. The enabling condition of a distributed action depends on the values of *rsc*, *serv*, *bt* and *reach*. More specifically, a distributed action g is enabled in a certain state iff, in this state, the positions where its local actions execute are mutually in touch (*bt*) and, for each such position l:

- the channels that need to be read or written are located in positions that are in touch with the position of l (*bt*);
- the operations and resources necessary to evaluate the guard and perform the computations are available;
- location variables are only assigned positions that are within reach (*reach*);
- the guard evaluates to true.

Furthermore, the effects of an action on the system state are determined by the "interpretations" of the operations used to specify these effects *(serv)* at each of the locations where the action execution is distributed.

CommUnity, equipped with this context-sensitive semantics, provides us with the means to design systems that deal with situations where the availability of critical resources is not guaranteed. The absence of a critical resource is not regarded as a runtime error but rather as a blocking condition of the actions whose execution depends on this resource. By defining alternative actions that are enabled in these situations, we can specify how the system is required to operate in such situations.

For instance, in order to model a filter that performs the filtering activities locally if migration to the database host is not possible, we only need to introduce the action

```
[]    stay@lf:  q=1  →  q:=2
```

in *MobileFilter*. This action can be executed in the same system state as *move* and, hence, if the action *move* is blocked because the remote location *lr* is unreachable, the system can make progress through the execution of *stay*. If the location *lr* is reachable, then both actions can be executed and a non-deterministic choice will be made.

```
design FlexibleFilter is
inloc   lr, lc:Loc
outloc  lf:Loc
in      db:set(image)
out     img@lf:set(image), size@lf:nat
prv     s@lf:[0..4], q@lf:[0..2], op@lf:[set(image)->set(image)]
do      beg@lf: s=0 ∧ q=0 → s:=1|| q:=1|| op:=serv(filterop)
[]      move@lf: q=1 → q:=2
            @lc: true → lf:=lr
[]      stay@lf: q=1 ∧ lr∉reach → q:=2
[]      req@lf: s=1 ∧ q=2 → s:=2
[]      filt@lf: s=2 → s:=3|| img:=op(db)
[]      rel@lf: s=3 → s:=4|| size:=imgsize(img)
[]     end@lf: s=4 → skip
```

Fig. 5. A context-aware *Filter*

3.2 Context-Awareness

In order to obtain a more expressive model of context-aware computing, software designers should be able to take advantage of contextual information by explicitly defining how it affects the behaviour of the system. For instance, in the case of the filter, we would like to be able to express that the decision to download the images from the remote database is restricted to the situations in which the migration to the database host is not possible. This can be achieved as presented in Figure 5.

The design *FlexibleFilter* uses two new primitives – the special observables *reach* and *serv*. The observable *reach* is used for expressing that the remote execution of the filter is preferred to the local execution. This is achieved by defining that action *stay* is blocked if $lr \in reach$. Because this expression is evaluated at *lf*, the contextual information that is used is the one available there and, hence, $lr \notin reach$ means that *lr* is not reachable from *lf*. The observable *serv* is used for ensuring that the filtering activity, even when performed remotely, uses the interpretation of *filterop* available locally in the client host. To this purpose, we introduced a new private channel *op* that, at the beginning of the filtering activity, is assigned the local interpretation of *filterop* and keeps it with the filter, as part of its state. Moreover, the command associated to action *filt* was modified so that the filtering activity is performed with the computational service available in channel *op*.

Indeed, the abstract data type specification associated with a CommUnity design identifies the nature of the data and operations that may be required at the positions of the distribution topology, e.g. in terms of libraries or packages. Different positions may provide different implementations for these data types. It may also happen that a given position does not provide an implementation for all the operations that may be required for the execution of a given action. We know all too well that software installation often fails because required libraries are missing in the target platform...

This justifies that, in CommUnity, part of the context identifies the libraries available at every location *(serv)* and that given functions can be transmitted as data from one location to another, either because they are missing, or to make sure that a specific version is used instead of the default available at the target. Such facilities are already available in most platforms. For instance, one of the central and unique features of RMI is its ability to download the bytecodes (or simply code) of an object's class if the class is not defined in the receiver's virtual machine.

We have illustrated the use of application-independent observables in the specification of designs. If other characteristics of the environment are considered relevant for the design of the system, they have to be defined as part of its context type.

3.3 Context Types

A *context type* includes the fixed set of observables defined in 3.1 and an application-dependent set of other observables. Each observable is of the form $obs: s_1...s_n \rightarrow s$, where $s_1,...,s_n$, s are sorts of an abstract data type specification that includes the sort *Loc* of locations. These data sorts are used for structuring the required contextual data. Other operations may be defined for manipulating that data as required by the application.

Each observable represents a specific context concept. It identifies the nature of observations that are relevant for the system at hand and the way this information is accessed by the application. Dependencies between different types of contextual information can be expressed through axioms of the specification.

The integration of context-aware decisions in the behaviour of CommUnity designs is based on the simple use of terms built over observables in the guards and effects of local actions. In the evaluation of these terms, it is the location of the action that determines the position of the space where the required observations are made.

Consider the design of an image search system in which the choice of where to perform the checking of the images selected by the filter is based on their size, the processing power available in the remote and local machines, and the bandwidth available between the two hosts. This context-aware decision can be achieved by superposing the following mobility controller over the *checker*.

```
design FlexMobCont is
inloc  lr, lc:Loc
outloc l:Loc
in     sz:nat
prv    q@l:[0..2]
do     pre@l: q=0 → q:=1
  []   move@l: q=1 → q:=2
          @lc: crit(bdw(lr),ppw(lc),ppw(lr),sz) → l:=lr
  []   stay@l: q=1 → q:=2
          @lc: ¬crit(bdw(lr),ppw(lc),ppw(lr),sz) → skip
  []   pos@l: q=2 → skip
```

Fig. 6. A context-aware *Mobility Controller*

FlexMobCont models a controller similar to the one we designed for controlling the mobility of the filter. In order to accommodate the criteria for migration, we introduced an action *stay* and an input channel *sz* (accounting for the size of the selected images) and we modified the guard of *move*.

The observables *bdw* and *ppw*, the nature of their observations and the criteria for migration are defined by the context type *network&cpu*. This context type defines that, in a given position of the space, the system is interested in a measure of the bandwidth available between this position and all the others, delivered as a natural number. These values are constrained to be related with the observations of connectivity (*bt*) in the obvious way. It is also defined that every local context must have information about the processing power (*ppw*) available at every position of the space.

The structure of the observations of *ppw* is defined by *ppwData* and operations *newPpw, better* and *crit*. The operation *better* is used to decide if the checker should migrate to the database host. The criteria to perform the migration, modelled by the operation *crit*, are based on the estimated transfer time of the images: migration should be carried out if the transfer of the images will take too long (above *timeThereshold*) or if there are too many images to scan (above *sizeThereshold*) and the processing power available remotely is considered better than the one available locally.

Context types may also include derived observables – observables whose values are completely determined by the values of the other observables. This is extremely useful for defining higher-level notions of context based on simpler sensed contexts.

```
context type network&cpu is
    sensed observables
        bdw: Loc -> nat
            // bandwidth available between self and given position
        ppw: Loc -> ppwData
            // processing power available in the given position
    constrained by p:Loc
        bdw(p)=0 ≡ p∉bt
    sorts
        ppwData
            // defines the nature of observations of ppw
    operations
        newPpw: nat natPercentage -> ppwData
            // creates a ppwdata from the power of the processor and the
            // percentage of processing power in use
        better: ppwData ppwData -> bool
            // Is the first ppw "better" than the second one?
        crit: nat ppwData ppwData nat -> bool
            // Are the given conditions favourable for migration?
        factor: nat
        timeThreshold, sizeThreshold: nat
    axioms v1,v2,perc1,perc2,b,s:nat, p1,p2:ppwData
        (1) better(newPpw(v1,perc1), newPpw(v2,perc2)) ≡
                (v1/v2)>factor ∧ (100-perc1)*v1>(100-perc2)*v2
        (2) crit(b,p1,p2,s) ≡
                s*b>timeThreshold ∨ (s>sizeThreshold ∧ better(p2,p1))
```

Fig. 7. The context type *network&cpu*

For instance, we can extend the context type *network&cpu* with:

```
derived observervables
        migr: Loc Loc nat ->bool
        migr(l1,l2,s)=crit(bdw(l1),ppw(l2),ppw(l1),s)
```

This defines a new observable *migr* whose values have not to be sensed but rather inferred from *bdw* and *ppw*. Intuitively, *migr* indicates whether, according to the criteria defined by *crit*, the actual context is favourable for migration or not.

We can now use this new observable to design a controller with the same functionally of *FlexMobCont*: we only need to replace *crit(bdw(lr),ppw(lc),ppw(lr),sz)* by *migr(lr,lc,sz)* in the guards of actions *move* and *stay*.

Although the functionality expressed in the two designs is the same, they provide different support for evolution and reuse. Because the condition *migr(lr,lc,sz)* is less specific than *crit(bdw(lr),ppw(lc),ppw(lr),sz)*, if we use the new controller for the mobility of a component, we have more chances of being able to change the design decision adopted for migration just by replacing *network&cpu* by an appropriate context type. All that is required is that the new condition can be expressed in terms of the values available in the channel *sz* and the locations *lr* and *lc*.

4   Context Modelling

So far, we have addressed context modelling from the perspective of the software designer that is in charge of the application logic. Our focus has been on the definition of modelling primitives that allow software architects to represent and organise the contextual information in which a system is interested and to take advantage of contextual information in the specification of system components and connectors.

The use of contextual information by an application assumes the existence of another system that senses the current context and delivers it to the application. In this section, we address context modelling from the perspective of the development of context-sensing systems – the systems responsible for the gathering, management and delivery of contextual information.

We start by analysing the role of context types in the development of context-sensing systems. Our view is that there exists one context-sensing system working on behalf of each context-aware application. In situations in which several applications are interested in the same contextual data, this does not mean that the sensing work has to be replicated because, for instance, the corresponding sensing systems can be components of an infrastructure that centralises the collection of all contextual data.

From the perspective of context-sensing systems, context types play the role of requirement specifications. They define what must be sensed, how the sensed data must be abstracted and the interface offered by the sensing system to the application layer. This interface consists of the *observables* through which it is possible to gain access to contextual data (both sensed and derived) and the *operations* through which it is possible to manipulate this data. Because the sensing system provides an encapsulation of contextual data as an abstract data type, all the operations that manipulate contextual data have to be provided by this system.

As specifications of requirements for context-sensing systems, there are important issues that context types do not address. One of these issues is the type of sensing that should be adopted for each sensed observable – *on demand* or *continuous*. In the case of *on demand* sensing, the information about the actual context is collected only when there is a request issued by the application, which waits for this information to proceed. In the case of *continuous* sensing, the sensing system is supposed to be proactively collecting the contextual information. Because this tends to be a costly activity, and different applications typically have different needs, it is important that designers have the means to describe at which frequency new data has to be obtained.

Mechanisms for expressing this kind of requirements can be easily integrated with the notion of context type, giving rise to what we designate by *context model*. An example of a context model for the image search system is presented in Figure 8.

```
context model network&cpu is
      contex type network&cpu
      on-demand
          ppw: Loc->ppwData
      continuous
          bdw: Loc->nat with frequency 50:natPercentage
```

Fig. 8. The context model *network&cpu*

In a context model, sensed observables are grouped according to the type of sensing they require. For observables that require continuous monitoring, the frequency at which data should be gathered is also defined using data types, keeping the level of abstraction (it would not make sense to ask designers to provide real time requirements for their high-level designs).

Another important concern in context modelling is to guarantee that the application and the context-sensing system have a common semantic understanding of the sensed information. This requires context models that support the definition of what has to be sensed in a precise way. Because the models we proposed are not powerful enough, we envisage their extension with mappings to standard ontologies representing the diversity of environment characteristics that is reasonable to sense in specific domains. The idea is for these mappings to establish the semantic understanding of each sensed observable of the context type. Unfortunately, despite recent developments in the area of the Semantic Web in this direction [19,21], such standardised ontologies are not yet available.

5   Concluding Remarks

In this paper, we addressed the integration of context-awareness in the set of aspects that systems architectures should be able to deal with. Having adopted an infrastructure-centred view of context-awareness development, we focused on the definition of modelling primitives that allow software architects (i) to represent and organise the contextual information that a system requires and (ii) to take advantage of contextual information in the specification of the components and connectors of the system.

Our proposal is based on the extension of system architectures with a new design element – *context models*, which supports the modelling of the context of a system as a first-class entity separable from its application logic.

Taking an example in which mobility is used as a tool to adapt to variations in the execution environment, we illustrated how CommUnity supports the design of components and connectors that take advantage of contextual information to adapt their behaviour. Adaptable behaviour is specified essentially through the specification of sets of alternative actions – actions that are enabled at the same system's states but not in the same context.

A complementary and important approach to adaptation in software architectures is the one that addresses adaptation at the configuration level through dynamic reconfiguration. Most of the work devoted to adaptation in software architectures focuses on this kind of adaptation (e.g., [4,12,18]). However, existing approaches fail to give a first-class status to the notion of context. Either they are developed having in mind specific aspects of the execution environment (essentially, performance-oriented aspects) or they support implicit definitions of context, hard-wired in different parts of the system architectural description. For this reason, we plan to investigate structural adaptation of systems architectures that include context models as design elements.

A related approach that is important to mention is the conceptual model for context-aware architectures proposed in [17]. In this work, an infrastructure-centred view is not adopted. Instead, context sensing is viewed just as an aspect of the system; components and connectors are themselves involved in the gathering of context information.

Because context models can be understood independently of the rest of the architecture, they were also investigated in this paper as specifications of requirements for context-sensing systems. This is an important perspective because it contributes to the understanding of the abstractions that should be provided by the middleware infrastructures that support the development of context-aware applications. As mentioned in [13], most existing infrastructures are built upon informal context models that lack in expressive power.

Context modelling concepts and techniques have also been investigated in the field of Pervasive Computing where some formal models of context have been proposed [13,20]. Compared with ours, these models are more powerful: for instance, they address uncertainty in and quality of contextual information. However, because these models were developed with different aims, they do not provide adequate support for defining abstract notions of contexts as required for the high-level design of context-aware systems. For instance, the aim of the context model of [20] is to provide a uniform representation of contextual information in context infrastructures for entities such as context providers, synthesizers and consumers. The language used in [13] is an information modelling technique suited for describing the context information available through a context infrastructure. Based on these fine-grained models, higher-level concepts can be defined and used as programming abstractions.

As far as modelling techniques are concerned, ContextUnity [22] is the approach most closely related to ours. In ContextUnity, systems are also designed by assuming that contextual information is transparently maintained. However, although the model of context is, as in CommUnity, explicit and separable from the behaviour specification, it cannot be externalised and modelled as an independent system dimension. In ContextUnity each component of the system is regarded as an autonomous agent and has a specific notion of context that is defined by a set of observables whose values depend exclusively on variables of other components in the system. As we have seen, context information in CommUnity is orthogonal to the decomposition of the system in components; it refers to any collection of characteristics and properties of the environment that are relevant to the system and *are not under its direct control*. This, we believe, adds flexibility and adaptability to system models as context-awareness is addressed as an independent architectural concern.

Acknowledgements

This work was partially supported by the EC through the IST-2001-32747 Project AGILE – *Architectures for Mobility* and by FCT through the POSI/EIA/60692/2004 Project MICAS – *Middleware for Context-aware and Adaptative Systems*. We wish to thank our partners in both projects for much useful feedback.

References

1. IST Global Computing Initiative, http://www. cordis.lu/ist/fet/gc.html.
2. M.Acharya, M.Ranganathan and J.Saltz, "Sumatra:A Language for Resource-aware Mobile programs", *Mobile Object Systems: Towards the Programmable Internet*, 1997.
3. L.Capra, W.Emmerich and C.Mascolo, "CARISMA:Context-aware Reflective mIddleware System for Mobile Applications", *Trans. Softw. Eng. Journal*, **29**(10), 929-245, 2003.
4. M.Castaldi, A.Carzaniga, P.Inverardi and A.Wolf, "A Light-weight Infrastructure for Reconfiguring Applications", *Software Reconfiguration Management Workshop*, LNCS 2649, Springer, 2003.
5. K.Chandy and J.Misra, *Parallel Program Design - A Foundation*, Addison-Wesley, 1988.
6. G.Chen and D.Kotz, "A Survey of Context-Aware Mobile Computing Survey", Dartmouth CS-TR-2000-381, 2000.
7. G.Chen and D.Kotz. "Context-sensitive resource discovery", *Pervasive 2003*, 243-252, 2003.
8. A.Dey, D.Salber and G.D.Abowd, "A conceptual framework and a toolkit for supporting the rapid prototyping of cw applications", *Human-Computer Interaction*, **16**(2-4), 97-166, 2001.
9. J.L.Fiadeiro, *Categories for Software Engineering*, Springer 2004.
10. J.L.Fiadeiro, A.Lopes and M.Wermelinger, "A Mathematical Semantics for Architectural Connectors", *Generic Programming*, LNCS 2793, 190-234, Springer, 2003.
11. N.Francez and I.Forman, *Interacting Processes*, Addison-Wesley, 1996.
12. D.Garlan *et al*, "Software Architecture-based Adaptation for Pervasive Systems", *Trends in Network and Pervasive Computing*, LNCS 2299, Springer, 2002.
13. K.Henricksen and J.Indulska, "A Software Engineering Framework for Context-aware Pervasive Computing", *Pervasive 2004*, 77-86, 2004.
14. A.Lopes, J.L.Fiadeiro and M.Wermelinger, "Architectural Primitives for Distribution and Mobility", *Proc. FSE-10*, 41-50, ACM Press, 2002.
15. A.Lopes and J. L.Fiadeiro, "Adding Mobility to Software Architectures", *ENCTS* **97**, 241-258, Elsevier Science, 2004.
16. A.Lopes and J.L.Fiadeiro, "Algebraic Semantics of Design Abstractions for Context-Awareness", *Algebraic Development Techniques*, LNCS 3423, 79-93, Springer, 2005.

17. J.J.Martínez and I.Ramos, "A Conceptual Model for Context-Aware Dynamic Architectures", *Proc. ICDCSW*, 2003.
18. P.Oreizy *et al*, "An Architecture-based Approach to Self-Adaptive Software", *Intelligent Systems* **14**(3), 54-62, 1999.
19. M.Roman, C.Hess, R.Cerqueira and A.Ranganathan, "GAIA: A Middleware Infrastructure to Enable Active Spaces", *Pervasive Computing* **1**(4), 74-83, 2002.
20. A.Ranganathan and R.Campbell, "An infrastructure for context-awareness based on first-order logic", *Pers Ubiquit Comput*, 7, 353-364, 2003.
21. A.Ranganathan *et al*, "Ontologies in a Pervasive Computing Environment", *Proc. IJAIC*, 2003.
22. G.-C.Roman, C.Julien and J.Payton, "A Formal Treatment of Context-Awareness", *FASE*, LNCS 2984, 12-36, Springer, 2004.

Modelling to Safety

Alek Radjenovic

The University of York,York YO10 5DD, UK
alek@cs.york.ac.uk

Abstract. In this position paper we outline the challenges that face safety critical systems. We identify the need to shift the validation emphasis from process
to product, and state how formal proofs would be of great benefit by providing
stronger evidence for safety case arguments. We also argue that a successful solution for the incremental certification problem could bring benefit to all levels
of system design. A better understanding of the non-functional behaviour and
methods for expressing, embedding into design, and managing properties that
play a role in this aspect of safety critical systems are urgently needed. We also
speculate that research into trusted components and compositional architectures
is vital for the future of safety critical systems design. In partnership with BAE
SYSTEMS, Rolls Royce, and QinetiQ, we have developed a framework and an
architectural description language that addresses these issues.

1 Introduction

Safety critical systems are a family of systems where safety is of paramount importance. Examples of such systems can be found in the avionics, automotive, space and
medical industries. They are predominantly driven by real-time embedded software
and are often referred to as the high integrity real time systems (HIRTS).

Safety is broadly defined as the freedom from accidents and losses [1]. Sometimes
there is no safe alternative to normal service, in which case, the system must be dependable to be safe. A dependable system is defined [2] as one that has the following
six attributes: *availability, reliability, safety, confidentiality, integrity, maintainability*.
We commonly use the term *dependable system* as one for which reliance may justi-
fiably be placed on certain aspects of the quality of service that it delivers. Dependability is thus concerned primarily with fault tolerance (i.e., providing an acceptable
level of service even when faults occur). It is not difficult to see that many of the attributes above are highly desirable in numerous other categories of modern software
systems and how the results of research into these attributes could be applied to software engineering whose primary concern is not safety. For example, availability of a
web service is not critical in the same sense as the availability of landing gear in an
aircraft. It is, however, critical from the business perspective and – highly desirable.
Another example would be a reliable banking system. Not really the same meaning as
a reliable car at high speeds, but nevertheless – highly desirable.

HIRTS software, like most other classes of software today, is becoming increasingly large and complex. Typical problem is that of poor visibility of the underlying

R. Morrison and F. Oquendo (Eds.): EWSA 2005, LNCS 3527, pp. 162 – 167, 2005.

architecture which blurs the dependency links between the requirements specifications, design-time artefacts and the implemented system. Under the circumstances, maintenance of the system is becoming ever more difficult. Even minor modifications require huge investment in time and money. It is often said that the cost of change is hugely disproportionate to the size of change.

Safety is a system property, not a component property, so any safety analysis needs to consider the entire system and not simply its components. Consequently, research into software and system architectures and modelling is regarded as crucial in the safety critical systems domain.

2 Challenges

Many safety critical applications demand a level of dependability that cannot be established by the state-of-the-art testing technology [3]. This being the case, the validation emphasis has shifted from the analysis of the *product* to the analysis of the development *process* of the product [4] (see, for example, the well-known ARINC DO-178B standard [5] for software in airborne systems). If results of the software architecture research are to become widely deployed, this emphasis will have to change. System design will have to consist of the reuse and integration of pre-validated hardware/software components.

In many cases, such as in the avionics industry, systems need to be certified before they are deployed. If changes are made to the system, common sense would suggest that only the modified parts are certified again. Sadly this is not the case, due to the lack of visibility of what the impact of the change is. Current practice is that for all but the most insignificant changes the recertification process involves the full system. This is known as the *incremental certification problem*. It is often thought of as an issue during the maintenance phase of the product lifecycle. Recently, the most common cause for system modifications (or, upgrades) is hardware obsolescence. With current advances in the electronics manufacturing industry, the average shelf-life of a hardware component is rapidly decreasing. However, if a solution is found to the incremental certification problem, it could be applied at almost every level of system design and every stage of the product lifecycle, not only the maintenance. Constant changes in requirements during the early stages of design impose continuous source of change and headache for software architects, designers and developers. Were they to have assurance that the modifications (or, increments) they are making to the system architecture, design and implementation is controllable, and satisfies the system goals such as safety, the benefit would be profound.

A safety case for a HIRTS system plays one of key roles in certifying the system. There is no definitive statement of what constitutes a safety case but there appears to be a commonality (amongst various definitions) as to what the purpose of safety case is, and that is to present a clear, comprehensive and defensible *argument, supported* by calculation and procedure that a system will be acceptably safe throughout its life (and decommissioning). Typically a safety case will contain a high level argument (HLA) and supporting evidence (SE). The HLA sets out the principles on which the design is based and reasons why the design should satisfy the safety requirements. The SE provides detailed analysis of the implementation to show that the design has the predicted properties, and hence that the system meets its safety requirements. The safety case would benefit greatly if the evidence presented was based on some formalism, i.e. providing formal proof with basis in mathematics.

Correct operation of the system (as laid out in its requirements specification) is only one part of the validation problem. Establishing correctness of non-functional behaviour or quality attributes of the system proves to be arduous indeed. Methods for expressing, embedding into design, and managing properties that play a role in these aspects of safety critical system are urgently needed.

3 State-of-the-Art

Our research group, DARP (Defence and Aerospace Research Partnership) HIRTS is funded by the UK government and the Ministry of Defence, and partnered by BAE SYSTEMS, Rolls-Royce and QinetiQ. The work within our strand (Model Based Systems Engineering) takes an *architecture-centric* view of the development process, and emphasises the use of *contracts* as a way of controlling the dependencies between components (subsystems) in the architecture. Most of our case studies come from the civil avionics domain.

In order to address the challenges mentioned above, our approach was to explore and build on the current best practice. We have reviewed a number of wide spread modelling and software architecture technologies and came to a conclusion that all, by some distance, fall short of providing the necessary assurance needed for a safety critical system.

The Model Driven Architecture (MDA) [6] identifies design abstraction layering as essential and suggests ways of mapping between these layers. Such approach is necessary if one is to have visibility of architecture from the source code, or the other way around. MDA, however, claims that in the absence of consensus on hardware platforms, operating systems, network protocols, and programming languages, there must be a consensus on interfaces and inter-operability. Such view is narrow-minded and naïve, as it purely reflects on the functional characteristics of a system.

The Unified Modelling Language (UML) [7] is a great tool for visualising systems (or, parts of a system), as well as for a diagrammatical communication between various stakeholders, such as the requirements analysts, designers, engineers, and so on. It is now regarded as a useful lowest common denominator (much like SQL) between different vendors, but not much more beyond that. Its most serious drawback is its lack formalism, a grave reminder for the safety engineering community to steer away from it.

Another important approach is the IEEE 1471 standard [8]. This endeavour addresses the activities of creation, analysis, and sustainment of architectures of software-intensive systems, and the recording of such architectures in terms of architectural descriptions. It is, possibly, the most complete *conceptual* framework for the architectural descriptions. However, it is brutally cut off at the model level, and provides no recommendation on how to bridge the gap between the design and implementation.

We also looked into a number of ADLs (Architecture Description Language). AADL [9] (Architecture, Analysis and Design Language), formerly known as the

Avionics ADL, effectively tackles many issues present in complex embedded real time applications. On the other hand, modelling with AADL appears to be too intensive and detailed from the very start. The concept of layered abstraction is absent. Although attractive in many respects for hard real time systems engineering, the lack of lightweight modelling could prevent AADL from gaining widespread acceptance.

Acme [10] began as a common interchange format for architecture design tools. Currently, it provides a generic, extensible infrastructure for describing, representing, generating, and analysing software architecture descriptions. Acme has many traits of the cutting-edge research thinking and modelling tool vendors, the key one being extensibility – providing a platform as a starting point from which a specific approach can be developed. Nonetheless, the support it offers is not sufficient in the safety critical systems domain. A vital ingredient is missing: for Acme language to be regarded as formal, apart from syntax and semantics, it fails to define the underlying proof theory, i.e. rules for inferring useful information from a specification.

4   Where Next?

Our view is that two aspects of software design for safety critical systems are vital for its future. They are: *trusted components* and *compositional architectures*.

Broadly speaking, trusted components are those of which we can expect to behave correctly with a high degree of confidence. A trusted component will, as a rule, impose a set of *pre-conditions* on the user of the component (normally another software component). If these pre-conditions are met, then the trusted component will perform its declared function and, upon termination, satisfy a set of *post-conditions*. The post-conditions describe what must be true at the end of execution (if the pre-conditions were true). Trusted components may also declare *invariants* and *rely conditions*. The invariants describe what must be true at both the start and end of component execution, and the rely conditions describe what must be true throughout the execution [11].

Compositional architectures are, ideally, those that guarantee not to violate the principle of composition upon the integration of (trusted) components. This principle states that the properties established at the component level will also hold at the system level [12]. From the point of view of analysis of compositional architectures, two key factors are of greatest significance. Firstly, it is important to distinguish between properties and services of a component prior to the integration into the system, and the emergent ones generated by such integration. In many cases, the new services are more than a sum of the individual services. For example, the integration of the chassis and engine in an aeroplane gives rise to a new kind of service – the transport service. Secondly, the non-functional behaviour analyses need to target specific domains by means of domain modelling. In case of safety critical systems, the software architecture and modelling research needs to draw upon the vast pool of traditional techniques on how to safely compose systems. These techniques include PHA (Preliminary Hazard Analysis), FTA (Fault Tree Analysis), SHA and SSHA (System and Subsystem Hazard Analysis), FMECA (Failure Mode and Effect Criticality Analysis) and many others.

5 Contributions

In our endeavour to address the challenges facing the modern safety critical software we have developed an approach called Architectural Information Modelling (AIM) [13]. In this approach we hope to have addressed all issues that were outlined in the previous text. AIM incorporates support for many aspects of modern software engineering such as: software architectures and design, domain modelling and safety engineering. Its meta-model is divided into three distinct categories of system design as shown in the picture below (Fig. 1.).

As part of the development process, we have also defined a formal notation – the AIM architectural description language.

The *infrastructure* of AIM builds on the well established paradigm for software architectures using components, connectors and their configuration at its core. The *properties* help to describe the non-functional characteristics of these components, connectors and their configurations. Finally, the *constraints* limit the freedom of the designer according to the system and safety requirements and prescribe design rules according to the agreed architectural style.

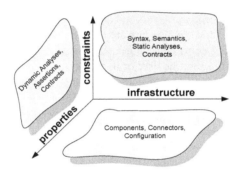

Fig. 1. AIM meta-model categories

In particular, we have found that the following nine top level constructs are essential for modelling systems in the HIRTS domain: Model, Environment, Class, Implementation, Collection, Constant, Type, Property and Contract [13].

AIM comes with a predefined architectural style (a collection of types for components, connectors, interfaces, and properties together with a set of rules for how elements of those types may be composed) well suited for the HIRTS domain. Like Acme, AIM is a fully extensible and open semantic framework allowing for other architectural styles to be defined, too. Furthermore, AIM is MDA-compatible by supporting multiple layers of abstraction. A lightweight, informal is supported for early stage design evaluation, leading to a rich formal model capable of mapping out a sound skeleton for system implementation.

We have also successfully performed simple mappings to MetaH (a predecessor to AADL), Acme and a limited set of UML constructs. We hope to be able to export AIM specifications to other notations and exploit external tools for model checking, theorem proofs, and various other kinds of analyses.

6 Conclusion

In this position paper we have outlined the challenges that need to be addressed in order to better manage the complexity and the development demands of the safety critical system. We have identified the need to shift the validation emphasis from process to product, and stated how formal proofs would aid in achieving this by providing stronger evidence for safety case arguments. We have also argued that a successful solution for the incremental certification problem could bring benefit to all levels of system design. Finally, better understanding of the non-functional behaviour and methods for expressing, embedding into design, and managing properties that play a role in this aspect of safety critical systems are urgently needed. We have also tried to indicate that research into trusted components and compositional architectures is vital for the future of HIRTS design.

References

1. Leveson, N.: Safeware: System Safety and Computers. 1995: Addison-Wesley
2. Avizienis, A., J.C. Laprie, and B. Randell.: Fundamental Concepts of Computer System Dependability. in Workshop on Robot Dependability: Technological Challenge of Dependable Robots in Human Environments. 2001. Seoul, Korea
3. Littlewood, B. and L. Strigini.: Validation of Ultradependability for Software Based Systems. in Predictably Dependable Computing Systems. 1995: Springer-Verlag
4. McDermid, J.A., et al.: Experience with the application of HAZOP to computer-based systems. in 10th Annual Conference on Computer Assurance. 1995
5. ARINC, Software Considerations in Airborne Systems and Equipment Certification, in DO-178B. 1992, ARINC: Annapolis, Maryland
6. OMG, MDA Guide Version 1.0. 2003, Object Management Group.
7. OMG, OMG Unified Modelling Language Specification v1.4. 2001, Object Management Group
8. IEEE-1471, Recommended Practice for Architectural Description of Software-Intensive Systems. 2000, IEEE.
9. SAE, Architecture, Analysis and Design Language (AADL) v1.0. 2004, SAE Aerospace
10. Garlan, D., R. Monroe, and D. Wile. Acme: An Architecture Description Interchange Language. in Proc. of CASCON '97. 1997
11. Conmy, P.: What is a Contract? 2004, Technical Report. DARP HIRTS
12. Kopetz, H.: Component-Based Design of Large Distributed Real-Time Systems. Control Engineering Practice - A Journal of IFAC, Pergamon Press, 1998. **6**: p. 53-60
13. Radjenovic, A.: Architectural Information Modelling: The Infrastructure and the LRAAM CAse Study. 2005, Technical Report. DARP HIRTS

A Distributed Intrusion Detection Approach for Secure Software Architecture

Paola Inverardi and Leonardo Mostarda

Dip. di Informatica, Università di L'Aquila,
Coppito 67100, L'Aquila, Italy
{inverard, mostarda}@di.univaq.it

Abstract. This paper illustrates an approach to add security policies to a component-based system. We consider black-box-components-based applications, where each component can run concurrently in a different domain. The problem we want to face is to detect at run time that a component might start interacting with the other components in an anomalous way trying to subvert the application. This problem cannot be identified statically because we must take into account the fact that a component can be modified for malicious purposes at run time once deployed. We propose a specification-based approach to detect intrusions at architectural level. The approach is decentralized, that is given a global policy for the whole system, i.e. a set of admissible behaviors, we automatically generate a monitoring filter for each component that looks at local information of interest. Filters then suitably communicate in order to carry on cooperatively the validation of the global policy. With respect to centralized monitors, this approach increases performance, security and reliability and allows the supervision of complex applications where no centralized point of information flow exists or can be introduced.

1 Introduction

This paper describes a specification-based approach to detect intrusions at architectural level. We assume to have a black-box-components-based application where all components run concurrently and interact each other exchanging services. At architectural level, we speak about intrusions when legitimate components perform unauthorized actions; e.g., a rogue client can be built by an attacker that uses his authorizations to subvert the application.

Intrusions at architectural level may be detected by using static approaches, e.g. by using model checking techniques. However, components can be dynamically modified for malicious purposes and the statically validated properties can be violated. Run-time tools monitoring for evidence of intrusions can provide a solution to these problems. Nowadays, several run-time monitors are available: they are referred to as Intrusion Detection Systems (IDSs), and their main task is to analyze the observable behaviors of a system in order to recognize malicious behaviors. The effectiveness of an IDS is usually measured in terms of: **detec-**

R. Morrison and F. Oquendo (Eds.): EWSA 2005, LNCS 3527, pp. 168–184, 2005.

tion efficiency: the amount of intrusions that are correctly recognized; **false alarms rate:** the amount of correct behaviors detected as intrusions.

There are three main types of IDSs detection techniques: *misuse, anomaly* and *specification-based. Misuse detection systems* [1] are explicitly programmed to recognize well-known attacks. These systems recognize intrusions by matching the pattern of observed data with the set of predefined (intrusion) signatures. They can perform focused analysis thus having a low false alarms rate. However, they cannot detect unknown types of attacks, since it is not possible to specify a signature for a still unknown vulnerability. Furthermore, IDS complexity grows with the number of well-known attacks. *Anomaly detection systems* assume that an attack will cause deviation from normal behaviors, thus detection can be done by comparing actual activities with known correct behaviors. Different approaches have been used to model normal behaviors: statistics-based [2], rule-based [3], immunology-based [4]. The advantage of this kind of systems is the ability of detecting novel attacks and the fact that it is not required specific knowledge about correct information flows. However, it is not easy to define what is a normal behavior, to set up anomaly thresholds, to have a good detection efficiency and moreover not all intrusions need to produce an anomalous behavior. *Specification-based systems* [5] use some kind of formal specification to describe the correct behaviors of the system. The detection of violations involves monitoring deviations from the formal specification, rather than matching specific well-know attacks. The advantage of this approach is the ability to detect previously unknown attacks at the expense of providing a formal specification of correct information flows.

Besides the problems mentioned above, all the described approaches when implemented suffer a number of further problems:

- the monitoring tools are subject to *tampering*, since they are software that can be itself target of attacks.   .
- correct monitoring of points where there is a high level of information flow may be problematic (loss of data);
- in complex systems no *centralized point* of information flow can exist, so distributed solutions are needed;
- IDSs have to be *scalable* with respect to the number of components to be monitored, i.e. augmenting the components number must not result in an increased execution response time of the monitoring tool.

This paper presents a specification-based intrusion detection approach to face intrusions at architectural level. The application to be monitored is composed by black-box components that run concurrently in different domains. We assume to know the services required/offered by each component that is name / formal parameters / returned values, (i.e. the component interface), the topology of the application in terms of potential interactions among components (the

---

[1] Tamper is a term to indicate *"any act that results in the improper alteration of the application code."* [6]

connectors) and the specification of the acceptable behaviors the system has to comply with. The latter is given by means of a language that defines the correct behaviors of the system.

We propose a polynomial algorithm that combines the specification and the architectural information in order to distribute the specification checking on the component where the information to be supervised flows. More specifically, this algorithm builds a set of local wrappers (filters), one for each component. Wrappers locally monitor the component behavior and communicate with each other in a peer-to-peer fashion to discover attacks scattered over several components. Moreover, in order to address the attacks to the security measures filters are able to detect filter *tampering* [6]. In the remaining of the paper we will use the terms wrapper/filter interchangeably.

We choose a specification-based monitoring as opposed to anomaly base detection since it permits to detect unknown attacks and reduces the false alarm rate. Moreover, since our approach to intrusion detection is distributed it allows the monitoring of complex applications where there is no central point of information flow. However, the distributed approach also brings obvious overheads in terms of message exchange.

The contribution of this paper is in proposing a way to automatically generate a set of local filters (one for each component) that detect components dynamic misbehavior. Our approach also permits to build a tamper resistant IDS [6], i.e. an IDS which is resistant to modification and observation. The approach we propose is architectural since it relies on architectural information about components (interface) and connections (topology).

2   Related Work

Most of the advanced tools for intrusion detection send distributed data to a centralized unit that relates them in order to detect violations. This centralized design poses problems of: *scalability, fault tolerance* and *security*. Attacks to and faults of the central unit can deactivate the monitoring of the distributed system. An increasing number of sensors that forward data can cause loss of information or increase the monitoring system reaction time.

Systems like NetSTAT [7], and Emerald [8], and GrIDS [9] try to solve the above problems by means of a layered structure. Data are locally processed and events that are part of distributed attacks are forwarded to an higher entity. Although such systems try to address the problem of scalability, nodes close to the root of the hierarchy can still be overloaded and they represent a single point of failure or vulnerability.

CSM[10] faces these problems by means of a peer-to-peer design. It has no centralized unit thus data are exchanged among peers to correlate them.

All the above mentioned tools recognize well-known kinds of attacks by means of intrusion patterns (misuse based). Patterns are usually defined at networking level and they are monitored by distributed sensors that sniff traffic. Such tools have dedicated hosts and a management network separated from the one used by the application data. This choice is dictated by the fact that monitoring systems are themselves software that can be *tampered*.

Our approach aims at lifting monitoring technology from the operating system and network level to the application architecture level. We choose a peer-to-peer design to address *fault tolerance* and *scalability*. Our wrappers reside on the same host of the component code; thus we cannot rely on separated host/network to avoid their *tampering*. However, in our monitoring tool filters that interact with a tampered filter can detect its anomalous behavior.

The idea to monitor distributed systems at application level is not new. The ORA organization[4] monitors applications in anomaly based fashion. They characterize the normal behavior of the components interaction by using an immunology approach. While they are able to detect previously unknown attacks, not all intrusions deviate from normal behavior. We choose a specification-based monitoring to overcome such problem and to reduce the false alarm rate.

The DIANA tool[11] uses a specification-based approach to monitor distributed programs in a decentralized way. Safety properties are specified on each distributed process by means of a variant of a past time linear temporal logic. Formula related to a particular process can refer to remote states of other processes by using particular operators. Remote state information is delivered only when there is an explicit interaction with that process. Therefore a process locally computes a formula by using the information of remote states it is aware of. This logic seems not adequate to express security behaviors, since it may well happen to monitor applications (part of) whose components do not explicitly interact but their local states contribute to discover an attack.

Ponder [12] is an object oriented and declarative language mainly adopted for Object-Oriented distributed systems. A set of agents deployed at different hosts allow the monitoring. This language is specifically tailored to define roles, subjects domains and policies. However agents could overload the host to be monitored and they can be target of *tampering*. Breach on the security measures can become a means to attack the distributed application to be monitored.

Our monitoring language defines the security policy and it is tailored to express distributed correlation of information at architectural level. We deal only with observable messages exchanged at architectural level. Given the policy to monitor, filters are automatically generated and deployed.

3   Enforcement Mechanisms and IDSs Specification Based

Earlier IDSs were only involved in monitoring activities and analyzing log files. Today's IDSs embed reactive utilities that are undertaken when an attack is detected. For instance an IDS can react to an attack by terminating the session, blocking or shunning the traffic, creating session log files or restricting the accesses.

The time required to detect an attack and the time to react to such attack are relevant parameters that characterize the effectiveness of an IDS. Ideally an attack should be detected when it is in progress, this would allow either to avoid the attack or to have a faster recovery. In the worst case an attack that is terminated can be unrecoverable and important information can be lost.

Our specification based IDS captures every message exchanged among the components of the system to be monitored. It verifies that the messages comply with the formal specification, then it releases the messages. An attack is detected when the IDS finds a mismatch between the observed messages and the formal specification. In this case it reacts with the following default actions. The *log reaction* in which all activities related to the attack are logged. The *enforcing reaction* in which IDS releases every captured sequence verifying the formal specification. In other words, if our IDS captures a sequence of messages that verify the specification, then it deliveries the messages to the related components. Therefore our monitoring system can be also seen as an enforcement mechanism (EM).

As defined in [13] enforcement mechanisms compare a formal specification with the system steps. When there is a violation of the formal specification an EM can either terminate the system execution or replace an unacceptable execution step with an acceptable one. Any EM is assumed to be isolated from the system and any input to the system must be forwarded to it.

However in a system composed by black-box components running in different domains an EM might not have the right to terminate the system execution. Therefore our enforcing mechanism replaces an unacceptable behavior with an acceptable one.

We use the formal specification introduced in [13] to build our EM on the basis of an automaton that specifies the policies to be enforced. Our contribution is the algorithm to automatically distribute the EM on each component that composes the system. The distribution phase creates one filter for each component. Each filter embeds only the part of control related to the local information of interest. The use of the automaton is twofold: on one side it permits to reduce the overhead of messages exchanged among the filters. On the other side it allows an acceptable tradeoff between detection time and expressiveness of the language used to describe the security policies. As described in [13], relevant security properties can be described by means of security automata. In the following section we categorize these security policies by means of definitions and examples.

4   Violations at Architectural Level

Systems must embed security features to resist to attacks. However, nothing is perfect. Even the best protected system must be monitored to detect security violations. In a component based system, we characterize attacks as: *interface attacks* and *trace attacks*. *Interface attacks* are carried out by requesting a service with bad formatted inputs: anomalous inputs can produce a buffer overflow or code injections, so that attackers can gain unauthorized accesses. *Traces attacks* aim at subvert the correct communication among components. In the following we list some subcases of *traces attacks*. *Sequence attacks* are related to the order in which messages are exchanged among components. For instance, a component may access a service before performing authentication, or a component may request exclusive access to a data base component without releasing it before exiting. *Synchronization attacks* are performed by synchronizing components in a suspicious way. This is the case in which two components require a write service offered by a data base component. This could lead the system in an erroneous state in which one of the component could not have access to the system any more. *Coordination attacks* concern an anomalous cooperation of a component to reach some global goal. For instance, in a collaborative writing system, a component cannot cooperate with another component in order to read or write a different piece of file. *Distributed attacks* are scattered over several sources. These attacks look innocents when local-component traffic is considered, but they result in a violation when data are related. An example of this type of attacks is given by a chain of requests among components.

We detect violations in a component based application by checking that the system behaviors match a well defined policy. Here, a *policy* is a set of rules that dynamically regulate the behavior of a system neither changing the components code nor requiring their cooperation. In particular, security policies define what actions are permitted or not permitted, for what or for whom, and under what conditions. Policies can define correct communications among components, access and protection to components, authentication, monitoring of the responses and correct use of services. To define policies, we provide an ad-hoc language based on state machines. We also provide an algorithm to automatically generate a set of wrappers, starting from the given policy and the system architecture. Our wrappers are distributed one for each component and embed the part of policies that define the component local interactions. Although wrapper can implement confidentiality, we mainly focus on policies related to communications, access, correct use of services, monitoring of the responses and protection of components.

5   The Model of the System

At the architectural level, a system is viewed as composed by a set of components communicating with each other. We consider distributed-black-box components running concurrently and communicating either asynchronously and/or synchronously. We know that messages exchanged among distributed components can always be totally ordered [14], thus, a global trace of the system can be obtained. In this Section, we will give the basic definitions which our frame relies on. In all these definitions, we will assume that a global system clock exists. However, this assumption is needed only for modelling purposes, and it will be relaxed in Section 6, where we describe how our filters distribution algorithm works.

We focus on architectural system traces, i.e. on strings containing all messages observed at architectural level. A message encodes information about the type of communication, i.e. a request or a reply, the kind of service and its parameters and the (returned) data. We also assume, without loss of generality, that all messages are uniquely identified. Two requests of the same service from two different components originate two distinct messages.

We introduce some definitions that will be used in the following.

Definition 1. *Let T be a string $m_1m_2m_3 \ldots m_im_{i+1} \ldots$. T is an* architectural system trace *if the following properties hold:*

- $\forall m_k \in T$ m_k *codifies a service request to a component or a valid answer to some request.*
- *if $i < k$ then $t(m_i) \leq t(m_k)$, where $t(m)$ denotes the global system time at which the message occurred.*

Definition 2. *A sequence of messages $m_{l_1}m_{l_2}m_{l_3} \ldots m_{l_i}m_{l_{i+1}} \ldots$ is a* sub-trace *of some system trace $m_1m_2m_3 \ldots m_im_{i+1} \ldots$ if $l_1l_2l_3 \ldots l_il_{i+1} \ldots$ is a subsequence of $1, 2, 3, \ldots, i, i+1, \ldots$*

Definition 3. *Two subtraces $s_1^a s_2^a s_3^a \ldots s_i^a s_{i+1}^a \ldots$ and $s_1^b s_2^b s_3^b \ldots s_k^b s_{k+1}^b \ldots$ are said to be* distinct *if and only if $\forall i, j$ $s_i^a \neq s_j^b$.*

Definition 4. *Given two distinct subtraces $T1$: $s_1^a s_2^a s_3^a \ldots s_i^a s_{i+1}^a \ldots$ and $T2$: $s_1^b s_2^b s_3^b \ldots s_k^b s_{k+1}^b \ldots$ of T, a merge trace $T1 \oplus T2$ is a subtrace of T defined by $s_1 s_2 s_3 \ldots s_j s_{j+1} \ldots$ where:*

- $s_r \in T1 \oplus T2$ *if and only if $s_r \in T1$ or $s_r \in T2$*
- *for each s_i and $s_j \in T1 \cup T2$ if $t(s_i) < t(s_j)$ then s_i appears before s_j in $T1 \oplus T2$*

The definition of subtrace permits to define for each component C a component local trace that is all messages locally sent/received by a component.

Definition 5. *Let C be a component and T an architectural system trace. $T_C = m_1^c\, m_2^c m_3^c \ldots m_k^c m_{k+1}^c \ldots$ is a* component local trace *of C if it is a subtrace of T and each m_i^c is a message that codifies either a request or a provided service of the component C.*

In our model, the architectural system trace is produced by messages exchanged among all the components. Each running component C_i in the system defines a, local to the component, subtrace T_{C_i}. These sets of local traces constitute a partition of the architectural-system trace. In other words, if T: $m_1m_2m_3 \ldots m_im_{i+1} \ldots$ is an architectural-system trace, $\{T_{C_1}, T_{C_2}, T_{C_3}, \ldots, T_{C_n}\}$ the sets of local traces observed by the components of the system, then $\bigcap_{1 \leq i \leq n} T_{C_i} = \emptyset$ and the merge of T_{C_i} is equal to T.

Our purpose is to analyze the system architectural trace T produced at runtime to detect if T contains subtraces that violate the defined policies.

We provide an ad-hoc language based on state machines to specify policies (see [15]). It allows the definition of constrains on the input data of the services, on the ordering of the messages, on the synchronization among requests and on the relations among messages scattered over several components(see Section 4). The defined policy can establish when a component can access a service and it permits to monitor the response of a component. In this paper we do not show syntax and semantics of the language [15].

Our language permits to define the following automaton [13].

Definition 6. *A secure automaton is 4-tuple $A = (Q, q_0, I, \delta)$ where: Q is a finite set of automaton states, $q_0 \in Q$ the initial state, I is a finite set of input symbols and $\delta(Q \times I) \to Q$ is a transition function.*

Definition 7. *A secure automaton $A = (Q, q_0, I, \delta)$ parses a sequence $T = m_1 m_2 m_3 \ldots m_i m_{i+1} \ldots$ one symbol at a time from left to right. Let $q_{i-1} \in Q$ be the current state of A and let m_i be the next symbol to read. A accepts m_i if there exists a transition rule $\delta(q_{i-1}, m_i)$.*

Definition 8. *Let $A = (Q, q_0, I, \delta)$ be a secure automaton and $T = m_1 m_2 m_3 \ldots m_i m_{i+1} \ldots$ be a sequence of symbols in I. Let q_0 be the starting state of A and m_1 be the first symbol to read. A accepts the sequence T if for each current state q_{i-1} and next symbol m_i, A accepts m_i. $q_i = \delta(q_{i-1}, m_i)$ is the new state of A and m_{i+1} the next symbol to read.*

Definition 9. *The language $\ell(A)$ recognized by $A = (Q, q_0, I, \delta)$ is composed by all sequences of symbols in I accepted by A.*

This acceptance criterion permits to recognize finite and infinite sequences of symbols(see [13]).

In the context of component based systems, the 4-tuple of the secure automaton is constrained by the following rules. I is a finite set of symbols that represent messages at architectural level. Messages are of the form: $!s$ denoting outgoing message and $?s$ incoming message from/to a component, respectively. δ represents the policy that defines the correct messages exchange among components. We call such secure automaton: *Global Secure Automaton*. Global, since the alphabet I is a subset of all messages exchanged among components.

In Figure 1, we show a component-based system composed of three different types of components. A database component $C1$ can accept a login event which corresponds to an authentication service, encoded as $?login$. The message $!fail$ models a failure answer that $C1$ can send to a non-authorized client while the

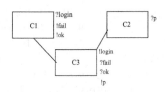

Fig. 1. Architectural view of the system

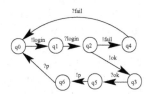

Fig. 2. Global secure automata

message $!ok$ is sent to an authorized client. A printer component $C2$ can accept incoming requests of print encoded as $?p$. A client component $C3$ requires login and print services encoded as messages $!login$ and $!p$, respectively and waits for incoming messages of successful/unsuccessful login encoded as $?ok/?fail$.

The global secure automaton (see figure 2) expresses a security policy in which a $!login$ request to the authentication component C1, once received, can be followed by either $!fail$ or $!ok$ messages. The service $!p$ can then be required only after a reception of an $?ok$ message.

The global secure automaton permits to monitor architectural system traces (see Definition 1). It performs a state transition for each observable message of the system and detects an attack when a message is not accepted.

Our main purpose is to automatically distribute the global secure automaton, so to monitor the distributed-component-based application in a peer-to-peer fashion. An algorithm produces a set of local secure automata that are assigned one for each component. Therefore, a local secure automaton can only observe the component local trace (see Definition 5) of the component it resides on. After the generation process each local secure automaton is implemented as a wrapper(filter) that envelops the component it supervises.

Notice that we consider deterministic automata. This permits to simplify the distribution algorithm and to reduce synchronization messages among filters. This choice is not a limitation, since, a non-deterministic automaton can be always translated to a deterministic automaton that accepts the same language. Moreover, we recall that a property is an high level description of the constraints imposed on the system components communications and not a complete description of the component-based-application behavior. In the remaining of the paper the notation $m^{C_i} \in C_i$ stands for messages locally sent/received by the component C_i.

6   Local Automata Generation

The monitor is conceived as a logically centralized process that makes a transition for each observable event of the system. A specification-based IDS can use the global secure automaton to realize the centralized monitoring by recognizing the languages defined by the security policies. Whenever these policies are violated an alarm is raised.

The algorithm to distribute the global secure automaton creates one filter for each component. The filter on a component C (in the following, we will denote it by $\Im_C$) implements a local secure automaton which, looking at the component local trace T_C (see Definition 5), detects a violation of the policies expressed by the global secure automaton. Obviously, by considering only the local-component trace of C $m_1^C m_2^C m_3^C \ldots m_k^C m_{k+1}^C \ldots$ is not sufficient to locally detect a violation of the policy. Therefore, $\Im_C$ has to parse an enriched trace that also contains context information provided by other filters. After the local parsing, $\Im_C$ can provide context information to other filters that need it. We call such information exchanged among filters *dependency information*.

Definition 10. *Let $\Im_C$ be the filter of the component C. Dependency informa-tion is of the form $!f(m, D)$ or $?f(m', S)$ where D and S range on the name of the application components. The message $!f(m, D)$, outgoing dependency, is sent by $\Im_C$ to filter $\Im_D$ in order to communicate that the C-component mes-sage m has been observed. The message $?f(m', S)$,incoming dependency, is an incoming information sent by filter $\Im_S$. With this information $\Im_S$ communicates to $\Im_C$ that it has observed a S-component message m'.*

Dependencies ensure that the merge (see Definition 4) of local-component traces result in a global trace of the system which satisfies the secure property expressed by the global-secure automaton. Hence, dependencies are a way to synchronize filters and to detect the violation of policies. Note that dependen-cies are sufficient to impose an order on messages; this allows us to relax the assumption that a global system clock exists (see Section 5).

A filter $\Im_C$ captures both local-component message and incoming dependen-cies ($?f(m, S)$) and outputs the outgoing dependencies ($!f(m, D)$) that will be used by other filters. In order to generate local automata we combine software architecture information with the global secure automaton. This combination is twofold: on one side permits to build local secure automata by projecting each transition of the global secure automaton (labelled with an architectural mes-sage, see Definition 6) on the component that accepts/sends the message. On the other side, it permits to enrich local secure automata with transitions that an-alyze and produce dependencies. Connections among components may be used to route context information messages through components filters [2]. Referring to the example in Figure 1 whenever $\Im_{C_1}$ needs to send a message to $\Im_{C_2}$ it has to route the message through the filter of C_3.

Informally, the algorithm for filters generation can be described as follows:

1. **Local automata generation**: For each component C, the set of automata $A_1 A_2 ... A_{n_C}$ is generated. These automata are the parts of the global secure automaton that processes events concerning interactions of the component C.

2. **Dependencies generation**:Let $A_1 A_2 ... A_{n_C}$ be the set of automata related to the component C. This step provides the needed context dependencies to ensure a complete and correct local message parsing. Furthermore, it connects the local automata $A_1 A_2 ... A_{n_C}$ of C in order to build a complete local secure automaton.

In the following we informally describe the algorithm and we illustrate its appli-cation by means of the example shown in Section 5. A more complete description is available in [16].

---

[2] The need of routing depends on the communication infrastructure on which the software architecture is built. For instance a component-based application may use communication layers that enable components to communicate with each other. In this case, a filter could send messages directly to another, which would avoid the overhead of routing messages via other filters.

6.1   Local Automata Generation

Given a global secure automaton $A = (Q, q_0, I, \delta)$, this step builds, for each component C of the system, a local secure automaton $\Im_C = (Q_C, q_{0C}, I_C, \delta_C)$. Informally $\Im_C$ is obtained by considering each rule $q_1 = \delta(q, m)$ defined in A. In the case that m is a C-component message such rule is reflected in a $\Im_C$-rule $q_1 = \delta_C(q, m)$, the states q, q_1 are added to Q_C and the message m is added to I_C. Therefore in the following we use two conventions: one is that we use exactly the same name q both for a state of the global automaton and the state of the filters where q has been projected. The other one is that, when it is clear from the context, we indifferently use either the rule $q' = \delta(q, m^C)$ or its $\Im_C$-projection $q' = \delta_C(q, m^C)$.

Looking at the global secure automaton A, the sequence of interactions that happen locally on a component C originates a local secure automaton $\Im_C$. In other words, $\Im_C$ does not include interactions among components that do not involve C. Therefore $\Im_C$ can result in a set of disconnected sub-automata $A_1 A_2 \ldots A_{n_C}$, each one modelling local interactions on C separated by interactions among different components.

The local automaton generation step is done locally to the component C. The time complexity is $O(|\delta|)$ where $|\delta|$ is the number of transitions of the global secure automaton. No new states are added, then the space complexity is linear.

Referring to the example in Section 5, after the local automata generation step the global secure automaton of Figure 2 is partitioned on each component of the system. Figure 3 shows such partition. For instance parts of the global automaton related to messages: $?login$, $!ok$ and $!fail$ constitute the local secure automaton on component $C1$, given that such messages are locally observed on that component. The same discussion can be done for the local secure automata of the components $C2$ and $C3$.

These local secure automata are not sufficient to validate the related component traces, therefore the next step shows how to add dependency transitions. Besides synchronization among local secure automata, dependencies are also used to link the disconnected automata $A_1 A_2 \ldots A_{n_C}$ of each $\Im_C$ (if any).

6.2   Dependencies Generation

The dependencies generation step takes as input the local secure automata and it adds dependencies information. Such information enforces the synchronization

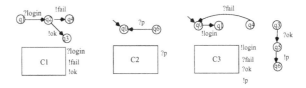

Fig. 3. Local automata generation

among the interested set of filters, so that merging the component local traces (see Definition 4) results in a trace accepted by the global secure automaton. For space reasons, we cannot provide a complete illustration of the dependencies generation step. Therefore we divide it into three phases and we sketch the basic idea of each phase. A complete and formal treatment of the whole step is described in [16].

Phase 1. In phase 1 the dependencies generation step provides the basic dependencies that are needed to synchronize a set of filters so that exactly one of them acquires the right to accept a local-component message.

A global secure automaton $A = (Q, q_0, I, \delta)$ can define a set of transitions exiting from a state q, with $q \in Q$. We consider the case in which from q two transitions exit: $q_1 = \delta(q, m^{C_1})$ and $q_2 = \delta(q, m^{C_2})$ with $m^{C_1} \in C_1$ and $m^{C_2} \in C_2$, and $q \neq q_1 \neq q_2$.

Local automata generation (see Section 6.1) ensures that the rules $q_1 = \delta(q, m^{C_1})$ and $q_2 = \delta(q, m^{C_2})$ are projected to the filters $\Im_{C_1}$ and $\Im_{C_2}$ respectively. Phase 1 adds the rules $q_1 = \delta_{C_1}(q, !f(m^{C_1}, C_2))$ and $q_2 = \delta_{C_1}(q, ?f(m^{C_2}, C_2))$ to $\Im_{C_1}$, and the rules $q_2 = \delta_{C_2}(q, !f(m^{C_2}, C_1))$ and $q_1 = \delta_{C_2}(q, ?f(m^{C_1}, C_1))$ to $\Im_{C_2}$.

From the point of view of A if it is in the state q then either the transition $q_1 = \delta(q, m^{C_1})$ or $q_2 = \delta(q, m^{C_2})$ can be applied. From the filters point of view such possibility is lost since these rules are independently applied by the two different filters residing on the two different components. The rules $q_1 = \delta_{C_1}(q, !f(m^{C_1}, C_2))$ and $q_2 = \delta_{C_2}(q, !f(m^{C_2}, C_1))$ are a means used by the filters to overcome this problem. Suppose that both filters $\Im_{C_1}$ and $\Im_{C_2}$ are in the state q. Each one of them can observe its local message, m^{C_1}, m^{C_2} respectively. In a single computation only one of them will participate in the (global) computation by parsing its message and leading to the state successor of q, that is either q_1 or q_2. However as far as the local automata $\Im_{C_1}$ and $\Im_{C_2}$ are concerned no matter who parses the message they must both move to the defined successor state, that is they will both reach either q_1 or q_2. For example, if $\Im_{C_1}$ observes the message m^{C_1}, it alerts $\Im_{C_2}$ of this observation by sending the dependency message $!f(m^{C_1}, C_2)$ and waits for an acknowledgment. If $\Im_{C_1}$ receives the $\Im_{C_2}$ acknowledgement, then this means that it has got the right from $\Im_{C_2}$ to move on and both filters move to state q_1. $\Im_{C_1}$ by consuming the message m^{C_1} by means of the rule $q_1 = \delta(q, m^{C_1})$. $\Im_{C_2}$ by consuming the dependency message $!f(m^{C_1}, C_2)$, by means of the rule $q_1 = \delta_{C_2}(q, ?f(m^{C_1}, C_1))$. In the case that both filters, at the same time, send the dependencies with each other then a synchronization protocol(see [16]) establishes that exactly one filter acquires the right to accept a component local message.

Phase 1 of the dependencies generation step considers a state q of a filter $\Im_C$ and its purpose is twofold: on one side it adds a set of transitions exiting from q labelled with outgoing dependencies. On the other side it adds a set of transition exiting from q labelled with incoming dependencies. The outgoing dependencies are needed to know the filters with whom $\Im_C$ has to synchronize, in order to acquire the right to parse a C-component message that labels a transition exiting from q. We call these outgoing dependencies *synchronization dependencies* and the protocol used by the filters to exchange these dependencies *synchronization protocol*. (see [16] for more details).

Phase 2. Phase 2 of the dependencies generation adds dependencies that are used by a filter to enable the parsing of local-component messages of other filters. A global secure automaton A can define a chain of rules $q_1 = \delta(q, m^{C_1})$ and $q_2 = \delta(q_1, m^{C_2})$, with $m^{C_1} \in C_1$, and $m^{C_2} \in C_2$, and $q \neq q_1$. The local automaton generation ensures that the rules $q_1 = \delta(q, m^{C_1})$ and $q_2 = \delta(q_1, m^{C_2})$ are projected on the filters $\Im_{C_1}$ and $\Im_{C_2}$, respectively. From the A point of view, this chain of rules defines a constraint among the messages m^{C_1} and m^{C_2}. That is, the message m^{C_1} must be accepted before the message m^{C_2}. However, from the local filters point of view, this constraint is lost, since the chain of rules is divided onto the filters $\Im_{C_1}$ and $\Im_{C_2}$. Therefore, the filter $\Im_{C_2}$ can autonomously accept the message m^{C_2} before the message m^{C_1} is accepted by the filter $\Im_{C_1}$. The problem is solved by adding dependencies. The dependencies generation adds to $\Im_{C_1}$ the rule $q_1 = \delta_{C_1}(q, !f(m^{C_1}, C_2))$ and to $\Im_{C_2}$ the rule $q_1 = \delta_{C_2}(q, ?f(m^{C_1}, C_1))$. Therefore $\Im_{C_2}$ can move to the state q_1, by means of the rule $q_1 = \delta_{C'}(q, ?f(m^{C_1}, C_1))$. However this rule can be applied only when the filter $\Im_{C_1}$ sends the outgoing dependency $!f(m^{C_1}, C_1)$. This is a means for filter $\Im_{C_1}$ to impose the right ordering among the messages m^{C_1} and m^{C_2}. We call such outgoing dependencies *enabling dependencies*, since they are used to enable the local-filter parsing when there is the right context condition.

Phase 3. Note however that, after the addition of such dependencies, some local automaton can still be disconnected. Phase 3 on one side links together the local disconnected automata $A_1 A_2 \ldots A_{n_C}$ through ε moves. On the other side it sets the initial state of all local automaton as the initial state of the global secure automaton.

The time-complexity to produce each local-automaton is $O(|\delta|^2)$ where $|\delta|$ is the number of transitions of the global secure automaton. The local dependencies generation does not add states with respect to the states of the global-secure automaton A. Therefore, the space-complexity is linear.

Figure 4 outlines the basic activities of a filter $\Im_C$ that is in a state q. In 4.1 a background thread buffers every C-component message in the message buffer and every incoming dependency in the dependencies buffer. In 4.2 $\Im_C$ picks up a C-component message m from the message buffer, if any. Steps 4.3-4.5 log and refuse m if it is recognized as an attack. On the contrary in 4.6 the filter $\Im_C$ tries to parse m by means of the rule $q1 = \delta_C(q, m)$. In 4.6b it starts the synchronization protocol in order to acquire the right to parse the message m. In the case that $\Im_C$ gains the right it applies the rule $q1 = \delta_C(q, m)$ and sends the enabling

1. a background thread buffers every C-component message in the message buffer and every incoming dependency in the dependencies buffer.
2. $\Im_C$-main process picks up a C-component message m from its message buffer, if any.
3. if m is not a C-local component message then it releases the message and logs a warning.
4. if m is a C-local component message that cannot be accepted in a successive state of $\Im_C$ then it trashes the message and raises an alarm.
5. if m is a message that cannot be accepted in the state q it logs a warning and it puts back the message on the buffer.
6. if m can be accepted by means of the rule $q1 = \delta_C(q, m)$ then
   (a) if $(q_1 = q)$ then it releases the message m and goes to step 7.
   (b) if $(q_1 \neq q)$ then it starts the synchronization protocol.
   (c) if it acquires the right to accept the message m then it sends the enabling dependencies, it applies the rule $q1 = \delta_C(q, m)$ and goes to step 7.
   (d) if $\Im_{C'}$, with $\Im_{C'} \neq \Im_C$ acquires the right to parse the message m' then
      – it puts back m on the local-component buffer.
      – it retrieves the rule $q' = \delta_C(q, ?f(m', C'))$ and it moves without non-local message observation.
7. it picks up an incoming dependencies from its local-dependencies buffer that can be accepted, if any.

Fig. 4. $\Im_C$-filter behavior in a state q

dependencies. Otherwise it moves through incoming dependencies. Finally step 4.7 checks and applies the dependencies that are stored in the dependencies buffer.

In the remaining of the paper we make use of a set of assumptions that, although not mandatory, allow the simplification of the presentation. We assume first of all that messages among filters are not lost and that messages sent between local filters are received in the same order they are sent. When drawing the local secure automaton multiple transitions from the same source and target are indicated by using one arrow with multiple labels.

We use the example in Section 5 to illustrate the whole approach. Figure 5 shows the local automata related to components $C1, C2$ and $C3$ as produced by the dependencies generation. Initially all local filters have state q_0. When the component C3 sends a $!login$ request to $C1$ the local secure automaton $\Im_{C3}$ captures the request. It observes that a $!login$ message can be accepted then it sends the $!f(!login, C1)$ dependency and the $!login$ message to $C1$. Finally, $\Im_{C3}$ moves to state q_1. The local filter on C1 receives the incoming message $!f(!login, C1)$ sent by $\Im_{C3}$ and it changes its state to q_1, since in q_0 it is waiting for an incoming message $?f(!login, C3)$. In state q_1 the filter on component $C1$ can accept the incoming $?login$ message and it changes to the q_2 state. We can observe that component C2 can provide a print service $?p$ only after some external events happened. These events are provided by $C3$ after a correct authentication is performed. At run time an attack is detected if a local automaton cannot accept a component local message, or if a local automaton is not able

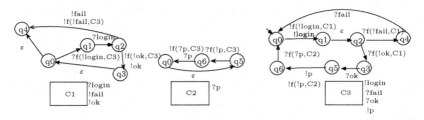

Fig. 5. Dependencies generation

to accept an external context information. In both cases, the information stored inside the filter gives details about the violation, providing a means to detect the source of attack. For example, in Figure 5 if component C3 requests the service $!p$ without previous $!login$, the local filter $\Im_{C3}$ captures the message and detects an error because it was waiting for a $!login$ request.

The overhead of messages generated by the filters is strictly related to the policies defined in the global secure automaton. A local automaton adds dependency messages when *non-interacting components* behavior has to be related. Let q be a state of the global secure automaton. Let $m_1 m_2 \ldots m_n$ be n messages, related to n different components residing on n different hosts $H_1 H_2 \ldots H_n$. Suppose that the messages $m_1 m_2 \ldots m_n$ label a transition exiting from the state q. In the worst case when a local secure automaton on the host H_i moves from a state q to a state q', with $q \neq q'$, then at most n dependencies can flow on the distributed system. In practice dependency synchronization messages are relatively small in size and, depending on the system architecture, it is possible to bound the number of the messages exiting from a state q related to different components/hosts.

Correctness and completeness of our algorithm derive from the following theorem that is described in [16].

Theorem 1. Let $A = (Q, q_0, I, \delta)$ be a global secure automaton, $\{C_1, C_2, C_3 \ldots C_i \ldots\}$ a set of components. Let $\Im_{C_i}$ be the automaton related to component C_i as produced by the algorithm. A accepts an architectural trace $m_1 m_2 m_3 \ldots m_i m_{i+1} \ldots iff$ all component traces T_{C_i} are accepted by $\Im_{C_i}$.

As discussed in Section 1 the main problem of security tools is tampering. Intruders can blind the security measures, so to violate the policies or use security measure against the system itself. In our approach, a component changing behavior is detected but problems can still arise if an intruder decides to attack by modifying both the filter's and the component's behaviors. Referring to (Figure 5), the intruder can change C3 so that it requests a printer service $?p$ without no previously $!login$ and can change accordingly filter $\Im_{C3}$. $\Im_{C3}$ is therefore changed so that it does not have anymore a $!login$ transition and the related signaling message, leaving only the transition from q_5 to q_6. In other words, the component and its related filter are changed to provide a different behavior. When $C3$ sends a $!p$ request, the local filter $\Im_{C3}$ does not detect any violation. The filter on component C2, $\Im_{C2}$, receives the correct $!f(!p, C2)$ signal and provides the printer service. The solution to this problem is to add further dependencies on the local secure automaton. For instance, $\Im_{C2}$ can be enriched to rely on the context information that the $?login$ message took place on filter $\Im_{C1}$. A new step (tampering step) can use local automata as generated by the dependencies generation step to add further dependencies. In other words this means to add redundant context information so that Theorem 1 is still true and both a component and related filter tampering can be detected.

7   Conclusion and Further Work

We have presented a distributed specification-based approach to detect intrusions at architectural level. Its peer-to-peer design allows the supervision of complex applications where no centralized point of information flow exists or can be introduced. This distributed solution presents several advantages with respect to centralized monitors. It is scalable, since the monitoring of an increasing number of components does not rely on a single point of data correlation, so to avoid problems of detection reaction time, loss of data and scalability. It provides an approach to face the problem of security measures tampering. A filter can detect a component that violates the policy, and other filters control and analyze the filter behavior to discover its tampering. The disadvantage of our approach concerns the potential message traffic increase due to the dependency messages exchanged among filters. This is the inevitable cost to pay to achieve a filters distribution which is correct and complete with respect to a centralized approach. However this overhead depends on the software architecture of the system to monitor and on the adopted security policies. Thus the suitability of the approach has to be measured taking into account these two factors.

At present our research proceeds in three directions. A prototypal version of the tool to generate local filters starting from a global secure automaton specification has been developed [15]. The approach has been applied to an industrial component-based application [17]. We are refining and extending the approach considering cases in which more than one component and the related filters are changed at the same time. We are also considering the use of context free languages to specify policies.

References

1. T.Eckmann, S., Vigna, G., Kemmer, R.A.: Statl: An attack language for state-based intrusion detection. Journal of Computer Security **10** (2002) 71–104
2. Javitz, H.S., Valdes, A.: The nides statistical component description and justification. Technical report - Columbia University (1994)
3. Vaccaro, H., Liepins, G.: Detection of anomalous computer session activity. In proc. of the 1989 Synopsium on Security and privacy (1989) 280–289
4. Stillerman, M., Marceau, C., Stillman, M.: Intrusion detection for distributed applications. Communications of the ACM (1999)
5. Ko, C., Ruschitza, M., Levitt, K.: Execution monitoring of security-critical programs in distribute system: A specification-based approach. IEEE (1997)
6. Aucsmith, D.: Tamper resistant software: An implementation. LNCS (1997)
7. Vigna, G., A.Kemmer, R.: Netstat: A network-based intrusion detection system. In proc. of the 14th Annual Computer Security Applications Conf. (1998)
8. A.Porras, P., G.Neumann, P.: Event monitoring enabling responses to anomolous live disturbances. In Proc. of 20th NIS Security Conference (1997)
9. Snapp, S.R., Dias, J.B.G.V., Goan, T., Heberlein, L.T., Ho, C., Levitt, K.N., Mukherjee, B., Smaha, S.E., Grance, T., Teal, D.M., Mansur, D.: Dids (distributed intrusion detection system) - motivation architecture and early prototype. In proc. 14th National Security Conference **1** (1996) 361–370

10. White, G.B., Fisch, E.A., Pooch, U.W.: Cooperating security managers: A peer-based intrusion detectionn system. IEEE Network (1996) 20–30
11. Sen, K., Vardhan, A., Agha, G., Rosu, G.: Effecient decentralized monitoring of safety in distributed system. ICSE (2004)
12. Dulay, N., Lupu, E., Sloman, M., Damianou, N.: A policy deployment model for the ponder language. IM2001, Seattle,IEEE Press. (2001)
13. Schneider, F.B.: Enforceable security policies. ACM Trans. on Information and System Security **3** (2000) 30–50
14. Lamport, L.: Time, clocks, and the ordering of events in a distributed system. Communications of the ACM **21** (1978) 558–565
15. Mostarda, L., Inverardi, P.: Distributed detection system for secure software architectures (desert) - a peer-to-peer tool for intrusion detection. http://www.di.univaq.it/mostarda/sito/default.php (2004)
16. Mostarda, L., Inverardi, P.: A distributed intrusion detection approach for secure software architecture - extended version. technical report http://www.di.univaq.it/mostarda/sito/default.php (2005)
17. Inverardi, P., Mostarda, L., Tivoli, M., Autili, M.: Automatic synthesis of distributed adaptors for component-based system. Submitted for publication (2005)

Deriving Architecture Specifications from KAOS Specifications: A Research Case Study[*]

Divya Jani[1], Damien Vanderveken[2], and Dewayne Perry[1]

[1] Empirical Software Engineering Lab, ECE,
University of Texas at Austin
divyaj@mail.utexas.edu, perry@ece.utexas.edu
[2] Dept. d'ingenierie informatique,
Universite catholique de Louvain
damien.vanderveken@swift.com

1 Introduction

The most difficult step in the design process of a system is clearly the transition from the requirements to the architecture. Requirements obtained from the various stakeholders must be transformed into an architecture that can be understood by developers. The power plant system we use in this study was derived from [1, 2]. We first created a goal-oriented requirements specification from the information available using the KAOS requirement specification language [3, 4, 5]. Since the description was not complete we often had to make do with inadequate data.

The first method used was developed by Axel van Lamsweerde (University of Louvain - Belgium) and is described in [6]. The various steps are explained in detail in Section 3.1 We describe some of the problems encountered during the derivation process. The second method used was that of Dewayne Perry and Manuel Brandozzi (University of Texas at Austin) [7, 8, 9]. The resulting architecture and some of the derivation issues are described in Section 3.2.

After obtaining both architectures we compared them and suggested some further work. In the case of the Perry/Brandozzi method we have made improvements to solve the problems we encountered and added the consideration of styles and patterns for non functional properties.

This case study [10] was structured as follows. First the authors together created the KAOS specification of the problem. Second Jani and Vanderveken then used the two methods to transform this specification into architecture specifications with Perry acting as mentor, arbitor and oracle in recording process issues and providing direction at critical points in the process. The authors together evaluated and compared the results.

[*] The research was supported in part by NSF CISE Grant CCR–0306613 "Transforming requirement specifications into architectural prescriptions".

2   Requirements Derivation Using KAOS

2.1   Goal Model

Given the fact that KAOS is a goal-oriented requirement specification method we logically began by trying to extract the goals of the system. A definition of the system was implicitly given in [1]. However the description of the powerplant monitoring system provided was partial and lacked details. So, throughout the requirement extraction process, we had to rely on experience and our common sense to create requirements that are as realistic as possible.

The following steps were followed to build the goal model. First of all, the informal definition of goals mentioned in [1] were carefully written down. From that, a goal refinement tree was built and completed by a refinement/abstraction process. The version we obtained at that point was still totally informal. Temporal first-order logic [11] was then used to formalize the goals and to ensure our refinement tree was correct, complete and coherent. The use of refinement patterns as described in [3] served as guidance. The milestone-driven pattern in particular was applied numerous times. It prescribes that some milestone states are mandatory in order to reach a final one. This pattern is presented in fig 1. The patterns were a great help to track and to correct incompleteness and incoherence. Furthermore they enabled us to save a huge amount of time by freeing us to do the tedious proof work.

Because of the iterative nature of the requirements gathering process, the goal model underwent subsequent changes. The reasons for that varied: coherence between the different models forming the KAOS specifications, enhancements, simplifications,etc.

The goal refinement tree is globally structured in two parts. This shape reflects the two main goals the system has to ensure to monitor the powerplant. The occuring faults have to be detected and the alarms resulting from those faults have to be managed. The roots of the two resulting subtrees are respectively FaultDetected and AlarmCorrectlyManaged. They are subsequently refined using the various patterns until the leaf goals are assignable to a single agent from the environment or part of the software.

As an illustration of the use of the milestone refinement pattern let's consider the goal AlarmRaisedIffFaultDetected with its formal definition

$$(\forall f : Fault, \exists!l : Location, \exists!a : Alarm)(Detected(f,l) \Rightarrow \Diamond Raise(f,a)) \quad (1)$$

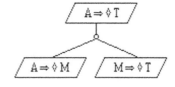

Fig. 1. Milestone refinement pattern

This goal is refined using the milestone refinement pattern by instantiating the parameters as follows:

$$A : (\forall f : Fault, \exists! l : Location)\,(Detected(f, l)) \qquad (2)$$

$$M : (\exists fi : FaultInformation)\,(f \equiv fi \,\wedge$$
$$Transmitted(fi, PRECON, ALARM)) \qquad (3)$$

$$T : (\forall fi : FaultInformation, \exists! a : Alarm)\,(Raised(fi, a)) \qquad (4)$$

The application of that pattern in particular results here from the fact that the information concerning the detected faults has to be transmitted to the ALARM to enable it to raise the proper alarm. This intermediate state is a necessary step to reach the final state, i.e., raising the alarm.

To have a system as robust as possible various goals were added to the goal diagram. Among these added goals, one class takes care of the correct working of all the sensors and ensures the data provided is consistent and coherent. The goals SanityCheckPerformed and ConsistencyCheckPerformed belong to this class. Another class – represented by the goal DataCorrectlyUpdated – makes sure the updates are well performed by the database. The purpose of some goals is to maintain the powerplant in a consistent state (e.g., FaultStatusUpdated, AlarmStatusUpdated). Communication has also been constrained in order to prevent any transmission problems and results in the refinement of the goal DataTransmittedToDB where refinement is shown in Fig. 2.

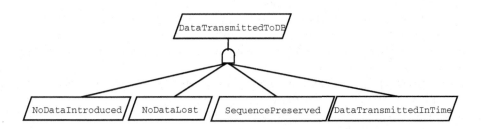

Fig. 2. Communication refinement subtree

The three first subgoals ensure the correctness of the transmission while the last one sets a time limit. This constraint varies througout the system depending on the importance of the communication channel. The FaultInformation has to be transmitted from PRECON to ALARM within 1 second while answer a request can take a little longer – 5 seconds. The three first subgoals have been formally refined as followed [3]:

---

[3] X stands for *SensorInformation*, *FaultInformation*, *AlarmInformation*, *FaultDiagnosis* and *AlarmDiagnosis*.

$$NoDataIntroduced:$$
$$\big(\forall x : Data\big)\big(Transmitted(X, \_, \_) \wedge x \in Transmitted(\_) \Rightarrow x \in X\big) \quad (5)$$
$$NoDataLost:$$
$$\big(\forall x : Data\big)\big(x \in X \wedge Transmitted(X, \_, \_) \Rightarrow x \in Transmitted(\_)\big) \quad (6)$$
$$SequencePreserved:$$
$$\big(\forall x, y : Data, \exists u, v : Data\big)\big(x, y \in X \wedge Transmitted(X, \_, \_)$$
$$\wedge Before(x, y, X) \Rightarrow u, v \in Transmitted(X) \wedge$$
$$Before(u, v, Transmitted(X)) \wedge x = u \wedge y = v\big) \quad (7)$$

They prescribe that no alteration has occured on the data transmitted i.e., no data has been introduced or lost and the sequential order has been preserved.

The formal definition of the last subgoal depends on the time constraint. If we consider for example the transmission of a FaultInformation – which has the strongest time constraint – the formalization is:

$$DataTransmittedWithinTimeConstraint:$$
$$\neg Transmitted(fi, PRECON, ALARM) \quad \Rightarrow \Diamond_{\leq 1s}$$
$$Transmitted(fi, PRECON, ALARM) \quad (8)$$

2.2   Object Model

Entities present in the objects were first derived from the informal definition of the goals. All the concepts of importance were modelled either under the form of an object or of a relationship. Attributes were then added to the different entities to characterize them. Some of the attributes were extracted from the problem definition but most of them proceed necessarily from the underlying domain from two main reasons.

First, certain goal definitions need the presence of specific attributes. For example the attribute WorkCorrectly of Sensor was needed by the goal Sanity-CheckPerformed.

Second, the definition of the properties of the various entities – expressed by invariants – requires specific attributes. As an illustration consider the following invariant of the object Alarm which expresses that all the alarms still active cannot have a deactivation time:

$$Activated = true \Rightarrow DeactivationTime = null \quad (9)$$

The purpose of certain attributes is to prepare for change. The reconfiguration function was not taken into account in the elaboration of the different models due to lack of time. However we believe that basically the only effect will be to modify the allowed range of temperature and pressure. Attributes representing the minimum, the maximum and desired value of both pressure and temperature were consequently added to the objects SteamCondenser and CoolingCircuit.

Last, a few attributes were added to build a more complete model. The justification was common sense. Among these are the attributes Type and Power of the object PowerPlant

The last step in the elaboration of the goal model was the formalization of the domain invariants characterizing the differents entities. The model was refined many times due to the iterative nature of the requirement extraction process.

The main characteristic of the model is that two different levels of representations are used for the concepts Sensor, Fault and Alarm. The first level refers to the object itself while the second one refers to its representation in the software. This distinction was introduced for robustness reasons. In fact it enables us to manage the case where the representation of the object is not correct which would be unfortunate but can happen. The two levels are constrained by an invariant prescribing that all the attributes have to be identical.

The representation of the three main objects – Sensor, Fault and Alarm – are linked together by a diagnosis relationship. The information provided by the sensor permits the detection of the faults and the description of a fault is the rationale for the raising of an alarm. Consequently the relationship FaultDiagnosis links SensorInformation and FaultInformation while AlarmDiagnosis links FaultInformation and AlarmInformation. Those two relationships are one-one. It is a modelling choice. We chose that a fault is the result of one and only one error detected by one sensor and that each fault raises one and only one alarm. The resulting simplicity and the ease of traceability is the reason for that.

2.3   Agent Model

The definition of the agents was extracted mostly from [1, 2]. We drew inspiration from the existing agents as well. Each leaf goal from the Goal Model was assigned to an agent. We made sure that every agent had the capacity to assume the responsibility for that goal. By capacity we mean that every agent could monitor or control, every single variable appearing in the formal definition of a goal the agent has to ensure. For further details refer to [5].

However a new agent was introduced : MANAGEMENT UNIT. Its purpose is to ensure that all the sensors are working properly. It was added for robustness.

Finally the operations needed to operationalize the differents goals were assigned to their responsible agents. This step will be explained later in the Operation Model section.

The agents PRECON, ALARM, COMM, DB and Sensor come from [1] though their names are different from there. PRECON is in charge of the detection of all the faults that might occur either in the cooling circuit or in the steam condenser. ALARM takes care of the alarm management. COMM ensures the reliability and the performance of all the communcication throughout the system. DB stores all the data persistently and answers all the requests concerning current values of the sensors, faults and alarms. The Sensor agent acquires the data from the field. The additional agent – MANAGEMENT UNIT – checks the sensors to see if they work properly.

The agents belong to one of two different categories: they are part of the software-to-be or part of the environment. For example, PRECON belongs to the former while Sensor belongs to the latter. This distinction in agents results also in goal differentiation. In fact the goals assigned to environment agents are expectations while the others are requirements. This led us to the introduction of the MANAGEMENT UNIT agent. Sensor is an environment agent and so all the goals assigned to it are expectations. But obviously we canot assume that the goals SanityCheckPerformed and ConsistencyCheckPerformed will be true without the intervention of reliable software devices. Moreover these kinds of tests should not be the responsibitlity of the Sensor from a conceptual point of view.

2.4   Operation Model

The operation model was the the last one to be constructed because it relies on a precise formal definition of the goals. The operations contained in the model were derived in such a way that they operationalize some goal present in the goal model. A complete operationalization of a goal is a set of operations (described by their pre-, trigger- and postconditions) that guarantee the satisfaction of that goal if the operations are applied. That is where all the difficulty lies: finding complete operationalizations. We extensively used the operationalization patterns described in [4] to derive complete operation specifications. It enabled us to save a lot of time on proofs. We found the application of the operationalization pattern very systematic.

Two patterns were particularly useful and we used them numerous times. The first one is the bounded achieve pattern described in Fig. 3. Its applicabilty condition (i.e., $C \Rightarrow \Diamond_{\leq d} T$) is pervasive. In fact most of our system's goals have that form. The operation specification prescribes that $\neg T$ becomes T as soon as $C \wedge \neg T$ holds for $d - 1$ time units. It is then straightforward to see that such a specification operationalizes the goal $C \Rightarrow \Diamond_{\leq d} T$.

The second most useful pattern was the immediate achieve pattern described in Fig. 4. Its applicability condition prescribes here that the final state T has to be reached as soon as C becomes true. In this case it is a bit more difficult to see why the satisfaction of the two operations guarantee the satisfaction of the goal (the interested reader can find a complete proof in [4]). The first operation

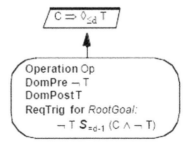

Fig. 3. Bounded achieve operationalization pattern

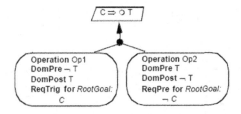

Fig. 4. Immediate achieve operationalization pattern

prescribes that as soon C becomes true the operation must be applied if $\neg T$ holds in order to reach the final state T. The second operation may be applied when C does not hold if the precondition T is true, making the postcondition $\neg T$ true.

Once all the operations were derived the were assigned to the agent responsible for the goal operationalized by those operations.

3   Architecture Derivations

3.1   Method 1: Axel van Lamsweerde

This method [6] prescribes the use of three different steps: abstract a dataflow architecture from the KAOS specifications; derive and refine the dataflow using styles to meet architecturals constraints; refine the resulting architecture using design patterns to achieve non-functional requirements.

Step 1: Abstract a data ow architecture The initial architecture is obtained from data dependencies between the different agents. The agents become software components while the data dependencies are modelled via dataflow connectors. The procedure followed is divided into two sub-steps.

1. Each agent that assumes the responsibility of a goal assigned to the software-to-be becomes a software component together with its operations.
2. For each pair of components C1 and C2, create a dataflow connector between C1 and C2 if

$$DataFlow(d, C1, C2) \Leftrightarrow Controls(C1, d) \wedge Monitors(C2, d) \qquad (10)$$

One can note certain features. Due to the fact that the COMM agent does not control any variables no arrow comes from it. In fact COMM carries all the data among the different components but does not do any modifications. Moreover there is a dataflow connector between PRECON and ALARM while the real dataflow goes through COMM. This situation also happen between Sensor and Precon. The real dataflow passes through DB but there is no dataflow derived.

We believe that the underlying cause is the presence of low-level agents – DB and COMM – performing low-level functionalities – storage and transmission of

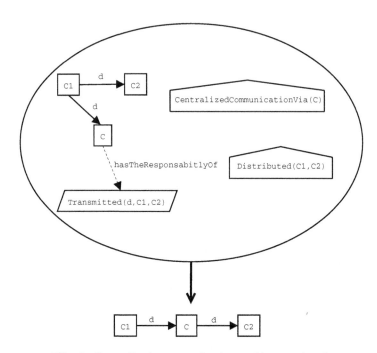

Fig. 5. Centralized communication architectural style

data respectively – in the requirements. They were however needed to achieve certain goals. It resulted in a rather strange architecture.

Step 2: Style-based architectural re nem ent to m eet architectural constraints In this step, the architectural draft obtained from step 1 is refined by imposing a "suitable" style, that is, a style whose underlying goals matched the architectural constraints. The main architectural constraint of our system [1, 2] is that all the components should be distributed. In fact, in the real system, only PRECON had to be built and integrated in to a pre-existing architecture characterized by centralized communications and by distributed components.

The only transformation rule mentionned in [6] did not match our architectural constraints so we had to design a new one on the basis of what was needed. The resulting transformation rule is shown in Fig. 5.

Once applied to the architecture every single communication is achieved in a centralized way through the communication module. The architectural constraints are now met.

Step 3: Pattern-based architecture re nem ent to achieve non–functional requirements The purpose of this last step is to refine further the architecture to achieve the non-functionnal requirements. These non-functional requirements (NFGs) can belong to two different categories: they are either quality-of-service or development goals. Quality-of-service goals include, among others, security, accuracy and usability. Development goals encompass desirable qualities of software such as M inim um C oupling, M axim um C ohesion and reusability.

Fig. 6. Fault-tolerant refinement pattern

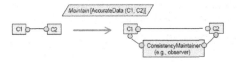

Fig. 7. Consistency maintainer refinement pattern

This step refines the architecture in a more local way than the previous one. Patterns are used instead of styles. The procedure is divided further into two intermediary steps.

1. For each NFG G, identify all the connectors and components G may constrain and, if necessary, instantiate G to those connectors and constraints.
2. Apply the refinement pattern matching the NFG to the constrained components. If more than one is applicable, select one using some qualitative technique (e.g., NFG prioritization).

Two refinement patterns were used on our system. The first is presented in Fig. 6. We wanted to have fault-tolerant communication between PRECON and ALARM because it is the core of the system. The most critical functions (i.e., the fault detection and the alarm management) are performed in these two component. That's why we wanted to make these modules as resistant as possible to any kinds of failure. One could note that the pattern was not applied exactly like it is defined in Fig. 6. The presence of the component COMM between PRECON and ALARM was however ignored because we believed it had no influence on the capacity of the pattern to achieve its goal.

The second refinement pattern is shown in Fig. 7. It was introduced because both Sensor and Management Unit access and modify the same data – SensorInformation. We wanted to make sure that all the modifications made from both sides are consistent.

3.2 Method 2: Perry and Brandozzi

This method converts the goal oriented requirement specifications of KAOS into architectural prescriptions [7, 8, 9].

The components in an architecture prescription can be of three different types - process, data or connector. Processing components perform transformations on the data components. Data components contain necessary information for processing. The connector components, which can be implemented by data and/or processing components, provide mechanisms for component interactions. All components are characterized by goals that they are responsible for. The interactions and restrictions of these components characterize the system. The following is a sample component -

Component PRECON
Type Processing
Constraints FaultDetected
   RemedyActionSuggested
   PeriodicalChecksPerformed&ReportWritten
Composed of FaultDetectionEngine
   FaultInformation
   FaultDiagnosis
   SensorInformation
   SensorConnect
Uses /

This example shows a component called PRECON. Type denotes that the component is a processing component. The constraints are the various goals realized by PRECON. Composed of defines the subcomponents that implement PRECON in the next refinement layer. The last attribute Uses, indicates the components interacted with and the connectors used for their interactions.

There are well defined steps to go from KAOS entities to APL entities. The following table illustrates possible derivations.

KAOS entities APL entities

Agent	Process component / Connector component
Event	-
Entity	Data component
Relationship	Data component
Goal	Constraint on the system / on a subset
	One or more additional processing, data
	or connector components.

In this method we create a component refinement tree for the architecture prescription from the goal refinement tree of KAOS. This is a three step process and may be iterated.

Step 1. In the first step we derive the basic prescription from the root goal of the system and the knowledge of the other systems that it has to interact with. In this case the software system is responsible for monitoring the power plant. Thus the root goal is assigned to the processing component "PowerPlantMonitoringSystem".

This goal is then refined into PRECON, ALARM, DataBase and Communication components. These refinements are obtained by selecting a specific level of the goal refinement tree. If we only take the root of the goal refinement tree, the prescription would end up being too vague. On the other hand if we pick the leaves, we may end up with a prescription that is too constrained. Therefore we pick a certain level of the tree which we feel allows us to create a very well defined prescription while avoiding a specification that overly constrains the lower level designs.

Step 2. Once the basic architecture is in place, we obtain potential sub components of the basic architecture. These are obtained from the objects in KAOS specification. We derive data, processing and connector components that can implement PRECON, ALARM, DataBase and Communication components. If in the third step we don't assign any constraints to these components, they are removed from the system's prescription.

The following are Preskriptor specifications of some candidate objects from the requirement specifications.

Component Fault
Type Data
Constraints ...
Composed of ...

Component FaultInformation
Type Data
Constraints ...
Composed of ...

Component SensorConnect
Type Connector
Constraints ...
Composed of ...

Component QueryManager
Type Processing
Constraints ...
Composed of ...

Since all the components derived from the KAOS' specification are data, we need to define various processing and connector components at this stage. At the next step we decide which of these components would be a part of the final prescription.

Step 3. In this step we determine which of the sub goals are achieved by the system and assign them to the previously defined components. With the goal refinement tree as our reference, we decide which of the potential components of step two would take responsibilities for the various goals. Note that this is a design decision made by the architect based on the way he chooses to realize the system. The components with no constraints are discarded, and we end up with the first complete prescription of the system.

Components like Fault were discarded from the prescription because they were not necessary to achieve the sub goals of the system. Instead of the Fault component we chose to keep FaultInformation. Different architects may make different decisions.

It is interesting to note that in our first iteration of the prescription Communication was a leaf connector with no subcomponents. It was responsible for realizing the necessary communication of the system. However the power plant communication was not uniform throughout the system. Different goals had different time, connection and security constraints for communication. In our first iteration we assumed that Communication component could handle these varying types of requirements on it. However then we realized that replacing the Communication component by more narrowly focused components was a step that helped illustrate these differences. Therefore we created the components UpdateDBConnect, FaultDetectionEngineAlarmManagerConnect and QueryD-BConnect. As the names suggest, each of these were responsible for the communication in different parts of the system. Therefore it was easier to illustrate the different time and security constraints needed for each of these.

The following are the prescriptions for the sub components

Component   UpdateDBConnect
Type   Connector
Constraints   Secure
   TimeConstraint = 2 s
Composed of /
Uses /

Component   QueryDBConnect
Type   Connector
Constraints   TimeConstraint = 5 s
Composed of /
Uses /

Component   FaultDetectionEngineAlarmManagerConnect
Type   Connector
Constraints   Fault Tolerant
   Secure
   TimeConstraint = 1 s
Composed of /
Uses /

Step 4. Achieving non-functional requirements An additional fourth step in the prescription design process focuses on the non-functional requirements. Goals like reusability, reliability etc can be achieved by refining the prescription. This step is iterated till all the non-domain goals are achieved.

For this system we introduced additional constraints on the Database and the connector between Alarm and Precon (FaultDetectionEngineAlarmManager-Connect). In the case of Database an additional copy of the Database was introduced to ensure fault tolerance. With the introduction of a copy additional issues arose. For example, we needed to ensure that if the main database recovers from a failure, all the changes made on the second database since the failure should now be made on the main database. Once that's done the control should be shifted to the main database. This and several other additional constraints were thus defined.

As a second step, we also defined two copies of Alarm and Precon. This again created additional constraints. For example, each time one copy of Precon fails, the other one should take over without affecting the functioning of Alarm.

Other constraints to be considered include no data lost, sequence preserved, data transmitted in x time, mediation, transformation, coordination, hardware interaction, software interaction, human interaction, interoperability, security, fault tolerance, consistency, recovery, post recovery, retrieval of information, update of information etc.

Step 5. Box diagram Once the architecture was created we added a box diagram illustrating the various components and connectors. The component tree created as a result of the three steps did not show how the various components are linked through the connectors. The box diagram helps in visualizing this and thus gives a more complete view of the architecture.

4   Problems and Issues

There were some issues common to both architectures. First neither architecture has means of addressing fault tolerance, reliability etc as architectural constraints. The architectures are derived only from the goal oriented requirements, and there is a possibility that for some cases fault tolerance etc may be introduced for architectural reasons. Neither method has a well defined way of dealing with this. Secondly, we often had to work with inadequate information on the functioning of the power plant. We were unable to find any information on certain requirements like performance. Therefore performance was not included. However in a real world power plant system performance is an extremely critical issue.

4.1   Architecture 1

Step 1 proceeded well in generating a useful data flow architecture. However, in Step 2 where architectural styles are applied, there were only a few sample styles to look at. The power plant architecture was relatively small and we were unable to apply many of these styles to the architecture.

The third step requires the use of patterns to achieve non-functional requirements. There were various sample patterns given, however the small size of the power plant architecture limited the choice of patterns to apply. In some cases the patterns were not well documented so it was difficult to understand their application. On the other hand there were cases where it was required to apply two or more patterns to the same components. It was difficult to decide how to combine the patterns to realize this.

Fig. 8. Interoperability refinement pattern

Another issue with the architecture was the creation of new components during the course of the derivation that had no operations. We also had to create some new connectors that did not have a complete definition.

Fig 8 and fig 6 show how to apply patterns to achieve interoperability and fault tolerance between components. However it is difficult to see how the patterns would be applied if components C1 and C2 needed to achieve both interoperability and fault tolerance. Another consideration is the order in which we apply these patterns to achieve a combination matters. There were no clear guidelines.

We were unable to find suitable patterns for some other non functional requirements. For example, the power plant architecture required certain time constraints on different functions, but there were not suitable patterns to incorporate these time constraints with the architecture.

To achieve fault tolerance some components were replicated as illustrated in the pattern. It was difficult to determine which and how many components should be replicated. There wasn't enough information available on the functioning of the power plant to assign higher priority to some components and lower to others. The final decision was made based on the limited information provided.

An additional problem was illustrating the need to ensure consistency between the two replicated components. The communication between the components would change with the introduction of replicated components; however, it was difficult to explain how.

The alarm component was replicated since it was critical to ensure smooth functioning of the power plant. However we could not define the method of communication between the two copies of alarm, nor the method used to ensure consistency. It was also difficult to determine how the communication between Alarm-Operator and Alarm-Communication would change with the presence of an additional component and how this would change the current connector.

We could not determine the need for interoperability due to the lack of detailed system information.

The final architecture we obtained used a communication component to facilitate all communication for the system. However the communication between components often had different features and constraints. There were hardware connections, software connections, redundant components, different time constraints and different reliability constraints. It was not possible to incorporate these differences in communication in the architecture. One possibility discussed was to define communication as a connector instead of a component.

4.2   Architecture 2

Our first hurdle was the very first step. The architect is given a large degree of freedom in choosing an initial overall structure. While this may be appropriate for an experienced architect, it was difficult for us to determine how to start and how much to try to do in the first step. It was also difficult to realize how much leeway was allowed for each of the steps. We were unable to find sufficient guidance on the various steps in the process. There were no examples where we could find both the complete goal tree and the complete component tree. This would have allowed us to compare the trees and understand better the progression required to create the architecture. Some of the questions were

- What decisions regarding the architecture are made at step 1. Do we simply assign a root goal or do we need to anticipate the next steps and have a basic structure thought out?
- Is it possible to have refinement where the tree had more than three levels?
- If all the sub goals (of a root goal) are realized by a component, does the root goal (for those sub goals) still need to be assigned to a component?
- Ideally in the second step KAOS objects are used to create sub components. Was it possible to use agents in this step also? Sensor Management Unit was an agent that we thought could be made a sub-component. However finally we used SensorInformation (which was an object) instead.
- Is it possible for a goal (and thus constraints) to be shared between sub components

Once the architecture was created we also added a box diagram illustrating the various components and connectors. The component tree created as a result of the three steps did not show how the various components are linked through the connectors. The box diagram helped in visualizing this and thus gave a more complete view of the architecture.

Once we obtained the component tree and the box diagram it provided us with different views. The tree seemed to indicate a hierarchy whereas the actual structure is quite different. The box diagram helped us realize the architecture as a network. Therefore there were different views of the system and structure based on the way we chose to look at it.

Additionally there were some components in the architecture that had no connectors. For example the AlarmInformation component under Alarm is a data component with various constraints on it, however it did not have a connector.

In the component tree and the resulting architecture there is no way to tell the data that is being passed through a connector. This made the architecture more difficult to understand. This information is particularly critical to describing the connectors. An alternative discussed for this problem was the possibility of having data as a constraint for a connector.

We also considered ways to explore the richness of connectors. Connectors can have different responsibilities like mediation, transformation and coordination. This richness would lead to a better design if we could portray this in the architecture prescription.

5   Comparison Between the Two Methods

The most significant difference is that the first architecture is more low level. The components are described together with the operations that they have to perform creating a more rigid design. The second method uses an architecture prescription language which tends to be more high level. This allows the designer to pick a better solution at a low level. However at the same time it provides less guidance in getting to the solution.

The first method provides a more 'network type' view showing the various relationships and interactions between the components. The second method resulted in a component tree which was more hierarchical in nature. We needed an additional box diagram to better explain the component interaction. However both views though different were useful.

The first method was more systematic in the beginning. There was a clearly laid out approach for going from requirements to an architecture. The initial steps were simple enough to consider the possibility of automation in the future. However in the second method one of our biggest hurdles was getting past the first step. It was difficult to determine the basic composition with which to start. This was probably due to the high level nature of this method.

As we continued with the architecture derivation the first method got a little more confusing. We had problems choosing the appropriate patterns, and applying combinations of patterns. There was inadequate documentation on them to help in the process. On the other hand the second method became more manageable once we decided on an initial structure.

An interesting difference was that in the first method there were no constraints on the various connectors. Instead the focus was on the data that is passed through those connectors. In the second method we were able to specify various constraints for each of the connector, but there was no way of specifying the data that is passed through. In both cases we were unable to specify the differences possible in the nature of various types of connectors. For example, connectors for fault tolerant components may provide mediation. There was no way to specify this in either case.

With respect to non-functional requirements, in the first method we applied them by choosing the appropriate pattern. However in the second method we created additional constraints on the components to realize the non-functional requirements.

The second method takes as input the requirement specifications in KAOS and provides as output an architecture prescription. Obtaining a architecture prescription was a challenging process. There were several points where we were unclear on how to proceed. Therefore some suggestions are proposed in this section to make the various derivation steps easier to follow. The biggest problem encountered was with the very first step. It was difficult to determine how much of the architecture needs to be in place when deciding the first step. We did not know how to pick the components to determine the root and the second level of the component tree.

One way of approaching this is that the root goal of the component tree is simply the name of the system that is being implemented. In order to determine the second level of this tree we look at the second level of the goal tree. This gives a good idea of some of the high level goals of the system. We also look at some of the main subsystems that the given system would need to interact with in order to realize these goals.

The next step is to determine how detailed we want the second level of the component tree to be. We can choose to keep the second step simple which would typically include basic manager type components and a main connector component. These components are further spilt into detailed subsystems later.

In the Power plant problem, the subsystems that the main system interacts with are used to determine the second level components. This makes the second level of the tree more detailed. In this case - Precon, Alarm and Databases are the major subsystems that the power plant interacts with so these form the second level of the component tree. A communication component is also present to ensure proper communication between these various subsystems. The agents in the goal model are a way to start looking for the various subsystems involved. In both cases we looked at agents that are subsystems not agents that are people.

It is important to note that in both processes there is always a connector element present at the second level

Once the basic tree is in place the remaining steps are easy to follow.

The next problem faced was that the architecture specifies the various connectors in the subsystem. We can specify the constraints on these connectors. However there is no way to specify the data being passed through them. Various components do specify the connectors they use however information regarding the data being passed is absent under the connector description. A data flow model for this method would be useful in this. Another possibility is specifying data as a constraint for various connectors. Data along with the constraints would form a complete connector description

Once the component tree was in place it was felt that there was still a missing element to understand the architecture completely. The component tree gave us a hierarchical type view of the system; but that was not adequate so we added a box diagram to give us a network type view. This is essential in understanding how the system worked. This diagram also helped in understanding the connectors of the system because it told us the way these connectors linked to components. This thereby helped in getting an understanding of the data that would be passed through these connectors. Understanding of the data passed is essential to getting a complete description of the connectors.

6   Conclusions

In this research we took a real world example of a power plant system and systematically obtained goal-oriented requirement specifications. We then created two architectures that satisfy the requirements. We analyzed and compared the results. Both architectures provided us with different but nonetheless useful views of the system. We used our example to create further well defined derivation methods making this critical step of the system design process easier.

Subsequently, this case study became the foundation for two masters theses: Jani explored how styles and patterns provide some non-functional constraints such as reliability and fault tolerance in the Perry/Brandozzi approach [12]; and Vanderveken investigated adding a behavioral view to van Lamsweerde's KAOS methods and precisely describing and applying transformation patterns. [13].

A good start, but much further work still needs to be done.

References

1. Coen-Porisini, A., Mandrioli, D.: Using trio for designing a corba-based application. Concurrency: Practical and Experience **12** (2000) 981–1015
2. Coen-Porisini, A., Pradella, M., Rossi, M., Mandrioli, D.: A formal approach for designing corba based applications. In: ICSE 2000 - 22nd International Conference on on Software Engineering, Limerick, ACM Press (2000) 188–197
3. Massonet, Ph., van Lamsweerde, A.: Formal refinement patterns for goal-driven requirements elaboration. In: FSE-4 - 4th ACM Symposium on the Foundations of Sofware Engineering, San Fransisco, ACM Press (1996) 179–190
4. Letier, E., van Lamsweerde, A.: Deriving operational software specifications from system goals. In: FSE-10 - 10th ACM Symposium on the Foundations of Sofware Engineering, Charleston, ACM Press (2002) 119–128
5. Letier, E., van Lamsweerde, A.: Agent-based tactics for goal-oriented requirements elaboration. In: ICSE 2002 - 24th International Conference of Sofware Engineering, Orlando, ACM Press (2002) 83–93
6. van Lamsweerde, A.: From system goals to software architecture. In Bernardo, M., Inverardi, P., eds.: Formal Methods for Software Architectures. Volume 2804 of Lecture Notes in Computer Science. Springer-Verlag (2003) 25–43
7. Brandozzi, M., Perry, D.E.: Transforming goal oriented requirement specifications into architectural prescriptions. In Castro, Kramer, eds.: STRAW 2001 - From Software Requirements to Architectures. (2001) 54–60
8. Brandozzi, M., Perry, D.E.: Architectural prescriptions for dependable systems. In: ICSE 2002 - International Workshop on Architecting Dependable Systems, Orlando (2002)
9. Brandozzi, M.: From goal oriented requirements specifications to architectural prescriptions. Master's thesis, The University of Texas at Austin (2001)
10. Jani, D., Vanderveken, D., Perry, D.: Experience report deriving architectural specification from kaos specification. Technical report (2004) Also avaiable at http://www.ece.utexas.edu/~perry/papers/R2A-ER.pdf.
11. Manna, Z., Pnueli, A.: 3. In: The Temporal Logic of Reactive and Concurrent Systems: Specification. Springer-Verlag (1992)
12. Jani, D.: Deriving architecture specifications from goal oriented requirement specifications. Master's thesis, The University of Texas at Austin (2004)
13. Vanderveken, D.: Deriving architecture descriptions from goal oriented requirements. Master's thesis, University of Louvain, Belgium (2004)

On the Systematic Conformance Check of Software Artefacts

Hylke W. van Dijk, Bas Graaf, and Rob Boerman

Delft University of Technology, Software Technology (EEMCS),
P.O. Box 5031, 2600 GA Delft, The Netherlands
{H.W.vanDijk, B.S.Graaf, R.Boerman}@ewi.tudelft.nl

Abstract. In this paper we present a systematic check of the conformance of the implemented and the intended software architecture. Nowadays industry is confronted with rapidly evolving embedded systems. In
order to effectively reuse design artefacts such as requirements, architectural views and analysis, as well as the code base, it is important to
have a consistent overview in each phase of the development process. In
this paper we propose a conformance check framework that combines a
colloquial engineering model and a conformance check system based on
commodity technology, albeit the model and the system can be used in
their own right. An academic experiment exemplifies the application of
our framework.

1 Introduction

The current trend in embedded systems is product families rather than single
products. Today's customers appeal to products that have a sense of uniqueness,
products that are compatible but slightly different than those of their friends.
The answer from industry is to set-up flexible product lines, which include a
range of disciplines: from product development to product manufacturing. The
efficacy of these product lines for evolving systems is mainly determined by the
amount and ease of reuse of existing artefacts.

The maintenance phase of a product has always been significant and will
increasingly be so. The growth of the complexity of systems is one reason, the
trend towards product families is another reason. From our participation in two
international industrial research projects [1,2] we learned that new products are
rarely developed from scratch and that reuse of existing development artifacts
is typically ad-hoc [3]. These observations triggered research in the field of conformance checking as a first step in enhancing the functionality of a product
or adapting it to a changed environment. The conformance check baselines a
consistent set of development artifacts and as such provides a starting point for
a more structured approach to reuse.

We address the problem of conformance checking by means of a conformance
check framework, describing the necessary steps. In order to be practically applicable in industry, it is required that such a framework suits the development organisation, builds on proven technology, and that its application is non-intrusive.

R. Morrison and F. Oquendo (Eds.): EWSA 2005, LNCS 3527, pp. 203–221, 2005.

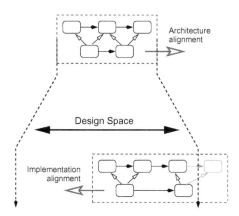

Fig. 1. Aligning architecture intention and implementation realisation

In general conformance checking could be applied on all related artefacts produced by the different domains of expertise in the software development process. In this paper we focus on the coordination between the domains of architecture and implementation.

The communication between the two domains is through views that are associated with a viewpoint [4], addressing a specific set of concerns. Views are developed in the architecture domain of expertise to specify the intentions, design restrictions, and design permissions for the eventual product implementation, i.e., the design space of Figure 1. Views can also be generated in the implementation domain of expertise [5]. These views predicate the properties of the actual implementation from an architectural perspective.

When views from the architecture and implementation domain are associated with a common viewpoint it is possible to identify discrepancies between the intended and implemented architecture. In Figure 1 there is apparently a mismatch, which can be resolved by either updating the architecture or the implementation. However, the semantic gap between the elements and relations used in architectural views and the programming language constructs available to implement them makes it difficult to reconstruct a view associated with an architectural viewpoint from an implementation.

In this paper we propose and experiment with, a conformance check framework (CCF) that combines a colloquial engineering model and a conformance check system (CCS). The CCS facilitates conformance checks through the definition of a design-space conformance viewpoint bridging the semantic gap between the implementation and architecture domain. Views associated with this viewpoint *can* be generated from the implementation and derived from the architectural views. The engineering model takes an architectural view on product development. It is based on the two principal categories of views described in literature [6,7,8]: runtime views and development views. We consider views from both categories in our experiments to attain a good coverage of the difficulties

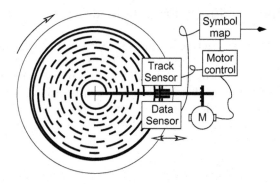

Fig. 2. Digital music box reader system

and possibilities of determining architectural conformance. We implemented the CCS using existing technology. Our experiments demonstrate the definition of conformance viewpoints and the visualisation of discrepancies between the intended (specified) architecture and the implemented (predicated) architecture. The CCF emphasises the role of conformance checks for maintainability of operational systems. Because of our academic interests, part of the result of our treatise will be an agenda for further research.

This paper is organised as follows. This introduction is concluded with the presentation of a running example. In Section 2 we present our conformance check framework, the two principal categories of views of the CCF and their relation are treated in detail in Section 3. Section 4 is devoted to a case study where we systematically conform a viewpoint from the set of runtime views and a viewpoint from the set of development views, thus implementing the CCS. In Section 5 we discuss our CCF, the applied technology, and related work. Finally, Section 6 presents conclusions on our work.

1.1 Running Example

The running example in this paper is the development of an academic system: a digital music box (DMB) that reads data from a paper disc (record). The record is a plotted spiral track of pulse-width modulated data bits. The disc rotates with a constant speed. The system tracks the spiral, reads the data bits, and then maps those bits to symbols. A string of symbols will be fed to an output device that transforms the string into audible music. Here we focus on the process of reading the record and the generation of the symbol stream. The physical system is composed of a traditional turn table and a set of simple light sensors that can be moved axially by a motor; the control is implemented on a simple micro controller. The controller is programmed in Java. Figure 2 gives an overview of the reader system.

2   Conformance Check Framework

Architecture is typically described using different views each addressing a different set of concerns. We therefore need to be explicit about the architectural view involved in the conformance check. For this purpose our framework includes an engineering model that involves the two principle categories of views for conformance checking: development views and runtime views. The model is complemented with a strategy for conformance checking and a generic conformance check system. The latter can be implemented with readily available technology.

2.1   Engineering Model

Our engineering model shows the architectural views involved in a product's life cycle. To position our engineering model, we consider a generic product model for embedded system development: the Vorgehensmodell (V-model [9]).

The V-model binds the analysis or design activities of product development with the synthesis or integration activities. Given a context with changing requirements and environment, and where new products are not developed from scratch, it is essential that the process model facilitates flexible interactions between different domains of expertise in the software development process. Thus generally, specifications flow forward from analysis to synthesis, whereas the return flow from synthesis to analysis carries predicated properties of the system.

We take an architecture centric position to product development. The architecture of a system provides a reasoning framework of that system; it is a common understanding of the involved stakeholders. Ideally the architecture

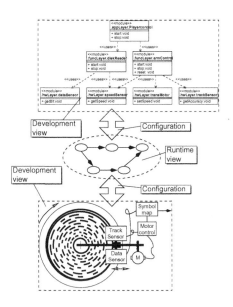

Fig. 3. Architectural views in the engineering domain

explicitly rationalises all important design decisions, in practice however architecture documentation mainly concerns the structural effects, manifested in the graphical presentation of the different architectural views [6, 4, 8].

The understanding of the *working* system takes a central position in the communication among stakeholders. This is indicated by the central role of the runtime view in Figure 3. The process view in Kruchten's "4+1" view model [6]; the different component-and-connector (c&c) views described in [8]; and also data and control flow diagrams known from structured analysis and design methods are all known examples of views that capture the structural organisation of a *working* system. Runtime views address the question: how does the system work? In order to arrive at a system functioning as presented in the runtime views, the periphery of the runtime views consists of views driving the actual *implementation* of software and hardware. Those views that capture the structural organisation of the implementation units are known as the set of *development views* and address the question (concern): how is the system developed? Examples of development views on the organisation of the software implementation units (modules) are decomposition views and uses views [8].

The compilation *configuration*, indicated by the double arrows in Figure 3, describes the integration of the constituent elements of a system, as described in the development views, into the working system, as described by the runtime views. It specifies the allocation of software modules of a development view to components of a runtime view and it additionally describes the allocation of that component to a hardware unit of the appropriate development view.

Figure 4 situates our engineering model in the V-model. It shows the two principal sets of views (the runtime view and the development view) and their configuration. Obviously development views are mainly used during coding and

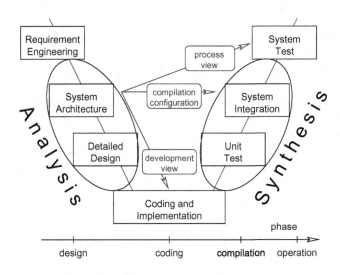

Fig. 4. V-Model engineering development model

implementation, runtime views are used to operate the system, compile configurations are used during the system integration (compilation) phase.

2.2   Conformance

Our engineering model suggests to check views from the set of runtime and development views, in order to arrive at a sufficient coverage of discrepancy detection between the specified and implemented system. A distinct constraint for a practical implementation of a conformance check system is the prevention of interference with ordinary system development. Therefore we regard the domains of architecture and implementation as autonomous activities, circumventing the use of an integrated development model.

practice, the implementation and architecture domains differ considerably with respect to the level of detail at which the involved concepts are defined. Implementation level constructs can be defined formally. At least there is a compiler that deterministically attaches meaning to implementation concepts. In the architecture domain, however, concepts do not typically have a universal, unambiguous meaning and their semantics is only specified, if at all explicitly, informally. Taking into account the fact that architectural decisions are typically made in the early phase in a product's life-cycle, we consider this a virtue of the architecture domain.

A conformance check between a specification and predication among two domains of expertise without affecting them requires the definition of a *common viewpoint*. The semantics of such a design-space conformance viewpoint must be clearly interpretable by both domains of expertise. Thus there must be a bidirectional *mapping* between the design-space conformance view and the domain-specific views. Mismatches between the design-space conformance views derived from the two domains-specific views identify potential discrepancies, or architecture violations. Whether a mismatch indeed implies a discrepancy involves more detailed knowledge of the relevant design decisions.

In Section 3 we develop design-space conformance viewpoints for a runtime view and a development view, plus their respective mappings from a typical set of architectural views and implementation views. Although implementation will mainly use the development views, it must obey the runtime views so as to facilitate their proper implementation in later stages of the product's life time. Predicated properties of the realised system contain the evidence that the development view has been properly implemented and that the runtime views can be realised in later stages of the product's life time. Our conformance check system (Section 2.3) gathers and extracts the specifications and the attributes in terms of the predefined conformance viewpoints, checks their conformance, and visualises the result.

In this paper we consider the architectural view as leading. From the perspective of an implementation there are three important situations for any entity or relation: *covered*, *excess*, and *deficit* [10]. A covered relation (or entity) has a corresponding relation in the architecture domain. An excess relation only exists in the implementation domain and a deficit relation only exists in the architecture domain. The result of a conformance check is a set of entities and relations that are attributed according to the three types above; the significance of mismatches found depends in general on the involved design decisions. Therefore discovery of mismatches should serve as a trigger to investigate further if they are allowed and possibly documented elsewhere. If not, they are considered to be discrepancies that reduce the conceptual integrity of a system and may result in unexpected dependencies, reducing the system's maintainability.

A conformance check can be used to evaluate specific concerns. As an example, we can locate the set of design-decision related to a selected quality attribute. The set of design decision determines a set affected views. This set of views can be used to define a design-space conformance view, the set of design decisions determines the impact of possible discrepancies found during a conformance check. An alternative use is to incorporate a conformance check in the system integration test set of a product, e.g., as part of the nightly build process.

2.3   Conformance Check System

The conceptual conformance check system (CCS) of Figure 5 outlines the process to identify discrepancies. A fact extractor derives views, associated with the design-space conformance viewpoint, from architecture and implementation domain artefacts. The subsequent comparison of the derived design-space conformance views is done based on a set of comparison rules. These rules are used for simple graph matching to identify mismatches, and more involved for selecting those mismatches that are actually related to discrepancies. Finally, a presentation filter visualises the comparison results.

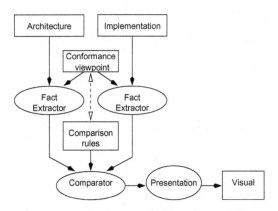

Fig. 5. Conceptual CCS

3   Deriving Conformance Viewpoints

In this section we describe how design-space conformance viewpoints can be derived for the two principle categories of architectural viewpoints. In particular we consider suitable (informal) semantics of the conformance viewpoints, their checkable mismatches, and their respective mappings from both the implementation and the architecture domain viewpoints.

3.1   Development Views

A development view describes a decomposition of the system in terms of implementation (e.g. source code) units, often called modules, and their dependencies. These modules, supposedly coherent units of functionality, are eventually assigned to development teams. Dependency relations between the modules of a development view are important, several types of them exists such as uses, allowed-to-use, and shares-data-with relations. Here we will focus on *use* dependencies.

Figure 6 depicts a development view of the digital music box architecture of Section 1.1 that reveals the use dependencies between the different modules. This view is part of the specification of the system, resulting from the architecting phase. The chosen viewpoint contains a module element and a use dependency relation, both indicated by UML stereotypes.

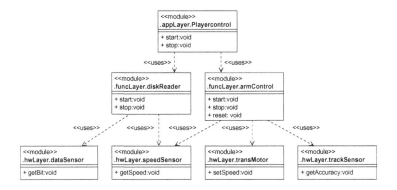

Fig. 6. Uses (module) view

Typically the implementation-level modularisation constructs do not match one-to-one with the architecture-level modules. Implementation engineers typically have reasons to further refine the provided decomposition of the development views. This is safe, provided the decomposition is registered, e.g., annotated. A simple, yet sufficient, method is to augment the implementation with *belongs-to* clauses that associate decomposed subsystems with a module of the architectural uses view. With the advent of integrated development environments dealing with these annotations is simple. Eclipse could, for instance, be easily changed such that this information is requested from the programmer in the wizard for defining a new class. Subsequently this information could be included in the header of the skeleton code generated by the wizard. The belongs-to clauses can be automatically retrieved during the fact extraction phase. Gathering these facts yields a design-space conformance view consisting of aggregates of implementation units. As an example consider Listing 1 where the following belongs-to relations are defined: BelongsTo($X; A$), BelongsTo($Y; B, C$).

Next to modules a uses view defines use relations [8]. The mere wording of use has conflicting interpretations [11]. As we strive for a clear definition of viewpoints, the meaning of "use" has to be clearly defined in order to determine the existence or possibly inexistence of a particular use relation. We start with the definition given by Clements et al [8]: "Unit A is said to use unit B if A's correctness depends on a correct implementation of B being present."

We take a pragmatic position by mapping the architectural use relation to a checkable tuple: a link plus an action that effectuates the link. The link is a reference to the used module and the action can be anything from a function call to an attribute access. This design-space conformance viewpoint only covers part of the architectural concept of using, as it does not take into account that the used module needs to be implemented *correctly*, it merely requires it to be present. Furthermore the architectural uses dependency does not necessarily require a direct reference in the implementation; more complicated indirect dependencies can also correspond to a use relation. In fact the design-space viewpoint captures calls and shares-date-with dependency relations, which are different specialisations of the depends-on relation.

A link from module X to module Y typically emerges as a reference, e.g., a declaration of an attribute of type B in class A, where A and B belong to X and Y respectively. The necessary action is determined by a method invocation or attribute access of that reference. Combining the links, actions and belongs-to relations, the example of Listing 1 contains the following use relations, as defined

```
// @belongsTo module X
Class A {
    private B objB;
    void A() {
      B = new B();
    }
    void doA(C objC ) {
        B.doB( C );
    }
}

// @belongsTo module Y
Class B {
    void doB( C objC ) {
        C.doC();
    }
}

// @belongsTo module Y
Class C {
    private A objA;
    void doC() {
        // stub
    }
}
```

Listing 1. Sample source code

by the design-space conformance viewpoint: $Uses(Y; X)$ and $Uses(Y; Y)$. The absence of a relation is not a property (fact), e.g. $Not\,Uses(X; Y)$.

3.2   Runtime Views

Runtime views on software architectures are frequently specified using component-and-connector (C&C) views [8]. The box-and-line diagrams created early during software design, usually are C&C type of views. C&C views are detailed runtime views addressing concerns such as concurrency and flow of data. Architectural components are loci of computation and state. Architectural connectors are loci of interaction. Both are architectural abstractions of elements that consume resources, either processing time or memory. A complete C&C view is an abstraction of a system during runtime.

To describe C&C views we adhere to the terminology of architecture description languages (ADL), e.g., [12]. Typically in C&C views components are associated with the connectors by means of attachments. Components and connectors habitat *processes* that interact with their environment through associated *interfaces*. In case of a component the interface is called a *port*, whereas in case of connector we call it a *role*. In order to establish interaction between two components over a connector we can attach component ports to connector roles, with the limitation that an attachment is only allowed if the component interacts using the port as interface and according to the expectations described by the connector role, i.e. port and role need to be compatible.

Figure 7 depicts a runtime view of the digital music box architecture of Section 1.1. It shows concurrently executing components as communicating-processes. The components interact through different types of connectors. Although UML is not the preferred modelling language, mapping of ADL constructs to UML is sometimes awkward, it can be done [13, 14]. Following an approach proposed by Garlan et. al. in [14], we represent component types and components by classes and objects, connectors by links (labelled with connector type names), and ports by link-roles (labelled with port type names). As we are only using relatively simple connectors we do not consider connector roles.

Components, ports, connectors, and roles are architectural concepts that may or may not have explicit counterparts in the development views or implementation. Source code is not merely a refinement of these architectural elements as in the case of development views, making the mapping between the architecture runtime views and implementation domain constructs indirect and more difficult.

The main concern of the C&C view in Figure 7 is concurrency. For such a view the components, processes, correspond to implementation mechanisms for concurrency and parallelism, such as processes, threads and tasks. For example in the case of a system implemented in Java, a component corresponds to a subclass of the thread class and all other classes it instantiates.

Connectors correspond to the mechanisms that allow these threads and tasks to interact, for instance inter-process-communication mechanisms, remote-procedure calls, or shared-data. As opposed to the architectural connectors these im-

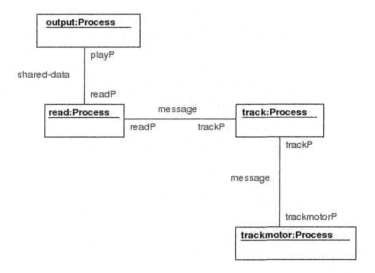

Fig. 7. Communicating-processes view

plementation-level communication constructs have an obvious direction. Therefore in the design-space conformance view we add a direction to the connectors defined in the architectural view. We need to consult the architect or the architecture documentation to discover the intentions. For message-based connectors the direction corresponds to the direction of the first message, i.e. from the component initiating the interaction to the other component. The direction of shared-data connectors is from the component writing in the shared-data to the component reading from the shared-data, assuming that components do not read *and* write to the shared-data, which in our case was a valid assumption.

4   An XML Implementation of the ccs

Our sample implementation of the ccs, depicted in Figure 8, uses readily available XML technology; the XLINKIT toolkit is the heart of our ccs.

Fact extraction involves two steps: a transformation of the sources (architecture and source code documents) onto XML format followed with a filtering and interpretation operation to populate the design-space viewpoint. In our experiment, the architecture has been described in UML, using its accompanying XML schema: XMI. The implementation has been coded in Java. The (static) facts about the implementation reside in the Abstract Syntax Tree (AST), which can be retrieved by replacing the code generation back end of a compiler. In this case we used an XML specification JAVAML [15] that is generated by a patched version of the Jikes compiler. Similar technology is available for many other programming languages [16].

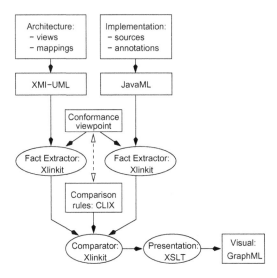

Fig. 8. Implementation of CCS

The filtering operation uses the XLINKIT technology [17] as a lightweight rule-based link generation tool. It combines current XML technology such as XPATH, XLINK, and XSLT. The XLINKIT rules that map architecture and implementation domain facts to the design-space conformance viewpoint (see Sec. 3) Figure 8, are specified in so-called CLIX [18] constructs.

The XLINKIT tool is also used as a comparator in the CCS. It takes the XML representations of the design-space conformance views and a set of CLIX comparison rules, which identify possible mismatches between the extracted conformance views and subsequently identify those mismatches that actually involve discrepancies. The result is a set of XLINK hyperlinks between the two conformance views. The comparison rules basically check the semantic consistency of the two design-space conformance views. The hyperlinks either represent evidence of a correct (covered relation) or an incorrect (deficit or excess relation) interpretation of the architectural views by the implementation domain.

Finally the information presentation phase takes the hyperlinks and produces a visual representation. This is done with an XSLT transformation engine. The result is in our case a graph, which is specified in GRAPHML, a flexible XML schema. Graph visualisation and layout tools are indispensable for the interpretation of the results, here we used GRAPHVIZ and YED.

4.1   Development Views

The uses view of Figure 6 was one input of the CCS. Derivation of the design-space conformance view from this UML model is straightforward because of the use of stereotypes to denote modules and use relations. Simple XPATH expressions suffice to generate a canonical XML model for the following phases in the CCS. A visual representation, through XSLT, is given in Figure 9(a).

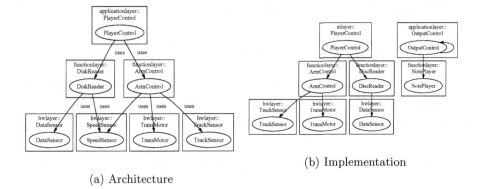

(b) Implementation

(a) Architecture

Fig. 9. Uses views

Recovering the design-space use-view from the implementation involves the interpretation of Java language constructs and the belongs−to annotations. Locating a module is simply done by retrieving the belongs−to attribute of identified classes in the sources. Locating a use-relation is more involved however. We demand *access* from a source class to a target class. It is insufficient for a source class to only maintain a reference to a target class or invoke a constructor for that target. Access involves the explicit invocation of a method in the target class or a field update of the target class. The CLIX expression to identify access is not very elegant, merely enumerating all possibilities. The resulting visualisation is given in Figure 9(b).

The comparison phase of the CCS co-locates facts from the conformance views extracted from the architecture and implementation domains. It binds entities from both domains through their names and determines covered, excess, and deficit relations. Note that in the current implementation we determine manually which mismatches actually involve discrepancies.

In the presentation phase of our CCS we map the entities and relations to a graph in which covered, excess, and deficit relations are coloured and shaped. The result is in Figure 10. The trapezoid shaped vertices and the edges with open delta arrowheads represent the deficit entities and relations respectively. Partly these relations originate from name mismatches, e.g. DiskReader and DiscReader. One entity has not been implemented: the SpeedSensor. The parallelepiped shaped vertices and the closed delta arrowheads represent the excess relations, e.g, showing name mismatches. But also real excessive relations emerge: NotePlayer and OutputControl. The covered relations use boxed vertices and sharp short arrowheads on the edges.

4.2   Runtime Views

The design-space conformance views resulting from the fact extraction in the architecture domain is given in Figure 11(a). It corresponds to the component-and-connector view in Figure 7. As explained in Section 3.2 we necessarily added

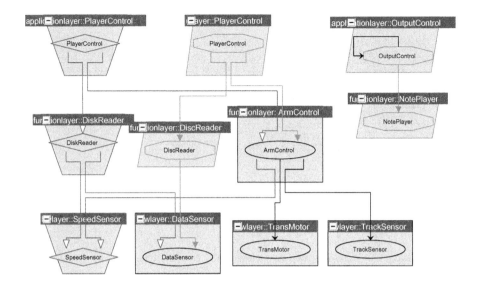

Fig. 10. Uses conformance view

direction to the connectors. In the design-space conformance view we represent components by rectangles and connectors by ellipses with arrows to indicate the direction.

Creating a C&C view from static sources is very application specific. For the transformation of sources to XML of the data gathering phase we use the same technology as for the development view. The filtering stage is now a multi-stage approach that extracts, combines, and interprets facts by cascading XLINKIT extracted reports. In this case we used two stages.

The first stage extracts associations from the source code and identifies autonomous threads of control. The associations identification reuses the CLIX rules of the static case. Autonomous threads are, in this case, defined as classes with a main-method or classes that extend the Java thread class. The second stage gathers the actual instantiated threads as well as interaction between thread instances. We recognise two types of communication links: a method call and a buffered stream with read and write access. The resulting graph is given in Figure 11(b).

Comparing the C&C runtime views of Figure 11 involves as before merging the namespaces. We have multiple mismatches here, as the names in the source code are derived from the names used in the *development* view. Furthermore implementation-level constructs used to implement interaction are often not named, e.g. procedure calls. Subsequently the components, connectors, and ports must be identified. Since the recovered C&C views from the sources lack ports and roles altogether we transform the conformance view by inserting ports and roles when appropriate. Comparing the design-space views results in the identification of covered, excess, and deficit constructs.

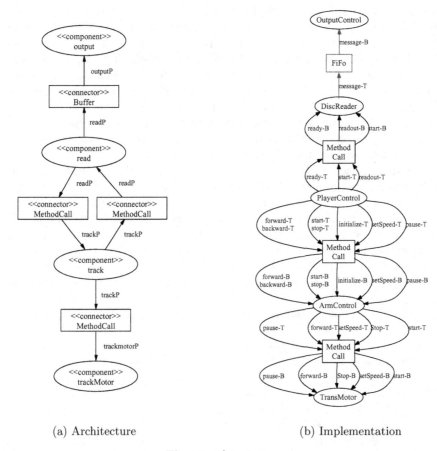

(a) Architecture

(b) Implementation

Fig. 11. c&c views

The resulting diagram is not shown, but considering the namespace mapping of the components (output $\mapsto$ OutputControl, read $\mapsto$ DiscReader, track $\mapsto$ ArmControl, and trackMotor $\mapsto$ TransMotor) of the two views in Figure 11 it is immediate that the connectors are more detailed in Figure 11(b). This is because it shows the different occurrences of interaction over each connector separately. Furthermore the PlayerControl component is an excess component not present in the architecture specification. It was intended as a connector between the read and track components, however in the implementation it included handling user interaction for which it required a separate thread.

5   Discussion

In this section we discuss issues that emerged in the execution of the experiment of the previous section.

Consistency and Technology Imperfections. The architectural views are expressed in UML, using stereotypes to identify modules and use dependencies. However, the current version of UML cannot enforce the consistent use of stereotypes, which potentially may yield false alerts in our CCS. Additionally UML does not offer support to conveniently specify all elements of component-and-connector views. For instance, the style we used to describe the component-and-connector views in UML does not represent connectors as first-class UML modelling elements, making it inconvenient to specify connector types and properties. The forthcoming UML 2.0 standard expectedly has better support for specifying software architectures.

Similarly, extracting the uses conformance view from the sources too depends on the applied (programming) style, e.g. usage of patterns, coding conventions, and so forth. Our systematic approach to conformance can be extended partly to the domain of consistency verification. Modelling style and programming style violations can be captured in rules that when checked provide insight in the overall consistency of the design or implementation [19] with respect to these rules. It is generally accepted that consistency is a desirable quality attribute.

There are two more unfortunates with our method of identifying use relations in the implementation domain. First it is unclear whether the implemented enumeration to locate use relations is complete and second the applied XPATH technology does not support a transitive closure function, which is necessary to handle nested access (e.g. A.B.C.foo()). The required breadth of the enumeration depends again on the programming style. For instance, the use of getter and setter methods circumvents the need to look for direct field access.

Intriguing research questions are to what extent we can include consistency checks in the mapping from the architecture and implementation domain views to the design-space conformance views and whether we can circumvent the need of enumerations in rules. The latter could be realised, for instance, by using canonical (intermediate) representations of artefacts?

Conformance Interpretation. In the conformance phase of the CCS, we merge the namespaces of the architecture and implementation domains. The current implementation uses string matching. Because of the human in the loop this is a workable situation. An alternative approach for string matching would be a graph matching and merging approach, in theory, because these algorithms execute in non-polynomial time. Graph matching thus automatically retrieves part of the mappings from the architecture and implementation domains to the design-space conformance viewpoint, e.g., compare the Figures 11 and 7.

Conformance checking identified covered, excess, and deficit constructs. This seems a sensible situation. However situations may occur that require more detail, i.e., specialisation of the identified constructs; an excess construct, for instance, may emerge due to namespace mismatches.

Research questions here involve means to specify, and possibly automatically resolve, conformance check results.

System Dynamics. Our CCF does not address the behaviour of the implemented system. Although various formalisms exist to describe the intended behaviour of a system, e.g., CSP and statecharts, these are not commonly used in practice [3]. Requiring such a view would therefore interfere with our prerequisite to develop a non-intrusive method for conformance checking. Furthermore, we use static views derived from the source whereas proper validation of the correct behaviour requires run-time information.

The runtime view conformance check has been executed based on a straightforward static code evaluation. This approach has drawbacks. Simple static evaluations consider the entire design space, including configurations that will not be reached in reality. Another option is to use run-time evaluations, however such a method is confined to the set of configurations of the executed test set. Alternatively sophisticated parsing and graph rewriting techniques could be used. In our implementation we rely on the consistent use of an architecture model with carefully chosen naming conventions. This yields static attachments that reveal the system configuration in the parse tree. Dynamic attachments cannot be retrieved this way.

The research question here is to find flexible parsing and logical reasoning techniques, maybe in combination with the use of runtime information.

More Related Work. Conformance checking is a systematic and quantitative approach that gives an indication of maintainability, whereas better known architecture evaluation methods such as scenario-based assessment methods (see [20]) and inspection methods (see [21]) are qualitative methods.

Methods for systematic architectural conformance checking have independently been compared in [22] and [23]. They categorise methods for architectural conformance checking, such as software reflexion methods [10] and their own expressive methods. In [22] design-space viewpoints are defined in a relational partition algebra, whereas in [23] a logic meta-modelling technique is used. Our CCF adopts the pragmatics of the efficient methods, while introducing a semantic interpretation of available artefacts.

An alternative would involve the use a code generation framework, such as the Ptolemy framework [24], extend the implementation language with architectural constructs as was done in ArchJava [25], or use an MDA-approach [26]. Such an approach directly connects architecture to implementation, improving consistency between the domains. However, this requires at least a change in the way of working of the implementation domain; it has to use a new language. This poses a barrier for implementing such an approach in practical settings.

6   Conclusions

In this paper we propose a conformance check framework (CCF) that systematically determines discrepancies between an intended architecture and the realised architecture. Illuminating these differences is a preparatory step for architecture-driven maintenance and evolution in which previously developed artefacts are reused for reasons of efficiency. Our CCF is non-intrusive. It coordinates the interaction between the architecture and the implementation domain of expertise, while regarding them autonomously. It uses readily available, possibly tailored, technology for the actual implementation of the conformance check system (CCS).

The CCF combines a colloquial engineering model and the CCS. The engineering model defines two principal categories of views on a system: runtime and development views. Checking the conformance of views from both categories requires different type of approaches. The engineering model also defines the concepts of the CCS. Two domains of expertise that independently develop view-based reasoning frameworks and a common design-space conformance viewpoint. The CCS relies on a clear definition of the design-space viewpoint and the mappings from the architectural and implementation views to this common conformance viewpoint.

The design-space viewpoint captures checkable concepts, which are the consensus between verifying abstract properties of the architecture domain and emerging properties of the implementation domain. Possible discrepancies between the domains are revealed as mismatches between the derived design-space conformance views and the impact of a mismatch on either of the domains; the severity of a mismatch is identified as part of the transformation from a domain specific viewpoint to the design-space viewpoint. We gave examples of design-space viewpoints for two principal categories of views and their mappings from architecture and implementation artefacts to this design-space viewpoint. The case study we executed uses and configures XML technology. Although the results are promising we encountered intriguing research questions, such as to what extent we can include consistency checks in CCF and how to use parsing and logic reasoning technology to implement the CCS.

Acknowledgement

This work has been sponsored in part by the Moose/Merlin ITEA projects. We thank the anonymous reviewers for their valuable comments.

References

1. MOOSE: software engineering MethOdOlogieS for Embedded systems (2004)
2. MERLIN: Embedded systems engineering in collaboration (2005)
3. Graaf, B., Lormans, M., Toetenel, H.: Embedded software engineering: state of the practice. IEEE Software **20** (2003) 61–69
4. IEEE-1471: IEEE recommended practice for architectural description of software intensive systems. IEEE Std 1471–2000 (2000)
5. van Deursen, A., Hofmeister, C., Koschke, R., Moonen, L., Riva, C.: Symphony: View-driven software architecture reconstruction. In: Proc. IEEE/IFIP Working Conf. on Software Architecture (WICSA'04). (2004) 122–134
6. Kruchten, P.B.: The 4+1 view model of architecture. IEEE Software **12** (1995) 42–50

7. Hofmeister, C., Nord, R., Soni, D.: Applied Software Architecture. Addison-Wesley (1999)
8. Clements, P., Bachmann, F., Bass, L., Garlan, D., Ivers, J., Little, R., Nord, R., Stafford, J.: Documenting Software Architectures:Views and Beyond. Addison-Wesley (2002)
9. IABG: Das v-modell: Vorgehensmodell zur planung und durchführung von it-vorhaben (1997)
10. Murphy, G.C., Notkin, D., Sullivan, K.: Software reflexion models: bridging the gap between source and high-level models. In: SIGSOFT '95: Proc. of the Symp. on Foundations of Software Engineering. (1995) 18–28
11. Stevens, P.: On associations in the unified modelling language. In: Proc. of UML 2001. Volume 2185 of Lecture Notes in Computer Science. (2001)
12. Garlan, D., Monroe, R.T., Wile, D.: ACME: architectural description of component-based systems. In: Foundations of component-based systems. Cambridge University Press (2000) 47–67
13. Medvidovic, N., Rosenblum, D.S., Redmiles, D.F., Robbins, J.E.: Modeling software architectures in the unified modeling language. ACM Trans. Softw. Eng. Methodol. **11** (2002) 2–57
14. Garlan, D., Cheng, S.W., Kompanek, A.J.: Reconciling the needs of architectural description with object-modeling notations. Science of Computer Programming **44** (2002) 23–49
15. Greg J, B.: JavaML - an XML-based source code representation for Java programs. http://www.cs.washington.edu/homes/gjb/JavaML/ (2000)
16. Al-Ekram, R., Kontogiannis, K.: An XML-based framework for language neutral program representation and generic analysis. In: Proc. of the European Conf. on Software Maintenance and Reengineering (CSMR 2005). (2005) 42–51
17. Nentwich, C., Capra, L., Emmerich, W., Finkelstein, A.: Xlinkit: a consistency checking and smart link generation service. ACM Trans. Inter. Tech. **2** (2002) 151–185
18. Michael Marconi, C.N.: Clix language specification version 1.0. http://www.clixml.org/clix/1.0/ (2004)
19. Nentwich, C., Emmerich, W., Finkelstein, A., Ellmer, E.: Flexible consistency checking. ACM Trans. Softw. Eng. Methodol. **12** (2003) 28–63
20. Dobrica, L., Niemelä, E.: A survey on software architecture analysis methods. IEEE Transactions on software Engineering **28** (2002) 638–653
21. Laitenberger, O., DeBaud, J.M.: An encompassing life cycle centric survey of software inspection. Journal System and Software **50** (2000) 5–31
22. Krikhaar, R.L.: Software architecture Reconstruction. PhD thesis, Universiteit van Amsterdam (1999)
23. Mens, K.: Automating Architectural Conformance Checking by means of Logic Meta Programming. PhD thesis, Vrije Universiteit Brussel (2002)
24. Davis, II, J., Hylands, C., Janneck, J., Lee, E.A., et al.: Overview of the ptolemy project. Technical Report UCB/ERL M01/11, University of California (2001)
25. ArchJava: Home. www.archjava.org (2005)
26. OMG: MDA. www.omg.org/mda (2005)

The Decision View of Software Architecture

Juan C. Dueñas[1,*] and Rafael Capilla[2]

[1] Department of Engineering of Telematic Systems, ETSI Telecomunicación,
Universidad Politécnica de Madrid, Ciudad Universitaria s/n, 28040 Madrid, Spain
jcduenas@dit.upm.es
[2] Department of Informatics and Telematics, Universidad Rey Juan Carlos,
c/ Tulipan s/n, 28933, Madrid, Spain
rafael.capilla@urjc.es

Abstract. Documenting software architectures is a key aspect to achieve success when communicating the architecture to different stakeholders. Several architectural views have been used with different purposes during the design process. The traditional view on software architecture defines this in terms of components and connectors. Also, the "4+1" view model proposes several views from the same design to satisfy the interests of the different stakeholders involved in the modelling process. In this position paper we try to go a step beyond previous proposals, to detail the idea of considering the architecture as a composition of architectural design decisions. We will propose a set of elements, information and graphical notation to record the design decisions during the modelling process.

1 Introduction

For years, the field of software architecture has been growing in width and depth; as key cornerstones of this evolution we could cite the discovery of architectural patterns, the agreed definition of software architecture in itself, the increasingly adopted lexical support for them (UML, for example), the generation of educated architects, the application of software architecture principles to the development of sets of systems (product lines and families), and so on. Very recently, the scope of work in the field has been widening even more by identifying quality attributes and their impact on the architecture of the systems, applying the architectures to distributed systems, and pieces in architecture that support the medium-term evolution of systems.

However, very recently the software architecture community has been facing its own limitations. The practical implementation of systems following the architectural approach proposed by this community is getting more and more complex, up to the extent of rendering the application of architectural approaches useless. Just an example of this fact is the perceived complexity (and instability) in the usage of platforms for enterprise computing; technologies such as J2EE have been available for several

---

* The work performed by Juan C. Dueñas has been partially undertaken by the FAMILIES project (Eureka 2023, ITEA ip00004), partially supported by the Spanish company Telvent and the Spanish Ministry of Science and Technology, under reference TIC2002-10373-E.

R. Morrison and F. Oquendo (Eds.): EWSA 2005, LNCS 3527, pp. 222–230, 2005.

years, but obtaining their promised benefits in practice seems still far of the average architect. Even more problems appear in the maintenance phase, due to the lack of explicit support for architectural decisions, as shown in [9].

In this position paper, we recall part of the original definitions of the software architecture [14][15], just to discover how poor has been supported one part of the architecting process. We also claim that the lack of coverage of this part of the architecture has lead to unmanageable complex architectures (such as those mentioned before); we propose to add some lexical support for this kind of key architectural information missed. At the far end of this vision, is the understanding of the architectural process as a decision making –and therefore a social and communication- process. Let us face it: building software architectures is taking design decisions but, once the architecture is there, these decisions evaporate.

2 Software Architecture Description

The software architecture of a system can be defined, using a well-known classical definition [15] as the structure of components, their relationships, and the principles and guidelines governing their design and evolution over time.

As for the representation of a system architecture composed by components and connectors, several graphical notations have been used, including UML. Also, different architecture description languages (ADL) (e.g.: ACME, C2, Wright, etc.) have been proposed and used to formalize the graphical notations describing the architecture. The need to describe the architectural products from different points of view [10] depending of the context and interests of the variety of stakeholders involved in the process has lead to define several views for each context and stakeholder. In this way, Kruchten's proposal [13] defines "4+1" views representing different viewpoints. These viewpoints shown in figure 1 are the following:

- **Logical view**: Represents an object-oriented decomposition of the design supporting the functional requirements of the future system.
- **Process view**: Represents the concurrency and synchronization aspects of the design and some non-functional requirements. Distribution aspects and processes (i.e.: executable units) of the systems as well as the tasks are represented in the process view.
- **Physical view**: Represents the mapping of the software onto hardware pieces. Non-functional requirements are represented in this view and the software subsystems are represented through processing nodes.
- **Development view**: Represents the static organization of the software in its environment. The development architecture view organizes software subsystems into packages in a hierarchy or layers. The responsibility of each layer is defined in the development view.
- **Use case view**: Represents the scenarios that reflect the process associated to a set of system's requirements. This view is redundant to the previous ones but it serves to discover architectural elements and for validation purposes.

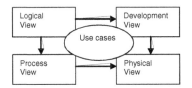

Fig. 1. The "4+1" view model (Kruchten)

The correspondence between the views of figure 1 can be performed to connect elements from one view to another. There are other classifications of views to be taken into account, and some of them have received widespread attention by the community of practitioners in the area (see [8] and [17]). In addition to this, other authors [12] propose a viewtype of the architecture associated to aspects. These authors introduce a conceptual model called *aspect architecture* which is considered as a software architecture viewtype. They propose a new UML diagram type called "concerns diagram" for modelling architectural views of aspects. Finally, in [5] the authors mention a new classification for architectural views called *viewtypes* for documenting purposes. A viewtype defines the types of elements and relationships used to describe the architecture from a particular point of view or perspective. More than defining new architectural views, they [5] try to modernize and make clear for the stakeholders the documentation generated during the architectural construction process. Also, they mention the need to record the rationale of the design decisions as part of the information needed when documenting software architectures but they do not mention how to record these design decisions in order to be used afterwards if needed.

The architectural construction process involves several elements and aspects for which the resultant software architecture constitutes the most visible part of the overall design process. Software projects involve several actors or stakeholders during the project lifecycle and the "view" of these stakeholders is quite different for each them. Therefore, the need to represent different views or viewpoints at the design level is a usual task [8].

There are many situations such as: the loss or non-existence of designs, reengineering legacy systems, evolution of architectural products, or even changes in the development team; in which it is mandatory to record the design decisions from which the software architecture was obtained at a first instance. Design decisions represent the cornerstone to obtain suitable software architectures because they represent the rationale that motivated the election of architectural patterns and styles, the functional blocks that represent systems and subsystems in the architecture, the relationships among them and the control of the architecture. Our position in this paper and following recent proposals [3] is to modernize the concept of software architecture making the design decisions explicit, and adding them a "new" viewpoint respect to the traditional approaches. Our proposal tries to detail the representation of this decision view in the architectural construction process. The traditional views of software architecture provide information enough to understand the pieces of the system under development, and also information useful to trace the requirements and features the system must fulfill, but, to date, there is no information about why a certain component or connector has been chosen, nor why other similar elements have been rejected in the architecture. Is this information about the "why" what we try to represent in the decision view.

3 Requirements for the Decision View in Software Architecture

Again on the software architecture definition, we have seen that the structure of the system's components and relationships is described using the traditional architectural views. Also in the software architecture there are "principles and guidelines" that are out of the scope of the traditional architectural views. Since the information about principles and guidelines is still required to create the system, current practice is to create natural language documentation (or even worse, keep the knowledge on the architects' minds).

But even for these less traditional topics there are proposals worth taking into account, although most of them come from the domain of requirements engineering, such as the NFR (non-functional requirements) framework proposed by Chung [4], that characterizes stakeholders and their relationships in order to structure the decision making process launched by the tradeoffs between conflicting quality requirements. Also, in this track we can allocate the well-known ATAM method [2] and derivatives. These methods are practical enough to be used in industrial settings; however, these methods focus on the decision making process based on stakeholders. There are reasons important in order to understand the decisions taken as a result of these decision making processes, that are not made explicit, and therefore the reasons for decisions can not be linked to the architectural information (the other traditional views).

Using version management on the architectural views (storing the changes made on each of the architectural views) is not a complete solution; first this method was attempted some years ago and lead to so many deltas (in configuration management terminology) that the method shown to be useless; even worse, if the deltas were not annotated with the knowledge that drive the architects to the next version, it was impossible to replay the process.

Recent advances for supporting traceability between requirements and architectures can also help in solving part of the problem [16]. In fact, for those decisions that come directly from requirements affecting architectural elements in a 1:1 relationship, the approach may be useful. But for the decisions affecting to large regions of the architectural models (this is the case with architectural significant requirements [11] and some quality attributes), the traceability mechanisms introduce much more complexity and therefore render useless.

There are other methods –albeit old- that may help in describing the decisions that guide the architecting process: the design space theory, the application of Quality Function Deployment, Design Decision Trees [1][7], etc. When these formalisms and methods were first applied to software architecture, the lack of unified notation for the other architectural views was a key problem; nowadays, the problem seems to be partially solved by using UML.

Some of the requirements stated then for the support of the decision view seem applicable right now [6]:

- **Multi-perspective support** to provide support to the different stakeholders.
- **Visual representation** so the decisions can be easily understood and "replayed".
- **Complexity control**: since in large systems the set of decisions is also large, some kind of mechanism (hierarchy, navigation, abstraction) is required in order to keep it under control. The "scalability" requirement is closely related to this one.
- **Groupware support**: this is now as an acknowledged fact that several stakeholders must interact in order to check and solve their conflicts.
- **Gradual formalization** because the decision making process is a learning process and thus the decisions evolve over time.

Once a lexical support for design decisions representation is found, the architecting process becomes a knowledge management process in which the product of the application of this knowledge produces the architectural models of the other views. We understand by "knowledge management process" that dealing with the explicit description of knowledge, the definition of the links from that knowledge to the organization that holds it and to any other element affected by this knowledge, and the support to the evolution of the knowledge and the links. Therefore, the process is able to explain why these elements have been chosen, which have been discarded and how this particular selection fulfills the system requirements. Some of the activities in this architectural-knowledge management process are:

- **Growth-refinement**: The design decisions are not isolated. As mentioned before, there is a gradual formalization that appears when architectural assessment activities are performed (both during the creation of the architecture and when architectural recovery and architectural conformance activities are done). The knowledge base formed by decisions is enlarged.
- **Dissemination and learning**: The knowledge base containing decisions is the key asset in order to learn the architecture process and this is precisely the point we try to illustrate at the beginning of this contribution: in order to cope with large or complex architectures, the ability to record and replay the decisions, provided by the explicit description of them is a key element.
- **Exploration-application**: the application of design decisions should get to the same architecture if the stakeholders, requirements and trade-offs are the same. Applying the same decisions on a different set of requirements would lead to a different architecture.

4   The Decision View of Software Architecture

The need to represent design decisions as a key aspect in the architectural construction process has lead us to propose a new view called the *decision view*. This new view has to be defined and represented in the architecture documentation so any of the stakeholders can use it later if needed.

Several reasons for record design decisions are: changes in the development team, design recovery needs, loss of designs, forward and backward traces between requirements and design products, etc. From our point of view, the explicit representation of design decisions becomes a key factor for building and communicating the software architecture.

Design decisions should connect requirements and architectural products in order to record and discover the rationale of the decisions taken during the design construction process. The information we believe a design decision should include for representing this using a UML notation or similar is the following:

- **Iteration Number**: Due that the software architecture is the outcome of an iterative process in which several design decisions are taken, we need to record the iteration of a particular decision.
- **Following Iteration**: It points to the following iteration in the design process, where iteration means the next step in the application of the design decisions, that renders an architectural model (maybe an intermediate model).
- **Decision Rule**: Represents the name of the decision rule taken by the architect. The motivation of the decision should be explicitly described here.
- **Decision Rule Number**: It numbers a specific decision rule
- **Following Decision Rule Number**: It points to the following decision rule and is used for tracing purposes or for tracking the decisions made.
- **Pattern / Style Applied**: Represents the pattern or style applied for a particular design decision. They are used to impose restrictions to a particular architectural element during the design construction process.
- **Associated Use Cases**: Represents the numbers or names of one or more use cases associated to a particular design decision. This is used to connect the architectural product to a set of requirements.

Figure 2 provides a graphical representation of a decision element which can be modelled employing a new UML element. This new element will serve to record and represent the design decisions with the information given above. Let us remark that, being a prospective work, the structure and lexical support for decisions is not definitive; in particular, the figure shows a sequential structure of decisions, but more complex topologies for interconnection may appear (binary trees [11] may be considered as a typical topology, although more complex decision networks may appear).

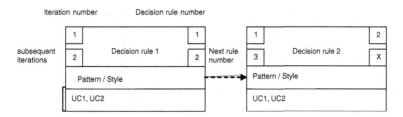

Fig. 2. Representation of the information included in the decision element

In this way, we can modify the figure proposed by Kruchten [13] to include the decision view as an intermediate element between requirements and other design views, such as figure 3 shows. The arrows in the figure indicate precedence or causality (so, for example, the decision view affects the physical view). The determination of the phase on which these views should be created is delegated to the development process. Also important to notice that this decision view is dealing with the software architecture, so it is likely that there is another decision view for requirements specification.

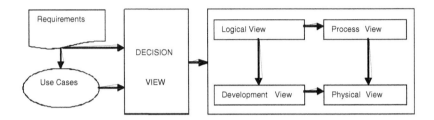

Fig. 3. The decision view model of software architecture

One key aspect when recording design decisions is how to associate these to architectural elements when we represent graphically the architectural products. For each of the iterations performed during the design process, we can assign a decision element (shown in figure 2) to each architectural element or work product. Adding backward traceability from the architectural element to the decisions that affect it may be helpful in the dissemination and learning activities mentioned in section 3. For subsequent iterations, the design decisions elements will expand to describe the rationale of the design decisions taken during the process.

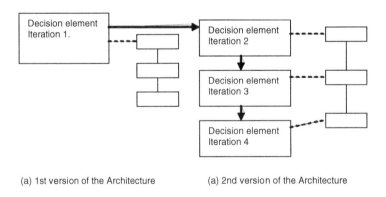

(a) 1st version of the Architecture   (a) 2nd version of the Architecture

Fig. 4. Decisions elements associated to architectural elements

Figure 4 shows an example of two iterations performed during an architectural construction process. The first iteration applies a layered style for the architecture and assigns a decision element for that. The following iteration applies other architectural styles and design decisions rules for each layer. The decisions elements shown in figure 4 are used to record and link the decisions taken.

5 A Proposal for the Implementation of the Decision View

In our proposal, so far, the key elements in the decision view are the links, or the relations between pieces of information, plus pieces of text for the rationale. The implementation of such should be the simplest if some kind of success in the industrial stage is sought. A principle just discovered in other branches of engineering may well be applied here: the quality and size of the links are more important than the qualities of the nodes. The practical application of this fact is that the decision view can be deployed as a hyperlinked documentation on top of the other views. We foresee two potential implementations for this network of knowledge: the provision of specific notations for decisions as extensions to the UML, supported by specific tools; and also the mapping of the knowledge structure to a web-based network that fosters the usage of the decision view as a communication and cooperation tool.

We are currently working towards this view; we expect that, once a knowledge base containing architectural decisions is created, and these decisions are linked between them and to the elements of the other architectural views, some activities performed in the development of the system can be supported by the navigation on that network of models. This way of understanding the software development can be called "building by browsing".

References

1. Alonso, A., León, G., Dueñas, J.C., de la Puente, J. A.: Framework for documenting design decisions in product families development. In Proceedings of the Third International Conference on Engineering of Complex Computer Systems, Como, Italia, September (1997).
2. Bass L., Clements P. and Kazman R.: Software Architecture in Practice, 2nd edition, Addison-Wesley, (2003).
3. Bosch, J.: Software Architecture: The Next Step, Proceedings of the 1st European Workshop on Software Architecture (EWSA 2004), Springer-Verlag, LNCS 3047, pp. 194-199 (2004).
4. Chung, L., Nixon, B., Yu, E. and Mylopoulos, J.: Non-functional requirements in software engineering. Kluwer Academic Publishers, (2000)
5. Clements P., Bachman F., Bass, L., Garlan D., Ivers J., Little R., Nord R. and Stafford J.: Documenting Software Architectures. Views and Beyond, Addison-Wesley (2003).
6. Dueñas, J. C., Hauswirth, M.: Hyper-linked Software Architectures for Concurrent Engineering. In Proceedings of Concurrent Engineering Europe 97, Erlangen-Nuremberg, Germany, pp: 3-10. Society for Computer Simulation. (1997)
7. Dueñas, J. C., León, G.: An introduction to evolution of large systems based on Software Architectures. In Systems Implementation 2000, IFIP TC2 WG2.4 Working Conference on Systems Implementation 2000, Berlin, Germay, February. Chapman and Hall, (1998) 128-139.

8. Gomaa, H., Shin, E.: A Multiple View Meta-modeling Approach for Variability Management in Software Product Lines. Eighth International Conference on Software Reuse: Methods, Techniques and Tools. LNCS 3107, Springer Verlag, (2004)

9. Graaf, L.: Maintainability through Architecture Development. F. Oquendo (Ed) Proceedings of the First European Workshop on Software Architecture, LNCS 3047, Springer Verlag, (2004)

10. IEEE Recommended Practice for Architectural Description of Software-Intensive Systems, IEEE Std 1471-2000 (2000).

11. Jazayeri, M., Ran, A., van der Linden (eds): "Software Architecture for Product Families", Addison-Wesley, (2000).

12. Katara M. and Katz S.: Architectural Views of Aspects. Proceedings of AOSD 2003, Boston, USA, ACM, pp.1-10 (2003).

13. Kruchten P. Architectural Blueprints. The "4+1" View Model of Software Architecture. IEEE Software 12 (6), pp.42-50 (1995).

14. Perry, D., Wolf, A.: Foundations for the Study of Software Architecture. ACM SIGSOFT Software Engineering Notes, 17/4, October (1992)

15. Shaw M. and Garlan D.: Software Architecture, Prentice Hall (1996).

16. Stuart, D., Sull, W., Cook, T. W.: Dependency Navigation in Product Lines Using XML. Third International Workshop on Software Architectures for Product Families, F. van der Linden (ed), LNCS 1951, Springer Verlag, (2000)

17. Woods, E.: Experiences Using Viewpoints for Information Systems Architecture: An Industrial Experience Report. F. Oquendo (Ed) Proceedings of the First European Workshop on Software Architecture, LNCS 3047, Springer Verlag, (2004)

Towards Context-Sensitive Intelligence

Holger Mügge[1], Tobias Rho[1], Marcel Winandy[1], Markus Won[1],
Armin B. Cremers[1], Pascal Costanza[2], and Roman Englert[3]

[1] Institute of Computer Science III, University of Bonn,
Römerstr. 164, 53117 Bonn, Germany
{muegge, rho, winandy, won, abc}@iai.uni-bonn.de

[2] Programming Technology Lab, Vrije Universiteit Brussel,
Pleinlaan 2, 1050 Brussels, Belgium
pc@p-cos.net

[3] Deutsche Telekom Laboratories,
Ernst-Reuter-Platz 7, 10587 Berlin, Germany
Roman.Englert@telekom.de

Abstract. Even modern component architectures do not provide for easily manageable context-sensitive adaptability, a key requirement for ambient intelligence. The reason is that components are too large – providing black boxes with adaptation points only at their boundaries – and to small – lacking good means for expressing concerns beyond the scope of single components – at the same time. We present a framework that makes components more fine-grained so that adaptation points inside of them become accessible, and more coarse-grained so that changes of single components result in the necessary update of structurally constrained dependants. This will lead to higher quality applications that fit better into personalized and context-aware usage scenarios.

1 Introduction

Most of the software sold nowadays are off-the-shelf products designed to meet the requirements of very different types of users. One way to meet these requirements is to design software that is flexible in such a way that it can be used in very different contexts. Thus, look and feel, functionality, and behavior have to be tailorable or even adaptive according to the task that needs to be fulfilled. Especially out of an organizational context most users have to tailor their software on their own. Taken into account that experiences in the use of computer systems in general increase exceedingly, tailorable and end user development applications become interesting topics. Component architectures were basically developed with the idea of higher reusability of parts of software. Furthermore, it is shown that they also build a basis for highly flexible software [1]. In this case the same operations that are used to compose software out of single components now can be applied to existing (component-based) software during runtime. Therefore, the basis for a tailoring language consists basically of three kinds of operations: choosing components, parameterizing them, binding

R. Morrison and F. Oquendo (Eds.): EWSA 2005, LNCS 3527, pp. 231–238, 2005.

them together. In this way very simple operations that can be easily understood by end users enhance the possibilities of tailoring software in a powerful way (cf. [2]).

2   Intelligent Dealing with Complexity

Still, there are several open questions according to how tailoring can be eased for end users. For instance, there is a need for a graphical front end that allows visual tailoring techniques. Here one problem is how invisible components can be presented to the users. In different studies it was shown (cf. [1]) that users are able to tailor their GUIs very easily. Nevertheless, the problem of finding an appropriate visual tailoring environment for both - visible and invisible components - is still unsolved.

A second problem is that tailoring becomes harder when more flexibility is needed. Flexibility in component architectures designed for tailorable applications is reached by a higher degree of decomposition [1]. That means, the more components are needed to design software, the more flexible it can be tailored as there are many fine-grained components that can be parameterized or exchanged.

Our goal is to design a stable basis for highly flexible software systems. Component architectures are appropriate in this case and thus concentrating on the second problem.

There are several approaches which may ease the use of software in different contexts. In our case we believe in a combination of tailorable software (user is in an active role) and adaptive techniques (software does adaptions by itself). This might be helpful to cope with the complexity problem. Combining both techniques means that tailoring activities are followed by automatic adaptions of the system which checks for dependencies within the composition and adjusts it.

Another point is the inspection of contexts: How do contexts look like and how can they influence the software system? The abstraction of different use contexts and their explicit description can reduce complexity of the components as context descriptions influence more the whole composition. If the context changes, users have only to switch the current context description which leads to changed functionality of the whole composition.

Furthermore, one source of complexity is that many applications run distributed and networked. In such systems (client-server, peer-2-peer) tailoring becomes even harder as adaptations on one client or one server might have dependencies on another part of the application which runs on a different machine. In such cases server components have to behave according to different clients. In section 3 we describe three basic techniques which can overcome these problems. After that we show how they can be integrated within one component framework in section 4.

3   Contributing Parts

We build our framework for CSI on top of three pillars: Generalized aspect weaving (3.1), adaptation of thread-local features (3.2), and structure elicitation and constraint checking (3.3).

3.1   LogicAJ

Modularization on component level fails on *crosscutting concerns*[3]. These can not be located in one place and are therefore scattered over several components. Examples are persistence, distribution[4], security[1] [5], synchronization and parallelization. Aspect languages modularize crosscutting concerns in a new construct: aspects. Aspects keep the code belonging to the concern in one place and describe where the code should be woven into the base program.

The following properties are necessary for an aspect language in an adaptive environment:

Expressiveness: In an evolving environment aspects must deal with an unanticipated structure of components and types. Aspects must therefore be highly generic to be independent from the lexical structure of a base program.

Static Type Safety: Expressiveness should not come with a loss of static type safety. Runtime checks and reflective techniques should not be used to avoid runtime errors in aspect execution and weaving[2].

Dynamic: Aspects need to be applicable and removable at runtime to react on changes of the application context.

Current aspect languages refer to fixed names for concrete entities of the base program, where reusable implementations would require role names that can be bound to concrete entities when the pattern (resp. aspect) is instantiated. Therefore, these implementations must be modified for every program and program modifications.

A generic aspect language allows aspects to use logic variables that can range over syntactic entities of the host language. In a Java-based generic aspect language, for instance, logic variables could match anything from packages and types down to individual statements, modifiers and throws-declarations. In particular, it is possible to create new code based on previous matches. In this respect, logic variables are more expressive than "*" pattern matching (e.g in AspectJ), where two occurrences of "*" do not represent the same value.

The modularization of crosscutting concerns by dynamic aspects enables the application to be configurable at runtime. Dependent on the context different aspects adapt the application.

---

[1]   authentication, secure socket code, ...

[2]   the application of the aspect to the base program.

For example consider a client application connected to a server with sensitive data. Depending on the current network connection different aspects are woven: If the connection is unsecured[3] the simple socket code is replaced with a ssl implementation. After detecting poor network performance a caching aspect is applied. Now the user maximizes the application window. An aspect adapts the content and shows based on the profile of the user more detailed information on the current task.

In a distributed environment these changes affect components which may also be used by other components in a different context. The next section (3.2) shows how we can deal with different component adaptations at the same time.

3.2   Dynamic Scoping

A definition is said to be dynamically scoped if at any point in time during the execution of a program, its binding is looked up in the current call stack as opposed to the lexically apparent binding in the source code of that program. The latter case is referred to as lexical scoping. An important property of dynamic scoping is that it fits naturally with multi-threaded programs when the new binding to a dynamically scoped variable is restricted to the current thread. Almost all programming languages in wide use employ lexical scoping but do not offer dynamic scoping. Notable exceptions are Common Lisp, various Scheme implementations, and recent attempts at introducing dynamic scoping into C++ [6] and Haskell [7].

We have achieved a similar level of usefulness when adding dynamic scoping for function definitions, and we have described two different working implementations of that idea in [8, 9]. A similar extension for Java looks as follows. Assume we have a method in a mobile application that performs an operation which may cause a large cost on the user's side. For example, it contacts a payed service on the network. The user may be interested in that method behaving differently depending on various contexts. For example, it should pop up a dialog that asks for authentication first for security reasons, it should simulate some useful response from the service in order to explore the possibilities, or it should just prevent the method from executing at all when lending the mobile device to some other user. An activation of such context-specific behavior looks as follows:

```
with {
  contactExpensiveService () {
    if askUser("Are you sure?") proceed();
    else throw new ServiceException();
  }
}{
  runApplication();
}
```

---

[3] For example, the connection uses an untrusted network and no VPN connection is active.

An important ingredient to make such context-specific behavior work is the `proceed` command that executes the original definition of the redefined method. This is reminiscent of `proceed` in AspectJ [3] and `call-next-method` in CLOS. Without such a `proceed` command, a dynamically scoped redefinition would only be able to completely replace an existing method (and this is an important difference to dynamically scoped variables).

According to the code above, the new definition for `contactExpensive Service`first asks the user for an acknowledgement and then either proceeds with execution of the original method or rejects its execution. Without a notion of dynamically scoped methods, such a behavior modification would only be possible by inserting appropriate `if` statements into the base code, leading to error-prone and hard-to-maintain code. With dynamically scoped methods, all the different contexts are cleanly separated within their threads and can be modified independently from each other. So in the case of method definitions, dynamic scoping again helps to avoid cluttering code with context-specific behavior.

3.3   Structural Constraints

Complex software usually comprises many variation points each with a number of different variants (as defined by van Gurp et al. in [10]). As a result increasing adaptability leads to a combinatorial explosion of potential adaptations. Separation of concerns as shown in sections 3.1 and 3.2 prevents the code from being polluted by scattered and intransparent conditional statements. But nevertheless the complexity shows up when the variation points are designed or the software is going to be configured, i.e. when one particular adaptation scenario has to be chosen. We need to know which variants can or should be combined and which must not or what consequences a certain adaptation implies.

This knowledge is not contained in the software per se. It is meta-information derived from application semantics or technical context for example and usually only given implicitly as Dolstra et al. point out in [11]. To tackle these issues, we integrate the framework PatchWork which allows for modelling complex structural conditions as explicit meta-data. It enables defining structure schemata relations between role sets with constraints imposed on them. Instances of a structure schema can be checked against these relational constraints and the software composition can be guided by the relational structure.

We demonstrate the usage of such structural meta-data with the following scenario: assume our software system comprises three functionalities a, b and c and offers the user two different and complete ways to access them, *menu-driven* and via *key shortcuts*. Both the functionality set and the set of access ways are configurable, hence they represent variation points [10].

Now, we want to enhance our software with a third way of user access via *speech recognition*. Figure 1 illustrates the performed adaptations. The table shows an instance of an underlying structure schema defining three role sets

Functionality (F)	User Access (U)		New way of access
	menu-driven	key shortcuts	speech recognition
a	$i_{m,a}$	$i_{k,a}$	$i_{s,a}$
b	$i_{m,b}$	$i_{k,b}$	
c	$i_{m,c}$	$i_{k,c}$	$i_{s,c}$

Fig. 1. Structural meta-data in the background supporting software adaptation

(functionalities F, user access ways U and implementations I), a ternary relation R between them, and a constraint on R which guarantees accessibility of each function by each user access way. The initial situation is depicted with solid lines in the table. Initially holds $F = \{a, b, c\}$, $U = \{menu\text{-}driven, key\text{-}shortcut\}$, and $I = \{i_{m,a}, i_{m,b}, i_{m,c}, i_{k,a}, \ldots\}$.

First, we add speech recognition as a new user access way. It is represented in our meta-data as a new player for the *user-access-ways role*, i.e. *speech-recognition* $\in U$. The underlying structure schema declares R to be total in $F \times U$, so we are forced to add valid tuples for each functionality to R, as shown in figure 1 with dotted lines.

In a *second* step we realize that functionality b is too complex to be accessed by speech recognition (i.e. there will be no element $i_{s,b}$ shown as the empty grey cell in figure 1). Hence, we must loosen our initial totality condition on R to allow that speech recognition does not offer access to all functionalities. We adjust the structure schema so that the constraint on R only demands totality in F so that it still guarantees at least one way of access for each functionality. Even though this may look like we simply give up a part of our initial requirements, we are forced to do that explicitly and consciously.

Finally as a *third* step we consider what happens when the usage context allows only to use speech recognition, i. e. $U = \{speech\text{-}recognition\}$. Now, totality of R in F is violated because the required tuple for b is missing. This could for example lead to automatically reducing the functionality set to $F = \{a, c\}$ so that the structural constraints hold again.

In reality the situation quickly gets more complex since one has to take into account contextual aspects like: device capabilities, access rights, location etc., therefore explicit modelling structural constraints becomes even more useful.

4   Summary

Our three approaches provide the following additional means to influence the behavior of component-based applications (see Figure 2): (1) LogicAJ helps im-

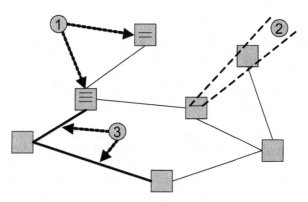

Fig. 2. Our approaches for an advanced component framework: (1) Generic aspect-oriented programming allows dealing with advanced crosscutting concerns; (2) dynamic scoping allows influencing the program's behavior from certain contexts without interfering with others; (3) PatchWork allows expressing and controlling structural constraints

plementing aspects that implement crosscutting concerns and are highly generic to be applicable in different contexts. (2) Dynamically scoped methods provide a mechanism for behavioral changes of an application that can be confined to thread boundaries without affecting other threads, leading to a natural mapping of contexts to threads. (3) Finally, elicitation of structural constraints and automatic checking of such constraints ensure that local changes to single components either do not violate coarse-grained, non-localizable dependencies, or else even trigger the subsequent automatic correction of dependents to adapt to the new environment.

These different approaches already substantially improve context-sensitive adaptability. However, a combination of these approaches has interesting synergistic effects: Dynamically scoped methods can be extended towards dynamically scoped activation of generic aspects while structural constraints are automatically maintained beyond traditional component-based means of adaptation. We have carried out first experiments to see whether our approaches indeed complement each other in this way, and the results thereof are very promising.

Security of adaptation is another important issue because new functionality may come from an untrustworthy source. Existing protection mechanisms must not be corrupted or by-passed and missing mechanisms should be added automatically.

Future work includes building a stable and secure software architecture that incorporates the ideas that we have sketched in this paper on the technology side, and carrying out user studies to understand to what extent end users are capable of dealing with our new abstractions.

References

1. Morch, A.I., Stevens, G., Won, M., Klann, M., Dittrich, Y., Wulf, V.: Component-based technologies for end-user development. Communications of the ACM **9** (2004) 59–66
2. Won, M., Stiemerling, O., Wulf, V.: Component-based approaches to tailorable systems. In Lieberman, H., P.F., Wulf, V., eds.: End User Development. Kluwer Academic (2005)
3. Kiczales, G., Hilsdale, E., Hugunin, J., Kersten, M., Palm, J., Griswold, W.G.: An overview of AspectJ. In Knudsen, J.L., ed.: ECOOP 2001 — Object-Oriented Programming 15th European Conference, Budapest Hungary. Volume 2072 of Lecture Notes in Computer Science. Springer-Verlag, Berlin (2001) 327–353
4. Silaghi, R., Strohmeier, A.: Better generative programming with generic aspects. (2003) 2nd International Workshop on Generative Techniques in the Context of MDA, OOPSLA 2003, Available as Technical Report, N IC/2003/80, Swiss Federal Institute of Technology in Lausanne, Switzerland, December 2003.
5. Viega, J., Bloch, J., Chandra, P.: Applying aspect-oriented programming to security. Cutter IT Journal **14** (2001) 31–39
6. Hanson, D.R., Proebsting, T.A.: Dynamic variables. In: Proceedings of the ACM SIGPLAN '01 Conference on Programming Language Design and Implementation, Snowbird, Utah (2001) 264–273
7. Lewis, J.R., Shields, M., Launchbury, J., Meijer, E.: Implicit parameters: Dynamic scoping with static types. In: Symposium on Principles of Programming Languages, ACM Press (2000) 108–118
8. Costanza, P.: Dynamically scoped functions as the essence of aop. In: ECOOP 2003 Workshop on Object-Oriented Language Engineering for the Post-Java Era, Darmstadt, Germany, July 22, 2003, ACM Press (2003)
9. Costanza, P.: A short overview of AspectL. In: European Interactive Workshop on Aspects in Software (EIWAS'04), Berlin, Germany. (2004)
10. van Gurp, J., Bosch, J., Svahnberg, M.: The notion of variability in software product lines. In: Proceedings of The Working IEEE/IFIP Conference on Software Architecture (WICSA 2001). (2001) 45–55
11. Dolstra, E., Florijn, G., Visser, E.: Timeline variability: The variability of binding time of variation points. In van Gurp, J., Bosch, J., eds.: Workshop on Software Variability Modeling (SVM'03). Number 2003-7-01 in IWI preprints, Groningen, The Netherlands, Reseach Institute of Computer Science and Mathematics, University of Groningen (2003)

Architecture Description for Mobile Distributed Systems

Volker Gruhn and Clemens Schäfer

University of Leipzig,Faculty of Mathematics and Computer Science,
Chair for Applied Telematics / e-Business*,
Klostergasse 3, 04109 Leipzig, Germany
{gruhn, schaefer}@ebus.informatik.uni-leipzig.de

Abstract. In this paper we motivate an Architecture Description Language (ADL) for mobile distributed systems based on the π-calculus. Different from other approaches, the non-functional properties, which are essential when mobile architectures are described, are treated in a flexible manner by inserting logical formulae for expressing and checking non-functional properties into π-calculus processes. A formal example is given to illustrate the approach before the constituents of the ADL are sketched.

1 Motivation

Modeling the architecture of mobile distributed systems using a domain-specific architecture description language (ADL) is considered as an useful approach [1], since the influence of mobility emphasizes the necessity to examine functional properties of software architectures as well as non-functional properties. This corresponds to the fact that "mobility represents a total meltdown of all stability assumptions ... associated with distributed computing" [2], which subsumes the problems software engineers have to face in practice when they build mobile distributed systems. Examples for these problems are network structures, which are no longer fixed and where nodes may come and go, communication failures due to lost links over wireless networks, or restricted connectivity due to low bandwidth of mobile communications links. These all have in common that they affect the non-functional properties of a system like performance, robustness, security, or quality of service. Besides non-functional properties, these intrinsic challenges of mobile systems may also affect the functional aspects of a system, since a mobile system may have to provide extra functionality (like replication facilities, caching mechanisms etc.) in order to ensure usability in situations where the aforementioned problems occur. With *Con Moto* (Italian for "in motion") we propose an ADL which enables system developers to address these issues during the early stages of system development in order to allow them to make appropriate design choices for mobile systems.

---

* The chair for Applied Telematics/e-Business is endowed by Deutsche Telekom AG.

R. Morrison and F. Oquendo (Eds.): EWSA 2005, LNCS 3527, pp. 239–246, 2005.

2   Introduction

ADLs have been area of research for many years. It is commonly understood that an ADL comprises three essential constituents: components, connectors and configurations [3]. Roughly speaking, components model the entities of software systems which perform computations or store data, connectors model the interaction of components, and configurations are connected graphs of components and connectors. Based on this understanding and the motivation given before, we can list the requirements for an ADL for mobile distributed systems:

- A mobile ADL must be able to model dynamic aspects of a system like the dynamic instantiation of components or the change of communication links during system execution.
- A mobile ADL should be able to model different communication channels with non-functional properties like reliability or bandwidth. This is necessary to analyze systems and to find possible problems that might arise when a connection fails. Therefore specialized connectors might be necessary.
- A mobile ADL should allow the composition of non-functional properties in order to be able to model the complex dependencies which are prominent in mobile distributed systems.
- A mobile ADL should be formally based, so that simulation and reasoning about the model is possible.

With Con Moto we strive to fulfill these requirements. The remainder of this paper is structured as follows. After an overview of the related work in section 3, an introduction in π-calculus (section 4.1) is given which acts as basis for the formal example in section 4.2, which illustrates the core concept of our considerations. After depicting the use of the formal model in Con Moto (section 5), a conclusion is drawn.

3   Related Work

ADLs in general have been topic of research in previous years. The necessity for modeling non-functional properties in architecture description has been recognized by Shaw and Garlan [4]. The classification work of Medvidovic and Taylor [5] present a sound compilation of properties of ADLs. From their work it becomes obvious, that none of the ADLs presented there is suitable for modeling dynamic aspects of mobile systems. In the past, this fact lead to the development of mobile ADLs which have recently been presented. The ArchWare project with its π-ADL [6] is one result of these efforts. Another mobile ADL can be found in the works of Issarny et al. [7]. Both present an ADL for mobile systems based on Milner's π-calculus [8]. These ADLs have in common that they are able model the dynamics of mobile systems, which is due to their theoretical foundation in the π-calculus. Although they vary in terms of elaboration and tool support, the fundamental difference—from the perspective of this paper—is the treatment of non-functional properties, which is absent in the π-ADL approach. Issarny addresses non-functional properties in her work, but the treatment of non-functional properties is bound to a global conformance condition, which must hold for a predefined set of non-functional properties assigned to components and connectors, and does not allow the composition of non-functional properties, which is novel in our approach. Currently, there is other research in the area non-functional properties of software systems. This work is mainly based on the Lamport's TLA+ language [9], which is a logic for specifying and reasoning about concurrent and reactive systems. Zschaler [10] presents a specification of timeliness properties of component based systems, but these as well as the underlying work of Aagedal [11], where the integration of TLA+ approach into architectural description is proposed, the models in TLA+ lack the support for mobility and are thus not regarded further.

4   System Model

4.1   Use of π-Calculus

Similar to the approach of Issarny et al. [7], we base Con Moto on a service-oriented interaction paradigm, i.e. a component abstracts a networked service which invokes operations of peer components and dually executes operations that are invoked. Processes are the foundation for grasping the functional aspects of the architectural description. Since we use Milner's π-calculus [8] for modeling, we give a very brief introduction into the monadic π-calculus (c.f. [12]) first: The simplest entities of the π-calculus are *names*. These can be seen as names of communication links and used by processes for interaction. These processes evolve by performing actions. Capability for actions are expressed as *prefixes*, of which we use three kinds[1]:

$$\pi ::= \overline{x}(y) \mid x(z) \mid [x = y]\pi . \tag{1}$$

The first capability is to send the name y via the name x, and the second to receive a name via x. The third is a conditional capability: the capability π if x and y are the same name. The *processes* and *summations* of the π-calculus are given by:

$$P ::= M \mid P \mid P' \mid !P \tag{2}$$
$$M ::= \mathbf{0} \mid \pi.P \mid M + M' \mid \mathbf{1}. \tag{3}$$

The semantics are as follows. $\mathbf{0}$ means inaction, the prefix $\pi.P$ means that P can be executed after π has been exercised; the sum $M + M'$ models a choice, the composition $P \mid P'$ is known as parallelism; $!P$ means replication. $\mathbf{1}$ is an extension by ourselves and has the notion of a "dummy" process: A process that can always

---

[1] We omit the non-observable action τ and binding of names for shortness.

be executed and does not perform any actions. We need this extension in our later example.[2] However, for modeling non-functional properties it is not enough to just exchange names between processes. We therefore make use of the polyadic π-calculus, which extends the monadic π-calculus in that way that tuples can be passed by actions instead of names. This leads to the following prefixes

$$\pi ::= \overline{x}(\widetilde{y}) \mid x(\widetilde{z}) \mid [x = y]\pi, \tag{4}$$

where no names occur more than once in the tuple $\widetilde{z}$ in an input prefix. In the following example we will use this polyadic π-calculus to illustrate our core idea. However, an formally exact treatment of this issue would require the usage of typed π-calculi, which we omit here for the sake of readability.

4.2   Formal Example

As in Issarny's work [7], we use processes given in π-calculus for expressing the functional properties of our architecture. We now extend the processes to cover also non-functional properties. The core idea behind this approach is, that every action in our processes can return its non-functional properties like execution time, memory consumption, availability etc. We will now introduce two components and their services and will show how their non-functional properties can be handled. However, we show the treatment only for abstract non-functional properties, since concrete properties would increase formal complexity, but would not contribute to the core idea.

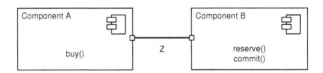

Fig. 1. Example components in UML-like notation

Assume the following scenario: as intuitively depicted in Figure 1 we have two components A and B. A offers the service $buy()$, whereas B offers the services $reserve()$ and $commit()$, which are subsequently invoked during the execution of $buy()$. Since $reserve()$ and $commit()$ have a certain set of non-functional properties, it is intuitively clear that the non-functional properties of $buy()$ should be a composition of the properties of $reserve()$ and $commit()$.

If we leave away all other aspects and just model the functional behaviour of A and B, we write in monadic π-calculus:

$$P_B \stackrel{\text{def}}{=} reserve(x).\overline{reserve}(x).\mathbf{0} \mid commit(x).\overline{commit}(x).\mathbf{0} \tag{5}$$

---

[2] Although **1** is formally not absolutely necessary for our modeling purposes, it enhances readability in the later examples. Formally we define the following reaction for our "dummy" process: $1.\pi \rightarrow \pi$.

```
component A: { provides { buy()      nfprop α() }
               requires { reserve() ensure β'()
                          commit() ensure γ'() } }
component B: { provides { reserve() nfprop β()
                          commit() nfprop γ() }
               requires { ∅ } }
connector Z: {                        nfprop ζ() }
```

Fig. 2. Example components in textual notation

$$P_A \overset{\text{def}}{=} buy(x).\overline{reserve}(x).reserve(x).\overline{commit}(x).commit(x).\overline{buy}(x).\mathbf{0} \quad (6)$$

The process P_B models the behavior of component B and the process P_A for the component A. For invocation of the service $buy()$ (which we assume is modeled by reading a value by $buy(x)$), an output $\overline{reserve}(x)$ is made to the processes in component B which models the invocation of $reserve()$. After $reserve()$ has returned (the input operation $reserve(x)$), $commit()$ is invoked similarly. Finally, $buy()$ returns. This is modeled by the output $\overline{buy}(x)$.

We now introduce the non-functional properties. The idea is as follows: Every service returns its non-functional properties when it terminates. In the textual notation in Figure 2, the keyword **nfprop** indicates a function which computes the non-functional properties of a given service (e.g. $\alpha()$ evaluates to the non-functional properties of $buy()$). These functions are defined for all services a component provides, which are listed after the keyword **provides**. Since non-functional properties have to be checked throughout the execution of the system (which refers to the global conformance condition in the work of Issarny), we also introduce a function for each service required by a component (indicated by the keyword **requires** in the example), which grasps the non-functional requirements for the service and therefore evaluates to true if these requirements are met. These functions are also given in the example after the keyword **ensure**. In our example, $\beta'()$ models the non-functional requirements for $reserve()$ in component A. For completeness, we now also model the connector Z, through which the services of B are invoked. This connector also has a function $\zeta()$ to determine its non-functional properties. We now integrate the functions for computing and checking non-functional properties into our examples 5 and 6:

$$P'_B \overset{\text{def}}{=} reserve(x).\overline{reserve}(\langle x, \beta()\rangle).\mathbf{0} \mid commit(x).\overline{commit}(\langle x, \gamma()\rangle).\mathbf{0} \quad (7)$$

$$P'_A \overset{\text{def}}{=} buy(x).\overline{reserve}(x).reserve(\langle x, p\rangle).[\beta'(p)]\mathbf{1}.$$
$$\overline{commit}(x).commit(\langle x, q\rangle).[\gamma'(q)]\mathbf{1}.\overline{buy}(\langle x, \alpha(p, q)\rangle).\mathbf{0} \quad (8)$$

Now, $reserve()$ is invoked as earlier. However, $reserve()$ returns a tuple, the name x as before and its non-functional properties p. Now, in the execution of $buy()$ it is checked, whether the requirement β' holds for the properties p. If this is the case, the process can continue by executing the "dummy"-process **1**. The same two steps are performed for $commit()$. Finally, the function α is evaluated in order to retrieve the composed non-functional property of $buy()$ and returned in the extended output statement. If we want to model the influence of the connector Z, we have to use its transfer function $\zeta()$ and apply it to the non-functional properties returned by $reserve()$ and $commit()$, i.e. we have to replace all occurrences of p and q with $\zeta(p)$ and $\zeta(q)$ respectively. Therefore, our process from 8 is transformed into

$$P_A'' \stackrel{\text{def}}{=} buy(x).\overline{reserve}(x).reserve(\langle x,p\rangle).[\beta'(\zeta(p))]\mathbf{1}.$$
$$\overline{commit}(x).commit(\langle x,q\rangle).[\gamma'(\zeta(q))]\mathbf{1}.\overline{buy}(\langle x,\alpha(\zeta(p),\zeta(q))\rangle).\mathbf{0} \quad (9)$$

Comparing the formulae 6 and 9, we see that the pure functional modeling of the behavior of component A could be evolved to a specification which includes abstract non-functional properties, allowing their composition and checking. This was achieved by subsequently applying transformation steps and enriching the formal functional specification.

5   Use of Model in Con Moto

In the following section we will discuss how the presented approach for modeling non-functional properties will be used in the ADL Con Moto. Here, models of software systems need to be given in a textual representation as indicated in Figure 2. However, in order to ease system composition, Con Moto will also provide a graphical representation which is based on concepts of UML 2.0 for modeling software architecture, which allows the use of components, ports and connectors. An example of a architectural diagram in UML style is given in the Figure 1.

In the textual representation, there is also the need for expressing the functional properties of the system, hence the invocations of processes, which can be compiled into π-calculus processes like those we used in the example. This is work which has to be done by the system designers, since the functional aspects are crucial for the modeling of mobile systems. Additionally, the designers have to provide the functions evaluating and checking the non-functional properties.

The composition of the processes as in our example can be done automatically by the Con Moto environment, so that for the designer there is the clear separation between functional and non-functional aspects in order to keep modeling complexity at a low level. After the Con Moto environment has composed the functional and non-functional properties into a enriched π-calculus specification, there is the model which allows checking.

A general useful approach for checking π-calculus models for certain properties is to apply model checking techniques. There are rather straight-forward transformations which allow the generation of input for model checkers from π-calculus models. One transformation of this kind is presented in the work of Song and Compton [13]. They propose a formalism for converting π-calculus models into the Promela language used by the SPIN model checker [14]. Although in their paper, Song and Compton restrict their transformation to monadic π-calculus, an extension to polyadic and typed π-calculus is possible. Our approach of integrating conditions for non-functional properties can also be added to the approach presented in [13]. Although it should be noted, that mapping the free conditions to Promela makes restrictions of this language apply to our conditions. But we are confident, that the power of Promela is sufficient for our modeling purposes.

It should be emphasized that we did not make any conclusions about complexity of a Con Moto model with regard to model checking yet. It can easily be imagined that choosing certain non-functional property definitions can lead to a state explosion in the model checker which makes checking of the model impossible. Nevertheless, since a Promela representation of the model also allows the simulation of the model, certain aspects of the architecture can also be checked by simulation.

6   Conclusion

We presented a formal foundation for modeling non-functional properties in architectural description. The main contribution to the research is that it facilitates a general treatment of non-functional properties, ensuring compositionality aspects and flexible checking, which provides a powerful tool for specifying mobile dynamic systems. After motivating our approach we showed that it is possible to pass non-functional properties in π-calculus processes. Since we enriched these processes with checking conditions, it is possible to extend the existing approaches for mobile ADLs with a general treatment of non-functional properties and hence prepare the groundwork for our ADL Con Moto.

Ongoing work is to elaborate the formal underpinning of the chosen approach: The approach has to be written down in a formal correct way using polyadic typed π-calculus, and properties of the extended notion of π-calculus processes have to be proven. The mapping of π-calculus to Promela has to be finished in order to provide tool support. Furthermore, an Eclipse plugin is in work which will allow the integration of architecture modeling with Con Moto into the accepted development process. Summing up, we are confident, that these contributions can add substantial benefit to the early stages of mobile system design.

References

1. Gruhn, V., Schäfer, C.: An Architecture Description Language for Mobile Distributed Systems. In: Proceedings of the First European Workshop on Software Architecture (EWSA 2004), Springer-Verlag Berlin Heidelberg (2004) 212–218
2. Roman, G.C., Picco, G.P., Murphy, A.L.: Software Engineering for Mobility: A Roadmap. In: Proceedings of the Conference on the Future of Software Engineering, ACM Press (2000) 241–258
3. Medvidovic, N., Rosenblum, D.S.: Domains of Concern in Software Architectures. In: Proceedings of the 1997 USENIX Conference on Domain-Specific Languages. (1997)

4. Shaw, M., Garlan, D.: Formulations and Formalisms in Software Architecture. In van Leeuwen, J., ed.: Computer Science Today: Recent Trends and Developments. Volume 1000 of Lecture Notes in Computer Science., Springer (1995) 307–323
5. Medvidovic, N., Taylor, R.N.: A Classification and Comparison Framework for Software Architecture Description Languages. IEEE Transactions on Software Engineering **26** (2000) 70–93
6. Oquendo, F.: π-ADL: An Architecture Description Language based on the Higher-Order Typed π-Calculus for Specifying Dynamic and Mobile Software Architectures. ACM Software Engineering Notes **29** (2004)
7. Issarny, V., Tartanoglu, F., Liu, J., Sailhan, F.: Software Architecture for Mobile Distributed Computing. In: Proceedings of the Fourth Working IEEE/IFIP Conference on Software Architecture (WICSA'04), IEEE (2004) 201–210
8. Milner, R.: Communicating and Mobile Systems: the π-Calculus. Cambridge University Press (1999)
9. Lamport, L.: Specifying Systems: The TLA+ Language and Tools for Hardware and Software Engineers. Addison-Wesley (2002)
10. Zschaler, S.: Formal specification of non-functional properties of component-based software. In Bruel, J.M., Georg, G., Hussmann, H., Ober, I., Pohl, C., Whittle, J., Zschaler, S., eds.: Workshop on Models for Non-functional Aspects of Component-Based Software (NfC'04) at UML conference 2004. (2004)
11. Aagedal, J.Ø.: Quality of Service Support in Development of Distributed Systems. PhD thesis, University of Oslo (2001)
12. Sangiorgi, D., Walker, D.: The π-calculus: a Theory of Mobile Processes. Cambridge University Press (2001)
13. Song, H., Compton, K.J.: Verifying π-calculus Processes by Promela Translation. Technical Report CSE-TR-472-03, University of Michigan (2003)
14. Holzmann, G.J.: The Spin Model Checker: Primer and Reference Manual. Addison-Wesley (2004)

Architectural Aspects of Architectural Aspects

Carlos E. Cuesta[1], María del Pilar Romay[2], Pablo de la Fuente[1],
and Manuel Barrio-Solórzano[1]

[1] Departamento de Informática, Arquitectura, C. Computación y Lenguajes,
Escuela Técnica Superior de Ingeniería Informática, Universidad de Valladolid,
Campus Miguel Delibes, Valladolid 47011, Spain
{cecuesta, pfuente, mbarrio}@infor.uva.es
[2] Departamento de Sistemas Informáticos,
Escuela Politécnica Superior, Universidad Europea de Madrid,
Villaviciosa de Odón, 28670 Madrid, Spain
pilar.romay@uem.es

Abstract. This document studies in some detail the recently developed concept of *aspect* at the architecture level. This concept introduces a novel kind of modularization and composition in software, and therefore it defines new structures which must be studied by Software Architecture, determining the architectural features of aspects. However the opposite strategy can also be considered; namely, a new conceptual model can be defined, including an architecture-level notion of aspect. This would provide a new abstraction to describe software structures, thus effectively providing an additional dimension in architecture description, and would enable the study of the specific compositional problems in this dimension. The document starts by addressing the relevance of this kind of study, and continues by discussing why the new notions are necessary. Then it continues by including a brief enumeration of the more relevant notions derived from this aspectual framework, with particular emphasis on their relationship with software components. Next the document explores the different forms in which these notions could be incorporated into the context of Software Architecture, revealing a rather extensive variety of approaches, and also the relationships and partial equivalences between them. The paper concludes by noting a number or open questions and futures areas of research within this context.

Eurythmia est commodus in conpositionibus membrorum aspectus
VITRUVIUS, DE ARCHITECTVRA

1   Introduction

Software Architecture has many facets and features. It is a discipline which studies the design decisions at an early stage of the software development process, the compromises between them, the effect of these decisions on analysis requirements and they way they propagate throughout this development process. It is also the branch of Software Engineering which considers systems and their subsystems as a whole, a place where it is possible to evaluate their global properties and their impact, and also to decide which of those properties are the driving forces in our design. It is also a point of

R. Morrison and F. Oquendo (Eds.): EWSA 2005, LNCS 3527, pp. 247–262, 2005.

view from which the software architect can conceive large-scale abstractions such as design variations, product families or architectural styles.

But above all Software Architecture is a discipline devoted to the study of modularization and composition, and their consequences. In this regard it is an incarnation of the principle of Separation of Concerns, which states that every concern or interest should be dealt with in a separate module. Once these modules have been defined, the structures combining them appear, and they must be studied toghether with their consequences. Hence the need for Software Architecture.

Recently the principle of Separation of Concerns has been used to provide a new approach to sofware development, which has become popular under the global name of Aspect-Oriented Software Development. Aspects are software entities encapsulating a given concern, just like modules; but the nature of their decomposition is quite different from the one which has been used before.

Though originally related to the implementation stage, aspects have now been extended to cover the whole of the software development cycle. They have been found particularly useful in the initial stages of software development, where they are known under the name of *early aspects*. This refers, basically, to their application in Requirements Engineering and Software Architecture.

The term *architectural aspect* was originally coined by Bedir Tekinerdoğan. It is no doubt intuitive by exploiting the analogy of implementation-level concepts, but this analogy can also be problematic, as it could be assumed as a direct one-to-one translation of the concepts in the AspectJ model [22].

This paper tries to study the notion of architectural aspects from the point of view of Software Architecture. This means that the expression is used in both senses here. We will describe the most important architectural features of existing aspectual models, and also describe some possible approaches to incorporate relevante aspectual notions and, more importantly, their relationships, into Software Architecture.

1.1   Some Open Problems of an Aspectual Nature

Recent research suggests that the degree of information hiding provided by traditional methods of encapsulation is still unadequate [7].The best known sympton is often identified with some kind of aliasing, and implies that some entity is able to access some location it was not supposed to. But the opposite problem also happens. Sometimes it is more difficult to provide a legitimate client with some required access, without making it public or permanent.While this applies to implementation-level modules, it is even more critical for modularization in-the-large. Components were originally conceived as the ultimate notion which would fulfill the promise of sofware reuse, and they depend heavily on encapsulation.But in spite of their ideal appareance, black-box components are not tenough. They must exchange flexibility for parameterization; consequently, now the greatest difficulty of their use is perhaps their configuration.

In the last decade, the need for grey-box components, which allow for some kind of principled adaptation under certain circumstances, has been ever more evident. This is the reason why reflection, traditionally considered as a complex and obscure feature of some experimental systems, is now present at the core of the most popular component platforms.Introspection is of critical importance in Java. Not only it is the essence of their basic *beans*; it is also a necessary step of every remote invocation.The role of reflection in the .NET Architecture is even more fundamental, as it is present on the internal definition of any entity and protocol in the platform. Again, the reason for this is the need to provide controlled access to internal features.

While not the only reason, this is also the main reason why aspect-oriented approaches had become so popular in the last years. They provide most of the capabilities of reflection with regard to the definition of grey-box components, and at the same time the concept itself is much easier to understand. The principle of separation of concerns is logical and easily accepted. It's just a matter of deal with one concern at a time, deferring their combination to a later step. Moreover, this reasoning is easily transported to other stages in the software process, and seems to bring the promise of a more efficient and comfortable development methodology.

The aspect-oriented research community is starting to study relationships between aspects and the properties of aspectual composition, something that should be studied at an architectural level. Even if the relationship was just pure, traditional composition, Software Architecture should be studying it. If it is not, and it is actually a novel concept, it should be added to the Software Architecture Body of Knowledge.

Recently, Rinard et al. [38] have presented an initial classification studying the features which define the relationship between aspects and objects. Though the study is situated at the implementation level, it is abstract enough to have already provided very useful insights on the nature of the interaction between aspectual and compositional entities. These insights can be easily extended to architecture-level aspects.

For instance, this interaction can be defined to *augment, narrow,* or *replace* the behaviour of the component, or also to *combine* it the the behaviour of the aspect. In turn, these behaviours can be designed to be *independent*, or to directly *interfere* with each other; their mutual influence can also be indirect; the aspect can *actuate* where the component only reads, or simply *observe* what is the component doing.

But once that aspects have been introduced in the compositional model, the most critical issue is that of their *composition*. Ideally, the composition of different concerns should provide a combined concern, but often this is not so simple. Moreover, the most usual kind of aspectual composition is held between aspects of the same concern. These aspects can describe complementary, opposite or partially conflicting strategies; therefore their interaction might be very complex and requires a detailed study.

In fact, a growing body of research is being devoted to the study of this important topic [4, 10, 13]; probably the first results in this direction were the ones achieved by Kienzle et al. [25] while considering the potential of aspects to be *reused* as conventional components. Their composition has to consider their dependencies; an aspect can be *independent, uni-directionally* (preserving or modifying) dependent and *circular* dependent with regard to another. The latter leads directly to composite aspects.

Kienzle and Guerraoui have also raised another critical question; namely, if certain behaviours and interaction schemes can effectively be *aspectized* or not [24]. Ironically, their study deals with the problems in the presence of concurrency, which was historically the first concern to be modularized as an aspect. However their conclusion in this case is to question the real need for obliviousness in intercepted components.

2   Structural Features of Non-architectural Aspects

In this section we will study in some detail the most interesting structural features of several existing proposals for aspect orientation, which are not situated at the architectural level. The purpose is twofold: first, we would clarify the notions in the concrete application of these ideas, outlining some basic models of aspect-orientation and the differences with many of their variants. But also this would help us to identify the main structural concepts in those models, providing a first impression of which of those concepts deserve to be translated to the architecture level.

First we will briefly comment on the distinction between the terms *concern* and *aspect*. Then we will describe in detail the most important concepts in the aspectual model, and finally we survey the most successful combinations of aspectual and component models; this would prepare us to later describe architecture-level models.

2.1   Concerns and Aspects

The Merriam-Webster Dictionary [1] lists six different meanings for the word *concern*. Among these, the more relevant in this context define it as a marked *interest* of regard, and a matter of consideration. An independent part of the global problem that the system under consideration is designed to solve. It has also a connotation, also present in other languages, which implies that it is a source of worry, some affair which cannot be simply ignored. Therefore, an eclectic definition, which would be valid even when considering it as a concept at the architecture level, could be *a specific area of active interest*.

But in English it has also another connotation which is unusual in other languages. A concern is also a *gadget* or contrivance: a small device or development, serving some practical purpose. This implies that a concern can be conceived not only as an area of interest, but also as the concrete module encapsulting this interest. This dual meaning is sometimes very useful, but it also introduces some confusion sometimes.

The word *aspect* has only four meanings, and two of them can be safely discarded. The original meaning of the term refers to the appearance or countenance of something. But this appearance implies also the perspective from which this object is seen. Therefore the word *aspect* has evolved to mean also a particular status or phase in which something is observed; one of its possibly many facets.

There is not a very strict distinction between these two terms in natural language. When applied to the field of computing, this has helped to popularize the term *aspect*, but it is also the source of a lot of confusion.

In the context of Aspect Orientation, a concern is conceived as an area of interest, a part of the problem to solve, or even a general feature or quality attribute to be achieved. Well known examples are non-functional concerns like security, fault tolerance or synchronization. On the other hand, an aspect is just a kind of module which is conceived to encapsulate the behaviour related only to an specific concern. In the conventional approach, the behaviour corresponding to a concern is *tangled* with other concerns, therefore making more difficult to reason and act upon them. Also, this behaviour has to be *scattered* throughout the system to be able to achieve a global effect. The purpose of the definition of aspects is to be able to modularize this concern-specific behaviour, therefore avoiding these two problems.

However, sometimes the term concern is used to refer to a module encapsulating a particular interest [44], and the term aspect is used to refer to a global facet of the system under discussion. In the remainder of this document, we will avoid this confusion by using the terms in the sense already noted. The only exception is the occasional use of the term *aspect* in two different senses, like in the title itself. When talking about an aspect *of* something, the term refers to a feature or property, in the global sense; in any other case, it refers always to an aspectual module.

Many authors relate the need for aspects to the presence of *crosscutting concerns*. Crosscutting means that it breaks through encapsulation barriers, ignoring or surpassing them. But of course this definition is relative, as it assumes that these encapsulation barriers already exist in the first place. In fact, it depends of the symmetry of the conceptual model [17]. Most popular aspectual models are asymmetric; they assume the presence of a dominant decomposition: traditional composition, basic functional modularization. That's why asymmetric aspects are assumed to be non-functional.

But in symmetric models [15, 37, 44], the notion of crosscutting does not make sense anymore. A concern is a dimension, and every module is supposed to be able to crosscut each other, merging together. There are only components, basic modules; the term of aspect is rarely used itself.

Asymmetric models must identify crosscutting concerns and then define aspectual entities to encapsulate them. Symmetric models just define modules to encapsulate concerns, without the need to consider whether they are crosscutting or not. That's the reason why symmetric models seem to be more elegant and adequate, especially at the architectural level. However, asymmetric models are easier to combine with existing approaches to software development, and therefore they are still more practical.

2.2   Concepts in Non-architectural Aspects

In this section we will briefly describe most of the novel concepts which have appeared in the context of aspect-oriented systems and platforms, or at least those which are relevant from an architecture-level point of view. Our main purpose here is to provide an independent and concise description for those, as many of them are too closely related or bound to a particular technological platform.

Most of these concepts were introduced in the context of the AspectJ language [22], an extension of Java which is not only considered as the most popular aspect-oriented platform, but it is also the one which has a patent on the term *aspect* [23]. Indeed, the term itself was coined in this context [28], even when it was not the first in using the concept. Therefore, the strict meaning of the expression *aspect-oriented* is restricted to this particular approach, although in the general sense it covers the many proposals using these notions. For the remainder of this document, we would refer to the AspectJ conceptual model as the *reference model*. This should not be interpreted as implying any architectual connotation, it just defines a starting point.

The basic concept in the reference model, and also in most of existing approaches to Aspect Orientation, is the notion of *join point*. In fact, the reference model itself has been described as a *join point interception model* [30]. Moreover, the particular interception mechanism is the distinguishing feature of most of these approaches. A join point is a point in a module's behaviour where additional behaviour, related to some specific concern, can be inserted. The thread of control is *intercepted* and deviated towards some aspectual module, where the relevant actions are specified. Eventually, control returns to the original module, which continues its behaviour from the join point. This pattern is not sequential; in a concurrent model, join points can be provided by synchronizations, rather than deviations [5]. The effect is the same, namely to *interleave* both behaviours, therefore inserting the new concern into the original module.

Join points are a consequence of the separation of concerns approach; concerns are independently described, but they must join together to define a single system. The combination process depends on the identification of common points between almost independent structures. The reference model is asymmetric because one of these structures is considered as the mainstream, and the rest as their extensions.

Another primitive element is known as the *advice*. It describes a piece of behaviour designed to be attached to join points, providing the support for some concern. It is not actually an aspectual notion, as it just defines some "optional" behaviour, and could appear as part of other models; but it is necessary to complement the previous concept, providing the active part of the interception. In most existing proposals, an advice can be inserted before or after a join point, or even instead of it.

The insertion of advices in join points does not provide a mechanism to guarantee separation of concerns. Usually a concern doesn't affect another in just one point; otherwise there would be no need to insist on separation. The relevant advice must be inserted simultaneously in several places, to scatter the additional behaviour. Therefore some kind of quantification abstraction is required, to refer to a set of join points at the same time. This set is known as *pointcut* in the reference model. The pointcut is defined by a *pointcut designator*, often a logical expression. Although at the implementation level this expression has often a lexical nature, this restriction should not be considered at the architecture level, where the nature should be mostly structural.

Considering all of the above, an *aspect* can be simply defined as a module gathering a set of advices related to the same concern, and the corresponding pointcuts which provide their linking with the relevant places in other components.

The attachment of advice to a concrete pointcut creates the mirror image of a method in the object-oriented paradigm; instead of being invoked by the main program, the advice is inserted by the pointcut in the point where it should be executed. At the architecture level, this reveals than an aspect is basically the same that a component, but substituing invocation by interception mechanisms.

Related to the notion of pointcut is the notion of *crosscut*. A pointcut just defines the set of join points in which a particular advice is going to be inserted. But usually more than an advice is required, and even more than a pointcut for each advice. A crosscut is the set of all the join points relevant to a particular concern, the intersection of all its pointcuts; therefore it indicates where this concern crosscuts another. Usually this notion is implicit, but some models make it explicit, particularly event-based aspects [14], which defines crosscuts using explicit events.

In the reference model, advices and pointcuts are mostly coupled; they are defined in the same aspect. This can be compensated by using abstract pointcuts and reflective capabilities, but is is still considered a limitation. Many variants try to decouple these notions. That's the case of JAC [35, 36], one of the first proposals in providing *dynamic aspects*. Dynamic aspects are attached and removed from the system at runtime, so they cannot be limited in the way they are bounded. So advices are joined in specific aspectual components named *wrappers*, and pointcuts are defined in a binding entity designated with the (perhaps misleading) name of *aspect-component*, which dynamically relates advices in wrappers to base components.

Those aspectual wrappers should not be confused with conventional wrappers [18]. Although they are obviously related concepts, their approach is rather different; while the former relies on some interception mechanism, and leave the existing connection structures unaffected, the latter use traditional composition to enclose the wrappees inside themselves, and achieve a total control of both their interaction and their visibility. In fact, their relationship is an interesting open problem at the architectural level.

The process of inserting advices into the corresponding join points, therefore combining aspects and components into a global behaviour, receives the name of *weaving*. The weaving can be implicit, provided by predicates defining pointcuts; or explicit, described as a mapping from aspects to components. The reference model chooses the first option; some other variants prefer the second one. Sometimes the specification of an explicit weaving is encapsulated in a specific element known as *connector*, which has the responsibility to manage this aspectual interaction [26, 30, 41]. These connectors must not be confused with architectural connectors.

The reference model provides also the additional notion of *introduction* or *intertype declaration*. It is simply an additional piece of behaviour which is inserted into a component, together with its entry point. It is simply an extension; differently from advice, introductions are not interleaved with the original behaviour, but just composed with it. The purpose of introductions is to provide a component with a new, independent concern. In particular, introductions are used to connect components which were previously unrelated, defining the ends of a new association.

Another slightly different notion is that of *hookset*, conceived by Eric Tanter et al [43] in the context of the Reflex language. Reflex is designed as a reflective language which uses an aspectual approach to define a model of partial behavioural reflection. Instead of inserting an advice into a join point, Reflex defines a *link* between a meta-object and a hookset; the effect is quite similar and can be used to provide aspect-orientation. Then a hookset is basically a pointcut; but the most interesting feature is that it is not intensional, but extensional. Instead of being defined by a predicate, it is created by composing other hooksets by using set-theoretic operations, starting with primitive hooksets, which essentially contain one join point definition.

As already noted, symmetric models usually don't use the term aspect, as this now implies the existence of components in a dominant decomposition. Instead they use several different incarnations of the most general notion of concern. Some approaches consider the system from the point of view of the different stakeholders, to later combine them using aspectual techniques. Probably the first incarnation of this idea was the notion of *viewpoints* [32], designed to capture requirements. Very similar, and even more influential, was the concept of *subject* [16], which tried to shift the emphasis from objects to the entities which use and act on them.

The notion of subject has evolved into two different, but related models. The work of Clarke et al. [9, 6] defines the concept of *theme*; basically, a modular part of a viewpoint, describing a particular concern from some concrete perspective. When a theme describes a crosscutting concern, which has a lot of interactions to some others, it can be shaped as a *composition pattern*. This is basically a generic structure, which is parameterized to be easy to combine with some others.

The other model takes a more radical approach; every concern is considered as a *dimension* to structure software, which can be used to define modules with different criteria. Dimensions are made first-class, and modules are defined for each one of them. These are known as *hyperslices*, and could be defined as symmetric aspects. One hyperslice can then be combined (merged) with another in another dimension, creating a composite *hypermodule* which is defined in a new, derived dimension. The process continues until a single hypermodule has been reached.

Some other related concepts refer to concrete weaving or compilation techniques, and thus they are not of particular interest at the architectural description level. These are notions like join point shadow, dynamic join point or morphing aspect. We will not consider them in the remainder of this document.

There are still some other relevant, but less extended concepts. Most of them refer to particular approaches to the above model, but some of them provide a different interception mechanism, like *composition filters* [2], or the support for better composition, like *superimpositions* [39]. They will be mentioned in subsequent sections. But the purpose of this section was to outline a general picture of the conceptual structure of aspect-oriented proposals, which will be complemented by subsequent sections.

2.3   On the Symbiosis of Components and Aspects

Even at the implementation level, many authors have noted that aspects and software components serve a similar purpose, namely, to encapsulate a given concern to be later able to reuse it. Beyond objects or classes, components try to fulfill the promise of software reuse by creating almost independent, coarse-grain entities which are conceived to be transportable. A well-designed component must provide a clearly defined function, and in this regard, it encapsulates a concern. Moreover, most of the modern component platforms include a set of pre-defined components and libraries, which are able to provide support for generic non-functional concerns, such as concurrency or transactional interaction, in a transparent manner. In this regard, the only real difference between these "traditional" components and the notion of aspects is the way they are decomposed into modules and composed in subsystems. The core distinction is not the kind of modules, but the relationship between them.

Therefore, aspects and components are not opposite abstractions, and they may be combined in the same context. Some existing platforms, such as JBoss [8], conceive then as orthogonal concepts, and allow to freely combine them. For instance, an aspect can be used to provide a component with the transactional features provided by another, instead of using the conventional interface. But there have also been several attempts to merge both concepts in an unified model, instead of maintainting them separate.

Next we will briefly comment on six of these efforts, which are among the most evolved aspectual models. These are of particular interest, as they provide some hints about the way aspectual concepts could be considered in the context of Software Architecture. Although components of this kind are not exactly architectural components, there are yet enough similarities between them to provide a good comparison.

The first one is also the most evolved and influential of them. There are several different proposals, which we group under the name of the *aspectual component model*. It was originally conceived as a regular component model, known as *adaptive plug & play components*. It was designed to allow external adaptation and composition, and it is reminiscent of several Architecture Description Languages. The evolution of this model led towards the definition of *aspectual component* [26], still the best known among them. With just a minimal modification, they allow for the specification of aspects within the same model. The main purpose of this approach is to allow aspects to be considered as regular components; so they can be intercepted themselves, and also they can use conventional composition mechanisms. The approach has since evolved; subsequent proposals have defined *pluggable composite adapters* and, finally, *aspectual collaborations* [27]. The latter emphasize their capability to describe complex interaction patterns by composing aspects and modules, and even collaborations.

The model defines a *collaboration* (or component) as a wrapper over some *participant*, which is a placeholder for a module. The collaboration defines *expected* methods in participants, which are equivalent to join points, and *aspectual* methods, which are equivalent to advices. It can also *attach* external participants, which can be collaborations themselves, then leading to a "Matrioska doll" model [27].

The main novelty of the aspectual component model was the concept of *connector*, which has been later adopted by other proposals. It provides the mapping which binds abstract participants to concrete modules, in a many-to-many relationship. In the last version, the mapping has been included as part of the collaboration itself.

Closely related to this family is *Caesar* [30]. This model is defined as a blend of aspectual components and the reference model; it has also been clearly influenced by JAC [36]. It provides a high-level structural module over the join point interception model, which is known as *aspect collaboration interface*; it is basically a less-coupled version of an aspectual collaboration, which defines provided and expected facets. The model includes *aspect implementations* to define provided facets; their combination with the interface defines a *weavelet*. An evolved connector, known as *aspect binding*, defines the binding of expected facets to base entities; it can also provide a mapping for one-to-many wrappers, and even pointcuts and advices, similar to those in the reference model. This last feature is really reminiscent of aspect-components in JAC.

The third model is defined in *JAsCo* [41]. It is also conceived as a combination of aspectual components and the reference model; but the major concern here is to achieve a balance between invasive adaptation and black-box modularization. The model provides a mechanism to define an *invasive component adapter*; a structure which is able to control a component's external interaction and also to adapt its internal behaviour, but with some restrictions which respect encapsulation barriers.

The JAsCo model is defined as an extension of Java beans, but this can be safely generalized to apply to any component model. It just adds two elements to this model:

aspect beans and *connectors*. An aspect bean is basically the combination of an aspect and a component. It defines a set of advices, which are known as *hooks*, but it also defines regular methods, and it is able to send events. This means it is still a component, and therefore it can be composed to other components in the conventional way. *Connectors* are the kind of explicit weaving mechanism which was already explained in section 2.2; they simply map hooks in aspect beans to methods in components, in a many-to-many relationship. The model is simple, but well balanced.

A very evolved variant of the JAsCo model is the component model in FuseJ [42]. In this proposal, "there are no aspects" and everything is a component. The model itself is reminiscent of the structure of many ADLs. Every component defines a set of *gates* composing an interface, and those gates are linked together by using *connectors*. This connectors specify a mapping between gates and their properties, which can define their interaction as regular or aspectual. This interaction determines aspect orientation.

The fifth model is that of Jiazzi [29]. It is a framework designed to provide compositional primitives to the Java language, which are basically architectural in nature. Like a typical ADL, it provides external linking and hierarchical composition, creating *compounds* by combining *units*. The model includes the definition of mixin-like components, conceived to extend basic units; together with the support for cyclic linking, this allow independent features which crosscut unit boundaries to be packaged in separate components. Combined with external linking, this can substitute feature addition and other external patterns. In summary, instead of being an aspectual model designed to use components, Jiazzi defines a component model which provides an indirect support for aspect orientation, which could be defined to be language-independent.

The approach of Jiazzi is reminiscent of open classes and some existing architecture-related proposals, like *mixin layers* [40], which are used to modularize collaborations between components. The mechanism is also similar to that of *role-model components* [45], which use a mixin to implement each of the roles in a component.

Finally, we should briefly mention the recent proposal of *open modules* [4]. These are aspects defined with a strong encapsulation interface. The argument is that grey-box components of the type discussed above compromise safety and security, and advocate the use of some access control mechanism. Open modules are basically components which also define *exported pointcuts* in their interface. This means that the component is exposing a number of join points just in case some aspect needs to intercept them; they are optional extension points which can be used or not. The rest of the component is encapsulated, and cannot be intercepted except under special circumstances.

3   Models for Architectural Aspects

Although the concepts of Aspect Orientation are relatively new, the number of essentially different proposals that use them is growing fastly. Most of these proposals are described at the implementation level, but also many of them could be easily translated to the architecture level. The purpose of this section is to consider the structural definitions already outlined in this document, and describe the form that a hypothetical (or even existing) model of architectural aspects could take.

There is not any mainstream proposal for the description of architectural aspects yet. In fact, there is a surprisingly large number of alternatives. Instead of describing a particular model, we provide an initial classification of aspect-oriented models with regard to their conceptual structure. This has been designed to cover the whole range of existing proposals, and should help us to identify the similarities between many of them, and also the relationships between several close, if not equivalent, approaches. We enumerate these appproaches in the remainder of this section.

1. *There Are No Aspects.* This model uses only conventional architectural elements, and therefore it suggests that there is no need to introduce any additional aspectual entity at this level. There are two different reasonings which could lead towards this option. One of them is to simply suggest that aspects are irrelevant and therefore there is no need to consider them at this level. The other approach decides not to define any aspectual notion, as it is not considered necessary, because aspect-oriented features are provided by some standard compositional mechanism. An example of this approach is Jiazzi [29], already exposed in the section 2.3.

2. *Architectural Aspects.* This model does consider aspects as relevant at this level, and define some explicit entity to gather their influence. This is, an architecture-level counterpart of implementation-level aspects is defined.

   (a) *Components as Aspects.* Instead of providing some additional abstraction, this approach prefers to use conventional components to play the role of aspects. This has the advantage of maintaining an uniform model. A good example of this approach is the proposal by Navasa et al. [31], which defines a two-layered coordination structure to support weaving.

   (b) *Connectors as Aspects.* This approach complements the previous one; it uses connectors instead of components to play the role of aspects. This makes sense, as aspects are often introduced by intercepting interaction, which is held by connectors. There exists some preliminary work in this direction [12], and it is also related to the *composition filters* [2] approach, although these filters are not exactly comparable to architectural connectors.

   (c) *Derived Components* This model provides some kind of second-class definition of an aspectual entity, which is conceived as a variant of the regular component. There is still only one kind of component, but some of them are provided with additional features. This approach has been considered mostly at the design level [3, 35]. Aspects are defined by *stereotyping* regular components.

   (d) *Aspectual Components.* This approach is close to the previous one. The model is still uniform and there is only one kind of component, but the component model itself is defined to include aspectual capabilities. Therefore even regular components have aspectual features. The best example of this approach is the JAsCo model [41], but the more strict approach of FuseJ [42] can also be included in this category. Curiously enough, Lieberherr's aspectual components approach [26] are not included, as it will be considered below.

   (e) *First-class Architectural Aspects.* This model is perhaps the most obvious choice. It just consists of providing a direct translation of the reference model [22] to the architectural level. The idea is to provide a component-like aspectual entity, a first-class architectural aspect. The model would be explicitly designed to be non-uniform and asymmetric, and require some kind of pointcut abstraction, similar to aspect-components in JAC [35, 36]. Curiously enough, currently there not exists a proposal for architectural aspects of this kind; the approach of open modules [4] could be however a first step in this direction.

3. *Aspectual Binding*. This model considers that there is no need to have an explicit aspectual entity. The distinguishing feature of aspect orientation is that it provides a novel kind of interaction, so the architectural model should only consider to provide a new kind of binding mechanism between components.

   (a) *Aspectual Interaction*. This model considers interaction as a low-level abstraction, and provides some explicit means to intercept it at the architectural level, thus providing aspect orientation. Again composition filters [2] appear in this category, which is somehow related to the idea of using connectors. The event-based approach of Douence et al. [14] might also be included.

   (b) *Aspectual Composites*. This is a refinement of the former; it tries to define a high-level structure encapsulating this kind of aspectual interaction. Therefore it uses an architectural approach for this problem. In this category we group proposals such as aspectual components [26], aspectual collaborations [27] or even Caesar [30]; they were described in the section 2.3. Clarke's compositional patterns [9] can also be included as a design abstraction.

   (c) *First-Class Aspectual Binding*. This model is a generalization of the previous approach. Binding is an architectural abstraction, and this novel kind of binding deserves a first-class concept. The best example of this approach is the work on *superimposition* by Katz et al. [21, 39]. Katzian superimposition is defined as a theoretical relationship which defines a high-level compositional structure. This approach has also been taken by our own work [11].

4. *Concern Models*. This is a symmetric model; it assumes that we have a regular ADL with standard compositional features, but with some internal concern model.

   (a) *Internal Concerns*. In this approach, concerns are explicitly considered in the internal definition of architectural abstractions, but this definition is fixed. Behaviour related to concerns can be specified as part of the specification. This is the approach defined by Kandé [19] in his *concern-based architecture*.

   (b) *First-Class Concerns*. This approach improves the former by including concern definitions as explicit entities at the architectural level. These are "symmetric aspects", which are part of the component definition. A component is described as a set of aspects, an explicit weaving and a common interface. This is the approach used in the PRISMA component model [37]

5. *Multiple Dimensions*. This is quite similar to the previous one. The main difference is that the concern model is not internal, but explicit. Concerns are large-scale entities which can be manipulated as such.

   (a) *Concern Views*. This approach defines the architecture of every concern in an independent view, and these views are later related using some mechanism. Obviously this approach is quite similar to architectural viewpoints, and therefore it is very consistent. The best example is given by *concern architecture views*, an approach which is also based on superposition [15, 20]. Clarke's themes have a similar philosophy [6, 9] can also be included in this category.

(b) *First-Class Dimensions*. This is the architectural equivalent of the MDSoC model defined by Ossher and Tarr [33, 44]. Every component has its own dimension in this model, and the architectural structure is only created as those dimensions are being merged. Although it is very expressive, the convenience of using this sort of approach has still to be determined.

4   Conclusions

Throughout this paper we have tried to outline the basic notions behind the concept of Aspect Orientation, and consider how these notions can be conceived in the specific context of Software Architecture. Even when both fields have a long history, they are also fairly young in their current incarnation; and although they are intrinsically related, their combination is still a recent idea. However, they have received a considerable attention and interest in the last years, and therefore the survey we have presented in previous sections must be necessarily incomplete.

In particular, there is a very interesting and important body of work concerning the use of formal methods to study the specification of aspect-oriented models and mechanisms. This kind of work has the advantage of describing the concepts independently of a particular language or platform, and therefore it provides very interesting insights about the real nature of the concepts under question.

There are still a good number of open structural problems in Aspect Orientation which would benefit a lot from an explicit architectural perspective. Moreover, architecture is a concern itself and it has even defined as an aspect. These fields have a lot of points in common, and they should be carefully explored.

For example, composition of aspects, the definition of priorities in this composition, and the resolution of structural dependencies between them are all structural issues which can be specified and studied by using architectural techniques. On the other hand, the concept of *dynamic aspects* [34, 35], which are added to or removed from the system's structure, provides an intriguing approach to describe a particularly complex kind of architectural dynamism.

As a testimony of the great interest which exists about this topic in the Software Architecture research community, we have consciously cited three of the papers in this workshop [15, 31, 37], which are devoted to this topic. The three of them are completely different, but they are all state-of-the-art contributions to these issues.

In summary, this is a novel field with a great number of open questions, and the opportunities for useful and relevant research abound.

Acknowledgements

The authors have benefit from very enlightening discussions on the topic of architectural aspects with several colleagues throughout the last four years. Although our approaches to the concept are quite different, both on perspective and origin, our greatest influence has been that of Rénaud Pawlak. We would like to thank him for "helping us to find our ways during our fruitful collaborations", to quote his own expression.

Even after our aspectual model had been established, our understanding of these concepts has always been challenged by those who had a different, but still interesting, vision. This has often helped us to widen our own perception. Specifically, we would like to thank Jenifer Pérez for our interesting discussions on PRISMA.

Of course, none of the above should be considered responsible for the opinions contained herein, which are only our own.

References

1. The Merriam-Webster Online Dictionary. http://www.m-w.com, 2005.
2. Mehmet Akşit and Bedir Tekinerdoğan. Solving the Modeling Problems of Object-oriented Languages by Composing Multiple Aspects using Composition Filters. In *ICSE'98 Workshop on Aspect Oriented Programming (ICSE-AOP'98)*, Kyoto, April 1998.
3. Omar Aldawud, Tzilla Elrad, and Atef Bader. UML Profile for Aspect-Oriented Software Development. In Omar Aldawud, editor, *Third Workshop on Aspect-Oriented Modeling (AOM/AOSD'03)*, Boston, March 2003.
4. Jonathan Aldrich. Open Modules: A Proposal for Modular Reasoning in Aspect-Oriented Programming. In Curtis Clifton, Ralf Lämmel, and Gary T. Leavens, editors, *Proc. Foundations of Aspect-Oriented Languages (FOAL 2004)*, pages 7–18, March 2004.
5. James H. Andrews. Process-Algebraic Foundations of Aspect-Oriented Programming. In Akinori Yonezawa and Satoshi Matsuoka, editors, *Reflection 2001: Third Intl. Conf. on Metalevel Architectures and Separation of Crosscutting Concerns*, volume 2192 of *Lecture Notes in Computer Science*, pages 187–209, Kyoto, Japan, September 2001.
6. Elisa L.A. Baniassad and Siobhán Clarke. Theme: An Approach for Aspect-Oriented Analysis and Design. In *26th Intl. Conf. on Software Engineering (ICSE 2004)*, pages 158–167, Edinburgh, Scotland, May 2004. IEEE Computer Society Press.
7. Andrew P. Black. Object-Oriented Programming: Regaining the Excitement. Speech at 12th European Conf. on Object-Oriented Programming (ECOOP'98), July 1998.
8. Bill Burke. JBoss AOP. http://www.jboss.org/developers/projects/jboss/aop, 2005.
9. Siobhán Clarke. Extending Standard UML with Model Composition Semantics. *Science of Computer Programming*, 44(1):71–100, July 2002.
10. Curtis Clifton and Gary T. Leavens. Observers and Assistants: A Proposal for Modular Aspect-Oriented Reasoning. In Gary T. Leavens and Ron Cytron, editors, *Proc. Foundations of Aspect-Oriented Languages (FOAL 2002)*, pages 33–44, April 2002. ISU-TR #02-06.
11. Carlos E. Cuesta, M. Pilar Romay, Pablo de la Fuente, Manuel Barrio-Solórzano, and Houman Younessi. Coordination in Architectural Connection: Reflective and Aspectual Introduction. *L'Objet*, 2005. To be published.
12. Carlos E. Cuesta, María del Pilar Romay, Pablo de la Fuente, and Manuel Barrio Solórzano. Aspectos como Conectores en Arquitectura de Software. In *II Jornadas de Trabajo Dynamica (Dynamic and Aspect-Oreinted Modeling for Integrated Component-based Architectures*, pages 63–72, November 2004.
13. Daniel S. Dantas and David Walker. Harmless Advice. In *12th Intl. Workshop on Foundations of Object- Oriented Languages (FOOL 2005)*, Long Beach, CA, 2005. ACM.
14. Rémi Douence, Olivier Motelet, and Mario Südholt. A Formal Definition of Crosscuts. In Akinori Yonezawa and Satoshi Matsuoka, editors, *Reflection 2001: Third Intl. Conf. on Metalevel Architectures and Separation of Crosscutting Concerns*, volume 2192 of *Lecture Notes in Computer Science*, pages 170–186, Kyoto, Japan, September 2001.

15. Imed Hammouda, Markku Hakala, Mika Pussinen, Mika Katara, and Tommi Mikkonen. Concern-Based Development of Pattern Systems. In Ron Morrison and Flavio Oquendo, editors, *Second European Workshop on Software Architecture (EWSA'05)*, Lecture Notes in Computer Science, Pisa, June 2005. *Included in this volume.*

16. William Harrison and Harold Ossher. Subject-Oriented Programming – A Critique of Pure Objects. In *Proceedings of 1993 ACM Conference on Object-Oriented Programming Systems, Languages, and Applications (OOPSLA'93)*. ACM Press, September 1993.

17. William H. Harrison, Harold L. Ossher, and Peri L. Tarr. Asymetrically vs. Symmetrically Organized Paradigms for Software Composition. IBM Research Report RC22685 (W0212-147), Thomas J. Watson Research Center, IBM, December 2002.

18. Urs Hözle. Integrating Independently-Developed Components in Object-Oriented Languages. In Oscar Marius Nierstrasz, editor, *ECOOP'93 – Object-Oriented Programming*, volume 707 of *Lecture Notes in Computer Science*, pages 36–56. Springer-Verlag, July 1993.

19. Mohamed Mancona Kandé and Alfred Strohmeier. Modeling Crosscutting Concerns using Software Connectors. In *OOPSLA'2001 Workshop on Advanced Separation of Concerns in Object-Oriented Systems (ASoC3)*, October 2001.

20. Mika Katara and Shmuel Katz. Architectural Views of Aspects. In *Proceedings of the Second International Conference on Aspect-Oriented Software Development (AOSD'03)*, pages 1–10. ACM Press, March 2003.

21. Shmuel Katz. A Superimposition Control Construct for Distributed Systems. *ACM Trans. on Programming Languages and Systems*, 15(2):337–356, April 1993.

22. Gregor Kiczales, Erik Hilsdale, Jim Hugunin, Mik Kersten, Jeffrey Palm, and William G. Griswold. An Overview of AspectJ. In J. Knudsen, editor, *Proceedings 15th European Conference on Object-Oriented Programming (ECOOP'2001)*, volume 1241 of *Lecture Notes in Computer Science*, pages 327–252, Budapest, June 2001.

23. Gregor Kiczales, John Lamping, Cristina Videira Lopes, J. Hugunin, Eric Hilsdale, and C. Boyapati. *Aspect-Oriented Programming*. U.S. Patent # 6.467.086, October 2002.

24. Jörg Kienzle and Rachid Guerraoui. AOP: Does it Make Sense?. The Case of Concurrency and Failures. In Boris Magnusson, editor, *Proceedings 16th European Conference on Object-Oriented Programming (ECOOP 2002)*, volume 2374 of *Lecture Notes in Computer Science*, pages 37–54, Malaga, June 2002. Springer Verlag.

25. Jörg Kienzle, Yang Yu, and Jie Xiong. On Composition and Reuse of Aspects. In Gary T. Leavens and Curtis Clifton, editors, *Foundations of Aspect-Oriented Languages (FOAL'2003)*, March 2003.

26. Karl Lieberherr, David Lorenz, and Mira Mezini. Programming with Aspectual Components. Technical Report NU-CCS-99-01, Northeastern University, Boston, March 1999.

27. Karl Lieberherr, David H. Lorenz, and Johan Ovlinger. Aspectual Collaborations: Combining Modules and Aspects. *The Computer Journal*, 46(5):542–565, September 2003.

28. Cristina Videira Lopes. AOP: A Historical Perspective (What's in a Name?). In Robert E. Filman, Tzilla Elrad, Siobhán Clarke, and Mehmet Akşit, editors, *Aspect-Oriented Software Development*, pages 97–122. Addison-Wesley, 2005.

29. Sean McDirmid and Wilson C. Hsieh. Aspect-oriented programming with Jiazzi. In William G. Griswold, Mehmet Akşit, and Karl J. Lieberherr, editors, *2nd Intl. Conf. on Aspect-Oriented Software Development (AOSD 2003)*, pages 70–79, Boston, March 2003.

30. Mira Mezini and Klaus Ostermann. Conquering Aspects with Caesar. In William G. Griswold, Mehmet Akşit, and Karl J. Lieberherr, editors, *Proc. 2nd Intl. Conf. on Aspect-Oriented Software Development (AOSD'03)*, pages 90–100, Boston, March 2003. ACM Press.

31. Amparo Navasa, Miguel Angel Pérez, and Juan Manuel Murillo. Aspect Modelling at Architecture Design. In Ron Morrison and Flavio Oquendo, editors, *Second European Workshop on Software Architecture (EWSA'05)*, Lecture Notes in Computer Science, Pisa, June 2005. *Included in this volume.*

32. Bashar Nuseibeh, Jeff Kramer, and Anthony C.W. Finkelstein. Framework for Expressing the Relationships Between Multiple Views in Requirements Specifications. *IEEE Transactions on Software Engineering*, 20(10):760–773, October 1994.

33. Harold Ossher and Peri Tarr. Multi-Dimensional Separation of Concerns and The Hyperspace Approach. In *Proceedings of the Symposium on Software Architectures and Component Technology: The State of the Art in Software Development*. Kluwer, 2000.

34. Renaud Pawlak, Jean-Philippe Retaillé, and Lionel Seinturier. *Programmation Orientée Aspect pour Java/J2EE*. Eyrolles, 2004.

35. Renaud Pawlak, Lionel Seinturier, Laurence Duchien, Gérard Florin, Fabrice Legond-Aubry, and Laurent Martelli. JAC: an Aspect-based Distributed Dynamic Framework. *Software – Practice and Experience*, 34:1119–1148, 2004.

36. Rénaud Pawlak, Lionel Seinturier, Laurence Duchien, Laurent Martelli, Fabrice Legond-Aubry, and Gérard Florin. Aspect-Oriented Software Development with Java Aspect Components. In Robert E. Filman, Tzilla Elrad, Siobhán Clarke, and Mehmet Akşit, editors, *Aspect-Oriented Software Development*, pages 343–369. Addison-Wesley, 2005.

37. Jennifer Pérez Benedí, Nour Ali, José Angel Carsí, and Isidro Ramos. Dynamic Evolution in Aspect-Oriented Architectural Models. In Ron Morrison and Flavio Oquendo, editors, *Second European Workshop on Software Architecture (EWSA'05)*, Lecture Notes in Computer Science, Pisa, June 2005. *Included in this volume*.

38. Martin Rinard, Alexandru Salcianu, and Suhabe Bugrara. A Classification System and Analysis for Aspect-Oriented Programs. In *Proceedings 12th Conf. Foundations of Software Engineering (SIGSOFT'04/FSE-12)*. ACM Press, November 2004.

39. Marcelo Sihman and Shmuel Katz. Superimpositions and Aspect-Oriented Programming. *The Computer Journal*, 46(5):529–541, September 2003.

40. Yannis Smaragdakis and Don Batory. Mixin Layers: An Object-Oriented Implementation Technique for Refinements and Collaboration-Based Designs. *ACM Transactions on Software Engineering and Methodology*, 11(2):215–255, April 2002.

41. Davy Suvée, Wim Vanderperren, and Viviane Jonckers. JasCo: an Aspect-Oriented Approach Tailored for Component-Based Software Development. In *Proc. 2nd Intl. Conf. on Aspect-Oriented Software Development (AOSD'2003)*, pages 21–29, Boston, March 2003. ACM Press.

42. Davy Suvée, Wim Vanderperren, Dennis Wagelaar, and Viviane Jonckers. There Are No Aspects. *Electronical Notes in Theoretical Computer Science*, 114:153–174, January 2005. Special Issue on Sofware Composition (SC'2004).

43. Éric Tanter, Jacques Noyé, Denis Caromel, and Pierre Cointe. Partial Behavioral Reflection: Spatial and Temporal Selection of Reification. In Ron Crocker and Guy L. Steele, Jr., editors, *18th ACM Conf. on Object-Oriented Programming, Systems, Languages and Applications (OOPSLA'2003)*, volume 38 of *ACM SIGPLAN Notices*, pages 27–46, December 2003.

44. Peri Tarr, Harold Ossher, Stanley M. Sutton, Jr., and William Harrison. N-Degrees of Separation: Multi-Dimensional Separation of Concerns. In Robert E. Filman, Tzilla Elrad, Siobhán Clarke, and Mehmet Akşit, editors, *Aspect-Oriented Software Development*, pages 37–61. Addison-Wesley, Boston, 2005.

45. Michael VanHilst and David Notkin. Using Role Components to implement Collaboration-based Designs. In *Proceedings 11th Intl. Conf. on Object-Oriented Programming Systems, Languages and Aplications (OOPSLA'96)*, pages 350–369. ACM, October 1996.

Author Index

Lecture Notes in Computer Science

For information about Vols. 1–3438

please contact your bookseller or Springer